THE DAY AFTER ROSWELL

COL. PHILIP J. CORSO (Ret.)
WITH WILLIAM J. BIRNES

GALLERY BOOKS

New York   London   Toronto   Sydney   New Delhi

G

Gallery Books
An Imprint of Simon & Schuster, Inc.
1230 Avenue of the Americas
New York, NY 10020

Copyright © 1997 by Rosewood Woods Productions, Inc.
Foreword copyright © 1997 Senator Strom Thurmond

First Gallery Books trade paperback edition June 2017

GALLERY BOOKS and colophon are registered trademarks of Simon & Schuster, Inc.

For information about special discounts for bulk purchases, please contact Simon & Schuster Special Sales at 1-866-506-1949 or business@ simonandschuster.com

The Simon & Schuster Speakers Bureau can bring authors to your live event. For more information or to book an event contact the Simon & Schuster Speakers Bureau at 1-866-248-3049 or visit our website at www.simonspeakers.com.

Manufactured in the United States of America

30 29 28 27 26 25 24

Library of Congress Cataloging-in-Publication Data is available.

ISBN 978-1-5011-7200-7
ISBN 978-0-6710-3695-9 (ebook)

Praise for Philip J. Corso and
THE DAY AFTER ROSWELL

"Plenty of new material . . . As far as Corso is concerned, the crash of an alien spaceship in the New Mexico desert was fact, and he presents information and theories not heretofore reported on what the military did with some unusual debris."

—Mary Kate Tripp,
Amarillo Sunday News-Globe (TX)

"If the details are accurate, [Corso] has apparently violated any number of security provisions and broken his oath of secrecy."

—Ben Martin,
Baton Rouge Advocate (LA)

"*[THE DAY AFTER ROSWELL]* does bring to the debate an incredible testimony from what appears to be an authoritative source."

—James Cummings,
Dayton Daily News (OH)

"An interesting read."

—Robert Kolarik,
San Antonio Express-News

"Full of controversy."

—Chris Tutor,
The Anniston Star (AL)

"Whether or not you believe in UFOs, or alien visitors, you might find yourself concluding that something extraordinary did happen in that New Mexican desert years ago and agreeing with the author that our lives have been changed forever by that event."

—Bob Raimonto,
Staten Island Advance (NY)

In memory of Lt. Gen. Arthur G. Trudeau. This great man was my superior as chief of U.S. Army Research and Development. He was a man of great courage; he put on a sergeant's helmet and fought with his men at Pork Chop Hill in Korea. He was deeply religious and went on "retreats" at Loyola. He was the most brilliant man I have ever known, who only gave me one standing order: "Watch things for me, Phil. The rest do not understand."

His accomplishments changed the world for the better. Any success I had I attribute to him and to his leadership.

Acknowledgments

I wish to thank the eighteen various U.S. Army installations from which I requested historical and background information on details of projects and studies in which I participated. They went beyond their normal activities to furnish the data I requested, which was invaluable in compiling this book. A list follows: Historical Reference Branch, U.S. Army Military History Institute, Carlisle Barracks, Carlisle Pennsylvania; Chief, Corps of Engineers, Washington, D.C.; Department of the Army R&D, The Pentagon; U.S. Army Missile Command, Command Historian, Redstone Arsenal, Alabama; U.S. Army Belvoir Research, Development and Engineering Center, Ft. Belvoir, Virginia; Space and Strategic Defense CMD, Redstone Arsenal, Huntsville, Alabama; Night Vision Electronic Sensor Center, Ft. Belvoir, Virginia; U.S. Army Research Laboratory Cmd.; Harry Diamond Laboratories, Adelphia, Maryland; Walter Reed Army Institute of Research, Washington, D.C.; Department of Army Historical Service Division, Center of Military History, Washington, D.C.; U.S. Army Corps of Engineers, Office of History, Ft. Belvoir, Virginia; Hdgs. U.S. Army Communications—Electronic Cmd., Research, Development and Engineering Center, Night Vision Electronic Sensors Directorate, Ft. Monmouth, New Jersey; Missile Command

USASS DC-H, CSSD-PA, Huntsville, Alabama; U.S. Army, Quartermaster Center, Ft. Lee, Virginia; Hdgs. U.S. Army Materiel Cmd., Research and Development, Alexandria, Virginia; Lincoln Labs, Lexington, Massachusetts; and Bell Laboratories, Westminister, Colorado.

I also wish to thank the modern military branch of the National Archives, Washington, D.C., and the Commissioner of Patents and Trademarks, Washington, D.C.

Thanks also to my friends Neil Russell and Dennis Hackin at Neil Russell Productions in Los Angeles for their understanding of this fascinating aspect of American history and their support, and to a special friend, Andrew Russell.

In addition, I offer thanks and gratitude for the understanding and support of my editor at Pocket Books, Tris Coburn, and our Editorial Director, Emily Bestler.

Last, but not least, the memoirs of Lt. Gen. Arthur G. Trudeau. He presented my copy to me personally, with instructions to use the contents as I saw fit.

*"Be sure you're right,
then go ahead."*

—DAVY CROCKETT

THE
DAY AFTER
ROSWELL

Introduction

MY NAME IS PHILIP J. CORSO, AND FOR TWO INCREDIBLE YEARS back in the 1960s while I was a lieutenant colonel in the army heading up the Foreign Technology desk in Army Research and Development at the Pentagon, I led a double life. In my routine everyday job as a researcher and evaluator of weapons systems for the army, I investigated things like the helicopter armament the French military had developed, the tactical deployment complexities of a theater antimissile missile, or new technologies to preserve and prepare meals for our troops in the field. I read technology reports and met with engineers at army proving grounds about different kinds of ordnance and how ongoing budgeted development projects were moving forward. I submitted their reports to my boss, Lt. Gen. Arthur Trudeau, the director of Army R&D and the manager of a three-thousand-plus-man operation with lots of projects at different stages. On the surface, especially to congressmen exercising oversight as to how the taxpayers' money was being spent, all of it was routine stuff.

Part of my job responsibility in Army R&D, however, was as an intelligence officer and adviser to General Trudeau who, himself, had headed up Army Intelligence before coming to R&D. This was a job I was trained for and held during World War II and Korea. At the Pentagon I was working in some of the most secret areas of military intelligence, reviewing heavily classified information on behalf of General Trudeau. I had been on General MacArthur's staff in Korea and knew that as late as 1961—even as late, maybe, as today—as Americans back then were sitting down to watch *Dr. Kildare* or *Gunsmoke,* captured American soldiers from World War II and Korea were still living in gulag conditions in prison camps in the Soviet Union and Korea. Some of them were undergoing what amounted to sheer psychological torture. They were the men who never returned.

As an intelligence officer I also knew the terrible secret that some of our government's most revered institutions had been penetrated by the KGB and that key aspects of American foreign policy were being dictated from inside the Kremlin. I testified to this first at a Senate subcommittee hearing chaired by Senator Everett Dirksen of Illinois in April 1962, and a month later delivered the same information to Attorney General Robert Kennedy. He promised me that he would deliver it to his brother, the President, and I have every reason to believe he did. It was ironic that in 1964, after I retired from the army and had served on Senator Strom Thurmond's staff, I worked for Warren Commission member Senator Richard Russell as an investigator.

But hidden beneath everything I did, at the center of a double life I led that no one knew about, and buried deep inside my job at the Pentagon was a single file cabinet that I had inherited because of my intelligence background. That file held the army's deepest and most closely guarded secret: the Roswell files, the cache of debris and information an army retrieval team from the 509th Army Air Field pulled out of the wreckage of a flying disk that had crashed outside the town of Roswell in the New Mexico desert in the early-morning darkness during the first week of July 1947. The Roswell file was the legacy of what happened in the hours and days after the crash when the official government cover-up was put into place. As the military tried to figure out what it was that had crashed, where it had come from, and what its inhabitants' intentions were, a covert group was assembled under the leadership of the director of intelligence, Adm. Roscoe Hillenkoetter, to investigate the nature of the flying disks and collect all information about encounters with these phenomena while, at the same time, publicly and officially discounting the existence of all flying saucers. This operation has been going on, in one form or another, for fifty years amidst complete secrecy.

I wasn't in Roswell in 1947, nor had I heard any details about the crash at that time because it was kept so tightly under wraps, even within the military. You can easily understand why, though, if you remember, as I do, the Mercury Theater "War of the Worlds" radio broadcast in 1938 when the entire country panicked at the story of how invaders from Mars landed in Grovers Mill, New Jersey, and began attacking the local populace. The fictionalized eyewitness reports of violence and the inability of our military forces to stop the creatures were graphic. They killed everyone who crossed their path, narrator Orson Welles said into his microphone, as these creatures in their war machines started their march toward New York. The level of terror that Halloween night of the broadcast was so intense and the military so incapable of protecting the local residents that the police were overwhelmed by the phone calls. It was as if the whole country had gone crazy and authority itself had started to unravel.

Now, in Roswell in 1947, the landing of a flying saucer was no fantasy. It was real, the military wasn't able to prevent it, and this time the authorities didn't want a repeat of "War of the Worlds." So you can see the mentality at work behind the desperate need to keep the story quiet. And this is not to mention the military fears at first that the craft might have been an experimental Soviet weapon because it bore a resemblance to some of the German-designed aircraft that had made their appearances near the end of the war, especially the crescent-shaped Horton flying wing. What if the Soviets had developed their own version of this craft?

The stories about the Roswell crash vary from one another in the details. Because I wasn't there, I've had to rely on reports of others, even within the military itself. Through the years, I've heard versions of the Roswell story in which campers, an archeological team, or rancher Mac Brazel found the wreckage. I've read military reports about different crashes in different locations in some proximity to the army air field at Roswell like San Agustin and Corona and even different sites close to the town itself. All of the reports were classified, and I did not copy them or retain them for my own records after I left the army. Sometimes the dates of the crash vary from report to report, July 2 or 3 as opposed to July 4. And I've heard different people argue the dates back and forth, establishing time lines that vary from one another in details, but all agree that something crashed in the desert outside of Roswell and near enough to the army's most sensitive installations at Alamogordo and White Sands that it caused the army to react quickly and with concern as soon as it found out.

In 1961, regardless of the differences in the Roswell story from the many different sources who had described it, the top-secret file of Roswell information came into my possession when I took over the Foreign Technology desk at R&D. My boss, General Trudeau, asked me to use the army's ongoing weapons development and research program as a way to filter the Roswell technology into the mainstream of industrial development through the military defense contracting program. Today, items such as lasers, integrated circuitry, fiber-optics networks, accelerated particle-beam devices, and even the Kevlar material in bulletproof vests are all commonplace. Yet the seeds for the development of all of them were found in the crash of the alien craft at Roswell and turned up in my files fourteen years later.

But that's not even the whole story.

In those confusing hours after the discovery of the crashed Roswell alien craft, the army determined that in the absence of any other information it had to be an extraterrestrial. Worse, the fact that this craft and other flying saucers had been surveilling our defensive installations and even seemed to evidence a technology we'd seen evidenced by the Nazis caused the military to assume these flying saucers had hostile intentions and might have even interfered in human events during the war. We didn't know what the inhabitants of these crafts wanted, but we had to assume from their behavior, especially their interventions in the lives of human beings and the reported cattle mutilations, that they could be potential enemies. That meant that we were facing a far superior power with weapons capable of obliterating us. At the same time we were locked in a Cold War with the Soviets and the mainland Chinese and were faced with the penetration of our own intelligence agencies by the KGB.

The military found itself fighting a two-front war, a war against the Communists who were seeking to undermine our institutions while threatening our allies and, as unbelievable as it sounds, a war against extraterrestrials, who posed an even greater threat than the Communist forces. So we used the extraterrestrials' own technology against them, feeding it out to our defense contractors and then adapting it for use in space-related defense systems. It took us until the 1980s, but in the end we were able to deploy enough of the Strategic Defense Initiative, "Star Wars," to achieve the capability of knocking down enemy satellites, killing the electronic guidance systems of incoming enemy warheads, and disabling enemy spacecraft, if we had to, to pose a threat. It was alien technology that we used: lasers, accelerated particle-beam weapons, and aircraft equipped with "Stealth" features. And in the end, we not only outlasted the Soviets and ended the Cold War, but we forced a stalemate with the extraterrestrials, who were not so invulnerable after all.

What happened after Roswell, how we turned the extraterrestrials' technology against them, and how we actually won the Cold War is an incredible story. During the thick of it, I didn't even realize how incredible it was. I just did my job, going to work at the Pentagon day in and day out until we put enough of this alien technology into development that it began to move forward under its own weight through industry and back into the army. The full import of what we did at Army R&D and what General Trudeau did to grow R&D from a disorganized unit under the shadow of the Advanced Research Projects Agency, when he first took command, to the army department that helped create the military guided missile, the antimissile missile, and the guided-missile-launched accelerated particle-beam-firing satellite killer, didn't really hit me until years later when I understood just how we were able to make history.

I always thought of myself as just a little man from a little American town in western Pennsylvania, and I didn't assess the weight of our accomplishments at Army R&D, especially how we harvested the technology coming out of the Roswell crash, until thirty-five years after I left the army when I sat down to write my memoirs for an entirely different book. That was when I reviewed my old journals, remembered some of the memos I'd written to General Trudeau, and understood that the story of what happened in the days after the Roswell crash was perhaps the most significant story of the past fifty years. So, believe it or not, this is the story of what happened in the days after Roswell and how a small group of military intelligence officers changed the course of human history.

CHAPTER 1

The Roswell Desert

THE NIGHT HUGS THE GROUND AND SWALLOWS YOU UP AS YOU drive out of Albuquerque and into the desert. As you head east along 40 and then south along 285 to Roswell, there's only you and the tiny universe ahead of you defined by your headlights. On either side, beyond the circle of light, there is only scrub and sand. The rest is all darkness that closes in behind you, flooding where you've been under a giant ocean of black, and pushes you forward along the few hundred feet of road directly ahead.

The sky is different out there, different from any sky you've ever seen before. The black is so clear it looks like the stars shining through it are tiny windows from the beginning of time, millions of them, going on forever. On a hot summer night you can sometimes see flashes of heat lightning explode in the distance. Somewhere it is light for an instant, then the darkness returns. But summer is the rainy season in the New Mexico desert, and thunderstorms assemble over you out of nowhere, pound the earth with rain and lightning, pummel the darkness with crashes of thunder, shake the ground until you feel the earth is breaking apart, and then disappear. The ranchers out there will tell you that the local storms can go on all night, bouncing off the arroyos like pinballs in play until they expend themselves over the horizon. That's what it was like fifty years ago on a night much like this. Although I wasn't there that night, I've heard many different versions. Many of them go like this:

Base radar at the army's 509th airfield outside the town of Roswell had been tracking strange blips all night on July 1, 1947. So had radar at nearby White Sands, the army's guided-missile base where test launches of German V2 rockets had been taking place since the end of the war, and at the nuclear-testing facility at Alamogordo. The blips would appear at one corner of the screen and dart across at seemingly impossible speeds for aircraft, only to disappear off another corner. Then they'd start up again. No earthly craft could have maneuvered at such speeds and changed direction so sharply. It was a signature no one could identify. Whether it was the same aircraft, more than one, or simply an anomaly from the violent lightning and thunderstorms was anybody's guess. So after the operators verified the calibrations of the radar equipment, they broke down the units to run diagnostic checks on the circuitry of the screen-imaging devices to make sure their radar panels were operating properly. Once they'd satisfied themselves that they couldn't report any equipment malfunction, the controllers were forced to assume that the screen images were displays of something that was truly out there. They confirmed the sightings with radar controllers at White Sands, but found they could do little else but track the blips as they darted across the screen with every sweep of the silent beacon. The blips swarmed from position to position at will, operating with complete freedom across the entire sky over the army's most secret nuclear- and missile-testing sites.

Throughout that night and the following day, Army Intelligence stayed on high alert because something strange was going on out there. Surveillance flights over the desert reported no sightings of strange objects either in the sky or on the ground, but any sighting of unidentified aircraft on radar was sufficient evidence for base commanders to assume a hostile intent on the part of "something." And that was why the Army Intelligence in Washington ordered additional counterintelligence personnel to New Mexico, especially to the 509th, where the activity seemed to be centered.

The radar anomalies continued into the next night as Dan Wilmot, owner of a hardware store in Roswell, set up chairs on his front porch after dinner to watch the streaks of lightning flash across the sky in the distance. Shortly before ten that evening, the lightning grew more intense and the ground shook under the explosions of thunder from a summer storm that pounded the chaparral off in the northwest of the city. Dan and his wife watched the spectacle from beneath the dry safety of their porch roof. It was as if each new bolt of lightning were a spear that rent the heavens themselves.

"Better than any Fourth of July fireworks," the Wilmots must have been remarking as they watched in awe as a bright oval object streaked over their house and headed off into the northwest, sinking below a rise just before the horizon where it was engulfed in darkness. The sky again became pitch black. By the time the next bolt of lightning shot off, the object was gone. A most unusual sight, Dan Wilmot thought, but it was gone from his sight and gone from his thoughts, at least until the end of the week.

Whatever it was that passed over the Wilmot house in Roswell also flew over Steve Robinson as he drove his milk truck along its route north of the city. Robinson tracked the object as it shot across the sky at speeds faster than any airplane he'd ever seen. It was a bright object, he noted, elliptical and solid rather than a sequence of lights like the military aircraft that flew in and out of the 509th airfield on the city's outskirts. It disappeared behind a rise off in the west toward Albuquerque, and Steve put it out of his mind as he pushed forward on his route.

To the civilians in Roswell, nothing was amiss. Summer thunderstorms were common, the reports of flying saucers in the newspapers and over the radio were simply circus sideshow amusements, and an object streaking across the sky that so attracted the Wilmots' attention could have been nothing more than the shooting star you make a wish on if you're lucky enough to see it before it disappears forever in a puff of flame. Soon it would be the July 4th weekend, and the Wilmots, Steve Robinson, and thousands of other local residents were looking forward to the unofficial start of the summer holiday. But at the 509th there was no celebrating.

The isolated incidents of unidentified radar blips at Roswell and White Sands continued to increase over the next couple of days until it looked like a steady stream of airspace violations. Now it was becoming more than serious. There was no denying that a traffic pattern of strange aircraft overflights was emerging in the skies over the New Mexico desert where, with impunity, these unidentifiable radar blips hovered above and then darted away from our most secret military installations. By the time the military's own aircraft scrambled, the intruders were gone. It was obvious to the base commanders that they were under a heavy surveillance from a presence they could only assume was hostile. At first, nobody gave much thought to the possibility of extraterrestrials or flying saucers, even though they'd been in the news for the past few weeks that spring. Army officers at the 509th and White Sands thought it was the Russians spying on the military's first nuclear bomber base and its guided-missile launching site.

By now Army Counterintelligence, this highly secret command sector which in 1947 operated almost as much in the civilian sector as it did in the military, had spun up to its highest alert and ordered a full deployment of its most experienced crack World War II operatives out to Roswell. CIC personnel had begun to arrive from Washington when the first reports of strange radar blips were filed through intelligence channels and kept coming as the reports continued to pile up with increasing urgency over the next forty-eight hours. Officers and enlisted men alike disembarked from the transport planes and changed into civilian clothes for the investigation into enemy activities on the area. They joined up with base intelligence officers like Maj. Jesse Marcel and Steve Arnold, a counterintelligence noncom who'd served at the Roswell base during World War II when the first nuclear bombing mission against Hiroshima was launched from there in August 1945, just about two years earlier.

On the evening of July 4, 1947 (though the dates may differ depending on who is telling the story), while the rest of the country was celebrating Independence Day and looking with great optimism at the costly peace that the sacrifice of its soldiers had brought, radar operators at sites around Roswell noticed that the strange objects were turning up again and looked almost as if they were changing their shapes on the screen. They were pulsating—it was the only way you could describe it—glowing more intensely and then dimly as tremendous thunderstorms broke out over the desert. Steve Arnold, posted to the Roswell airfield control tower that evening, had never seen a blip behave like that as it darted across the screen between sweeps at speeds over a thousand miles an hour. All the while it was pulsating, throbbing almost, until, while the skies over the base exploded in a biblical display of thunder and lightning, it arced to the lower left-hand quadrant of the screen, seemed to disappear for a moment, then exploded in a brilliant white fluorescence and evaporated right before his very eyes.

The screen was clear. The blips were gone. And as controllers looked around at each other and at the CIC officers in the room, the same thought arose in all their minds: An object, whatever it was, had crashed. The military response was put into motion within seconds: This was a national security issue—jump on that thing in the desert and bring it back before anyone else could find it.

Even before the radar officer called the 509th base commander, Col. William Blanchard, reporting that radar indicated the crash of an unidentified aircraft to the north and west of Roswell, the CIC dispatch team had already mobilized to deploy an immediate-response crash-and-retrieval team to locate and secure the crash site. They believed this was an enemy aircraft that had slipped through our radar defense system either from South America or over the Canadian border and had taken photos of top-secret military installations. They also wanted to keep civilians away just in case, they said, there was any radiation from the craft's propulsion system, which allowed it to make hairpin turns at three thousand miles an hour. Nobody knew how this thing was powered, and nobody knew whether any personnel had ejected from the aircraft and were wandering around the desert. "Bull" Blanchard green-lighted the retrieval mission to get out there as soon as possible, taking with them all the night-patrol equipment they could scare up, all the two-and-a-half-ton trucks that they could roll, and the base's "low-boy" flatbed wreckers to bring the aircraft back. If it *was* a crash, they wanted to get it under wraps in a hangar before any civilian authorities could get their hands on it and blab to the newspapers.

But the air controllers at the 509th weren't the only ones who thought they saw an aircraft go down. On the outskirts of the city, ranchers, families camping in the desert, and residents saw an aircraft that exploded in a bright light in between flashes of lightning and plummeted to earth in the direction of Corona, the neighboring town to the north of Roswell. Chavez County sheriff George Wilcox started receiving calls in his office shortly after midnight on the morning of the fifth that an airplane had crashed out in the desert, and he notified the Roswell Fire Department that he would dispatch them as soon as he had an approximate location. No sense pulling fire apparatus out of the station house to chase something through the desert unless they knew where it was. Besides, Wilcox didn't like rolling the trucks out of town just in case there was a fire in the city that needed all the apparatus they could throw at it, especially the pumpers.

However, finding the crash site didn't take long. A group of Indian artifact hunters camping in the scrub brush north of Roswell had also seen the pulsating light overhead, heard a burning hiss and the strange, ground-shaking "thunk" of a crash nearby in the distance, and followed the sound to a group of low hills just over a rise. Before they even inspected the smoking wreckage, they radioed the crash-site location into Sheriff Wilcox's office, which dispatched the fire department to a spot about thirty-seven miles north and west of the city.

"I'm already on my way," he told the radio operator at the firehouse, who also called the city police for an escort.

And by about four-thirty that morning, a single pumper and police car were bouncing through the desert taking Pine Lodge Road west to where Sheriff Wilcox had directed them. Neither the sheriff nor the fire department knew that a military retrieval team was also on its way to the site with orders to secure the location and, by any means necessary, prevent the unauthorized dissemination of any information about the crash.

It was still dark when, from another direction, Steve Arnold, riding shotgun in one of the staff cars in the convoy of recovery vehicles from the 509th, reached the crash site first. Even before their trucks rolled into position, an MP lieutenant from the first jeep posted a picket of sentries, and an engineer ordered his unit to string a series of floodlights around the area. Then Arnold's car pulled up, and he got his own first glimpse of the wreckage. But it wasn't really wreckage at all—not in the way he'd seen plane crashes during the war. From what he could make out through the purple darkness, the dark-skinned craft seemed mostly intact and had lost no large pieces. Sure, there were bits and pieces of debris all over the area, but the aircraft itself hadn't broken apart on impact the way a normal airplane would. And the whole scene was still shrouded in darkness.

Then, the staff cars and jeeps that had accompanied the trucks lined up head-on to the crash and threw their headlights against the arroyo to supplement the floodlights that were still being strung by the engineers. In the sudden intersecting beams of headlights, Arnold could see that, indeed, the soft-cornered delta-shaped eggshell type of craft was essentially in one piece, even though it had embedded its nose hard into the embankment of the arroyo with its tail high in the air. Heat was still rising off the debris even though, according to the base radar at the 509th, the crash probably took place before midnight on the 4th. Then Arnold heard the brief sizzle of a battery charging up and the hum of a gasoline generator. That's when the string of lights came up, and the whole site suddenly looked like a baseball field before a big night game.

In the stark light of the military searchlights, Arnold saw the entire landscape of the crash. He thought it looked more like a crash landing because the craft was intact except for a split seam running lengthwise along the side and the steep forty-five-plus-degree angle of the craft's incline. He assumed it was a craft, even though it was like no airplane he'd ever seen. It was small, but it looked more like the flying wing shape of an old Curtis than an ellipse or a saucer. And it had two tail fins on the top sides of the delta's feet that pointed up and out. He angled himself as close to the split seam of the craft as he could get without stepping in front of the workers in hazardous-material suits who were checking the site for radiation, and that was when he saw them in the shadow. Little dark gray figures—maybe four, four and a half feet in length—sprawled across the ground.

"Are those *people?*" Arnold heard someone say as medics rushed up with stretchers to the knifelike laceration along the side of the craft through which the bodies had either crawled or tumbled.

Arnold looked around the perimeter of light and saw another figure, motionless but menacing nevertheless, and another leaning against a small rise in the desert sand. There was a fifth figure near the opening of the craft. As radiation technicians gave the all-clear and medics ran to the bodies with stretchers, Arnold sneaked a look through the rip in the aircraft and stared out through the top. Jehosaphat! It looked like the sun was already up.

Just to make sure, Steve Arnold looked around the outside again and, sure enough, it was still too dark to call it daylight. But through the top of the craft, as if he were looking through a lens, Arnold could see an eerie stream of light, not daylight or lamplight, but light nevertheless. He'd never seen anything like that before and thought that maybe this was a weapon the Russians or somebody else had developed.

The scene at the crash site was a microcosm of chaos. Technicians with specific tasks, such as medics, hazardous-material sweepers, signalmen and radio operators, and sentries were carrying out their jobs as methodically and unthinkingly as if they were the Emperor Ming's brain-washed furnace-stoking zombies from the Flash Gordon serials. But everyone else, including the officers, were simply awestruck. They'd never seen anything like this before, and they stood there, overpowered, it seemed, by simply a general sense of amazement that would not let them out of its grip.

"Hey, this one's alive," Arnold heard, and turned around to see one of the little figures struggling on the ground. With the rest of the medics, he ran over to it and watched as it shuddered and made a crying sound that echoed not in the air but in his brain. He heard nothing through his ears, but felt an overwhelming sense of sadness as the little figure convulsed on the ground, its oversized egg-shaped skull flipping from side to side as if it was trying to gasp for something to breathe. That's when he heard the sentry shout, "Hey, you!" and turned back to the shallow rise opposite the arroyo.

"Halt!" the sentry screamed at the small figure that had gotten up and was trying desperately to climb over the hill.

"Halt!" the sentry yelled again and brought his M1 to bear. Other soldiers ran toward the hill as the figure slipped in the sand, started to slide down, caught his footing, and climbed again. The sound of soldiers locking and loading rounds in their chambers carried loud across the desert through the predawn darkness.

"No!" one of the officers shouted. Arnold couldn't see which one, but it was too late.

There was a rolling volley of shots from the nervous soldiers, and as the small figure tried to stand, he was flung over like a rag doll and then down the hill by the rounds that tore into him. He lay motionless on the sand as the first three soldiers to reach him stood over the body, chambered new rounds, and pointed their weapons at his chest.

"Fuck," the officer spit again. "Arnold." Steve Arnold snapped to attention. "You and your men get out there and stop those civilians from crossing this perimeter." He motioned to the small convoy of emergency vehicles approaching them from the east. He knew they had to be police or county sheriff. Then he called out, "Medics."

Arnold jumped to at once, and by the time the medics were loading the little creature on a stretcher, he was already setting up a perimeter of CIC personnel and sentries to block the site from the flashing lights and churning sand far in the distance to the south of them. He heard the officer order the medics to load the bodies on stretchers, pack them in the back of whatever two-and-a-half-ton GMC he could pull off the line, and drive them back to the base immediately.

"Sergeant," the officer called out again. "I want your men to load up everything that can be loaded on these deuce-and-a-halfs and sway that damn . . . whatever it is"—he was pointing to the delta-shaped object—"on this low-boy and get it out of here. The rest of you," he called out. "I want this place spotless. Nothing ever happened here, you understand? Just a nothing piece of scrub brush like the rest of this desert."

As the soldiers formed an arm-in-arm "search-and-rescue" grid, some on their hands and knees, to clean the area of any pieces of debris, devices, or chunks of wreckage, the huge retrieval crane that had been deployed from the air base hoisted the surprisingly light flying object out of its impact crater in the arroyo and swayed it above the long flatbed Ford that accompanied the convoy of army trucks. A small squad of MPs were deployed to face the civilian convoy of emergency vehicles quickly approaching the site. They fixed bayonets and lowered their M1 barrels at the whirlwind of sand directly in front of them.

On the other side of the skirmish line, Roswell firefighter Dan Dwyer, the radioman riding shotgun on the red Ward LaFrance pumper the company rolled that night along with the tanker, could see very little at first except for an oasis of white light in the center of darkness. His small convoy had been running lights but no sirens as they pulled out of the firehouse in the center of Roswell, rendezvoused with the police car north of town, and headed out to the site to rescue what he had been told was a downed aircraft. As he approached the brightly lit area of floodlights off in the distance—it looked more like a small traveling amusement park than a crash site—he could already see the soldiers in a rough circle around an object that was swinging from the arm of a crane. As the LaFrance got closer, Dwyer could just make the strange deltoid shape of the thing as it hung, very precariously, from the arm, almost dropping once or twice under the very inexperienced control of the equipment operator. Even at this distance, the sound of shouting and cursing was carrying across the sand as the crane was raised, then lowered, then raised as the object finally sat over the Ford flatbed trailer.

The police unit ahead of the fire truck suddenly shot out toward the brightly lit area as soon as the driver saw the activity, and immediately the area was obscured from Dwyer's vision by clouds of sand that diffused the light. All he could see through the thicket of sand were the reflections of his own flashing lights. When the sand cleared, they were almost on top of the site, swinging off to one side to avoid the army trucks that had already started back down the road toward them. Dwyer looked over his shoulder to see if any more military vehicles were headed his way, but all he saw were the first pink lines of sunlight over the horizon. It was almost morning.

By the time Dwyer's field truck pulled around to the area the soldiers had pointed out, whatever it was that had crashed was sitting on the flatbed, still clamped to the hovering crane. Three or four soldiers were working on the coupling and securing the object to the truck with chains and cable. But for something that had dropped out of the sky in a fireball, which was how the police described it, Dwyer noted that the object looked almost unscathed. He couldn't see any cracks in the object's skin and there were no pieces that had broken off. Then the soldiers dropped an olive tarp over the flatbed and the object was completely camouflaged. An army captain walked over to one of the police units parked directly in front of the fire truck. And behind the officer stood a line of bayonet-wielding soldiers sporting MP armbands.

"You guys can head on back," Dwyer heard the captain tell one of the Roswell police officers on the scene. "We've got the area secured."

"What about injuries?" the police officer asked, maybe thinking more about the incident report he had to fill out than about what to do with any casualties.

"No injuries. We have everything under control," the captain said.

But even as the military was waving off the civilian convoy, Dwyer could see small bodies being lifted on stretchers from the ground into army transport trucks. A couple of them were already in body bags, but one, not bagged, was strapped directly onto the stretcher. The police officer saw it, too. This one, Dwyer could tell, was moving around and seemed to be alive. He had to get closer.

"What about them?" he asked.

"Hey, get those things loaded," the captain shouted at the enlisted men loading the stretchers into the truck. "You didn't see anything here tonight, Officer," he told the driver of the police unit. "Nothing at all."

"But, I gotta . . ."

The captain cut him off. "Later today, I'm sure, there'll be someone from the base out to talk to the shift; meanwhile, let this one alone. Strictly military business."

By this time Dwyer thought he recognized people he knew from the army airfield. He thought he could see the base intelligence officer, Jesse Marcel, who lived off the base in Roswell, and other personnel who came into town on a regular basis. He saw debris from whatever had crashed still lying all over the ground as the flatbed truck pulled out, passed the fire apparatus, and rumbled off through the sand back on the road toward the base.

Dwyer took off his fire helmet, climbed down from the truck, and worked his way through the shadows around the flank of the line of MPs. There was so much confusion at the site Dwyer knew no one would notice if he looked around. He walked around in back of the truck, across the perimeter, and from the other side of the military transport truck walked up to the stretcher. He looked directly down into the eyes of the creature strapped onto the stretcher and just stared.

It was no bigger than a child, he thought. But it wasn't a child. No child had such an oversized balloon-shaped head. It didn't even look human, although it had humanlike features. It's eyes were large and dark, set apart from each other on a downward slope. It's nose and mouth were especially tiny, almost like slits. And its ears were not much more than indentations along the sides of its huge head. In the glare of the floodlight, Dwyer could see that the creature was a grayish brown and completely hairless, but it looked directly at him as if it were a helpless animal in a trap. It didn't make a sound, but somehow Dwyer understood that the creature understood it was dying. He could gape in astonishment at the thing, but it was quickly loaded onto the truck by a couple of soldiers in helmets who asked him what he was doing. Dwyer knew this was bigger than anything he ever wanted to see and got out of there right away, losing himself amidst a group of personnel working around a pile of debris.

The whole site was scattered with articles that Dwyer assumed had fallen out of the craft when it hit. He could see the indentation in the arroyo where it looked like the object embedded itself and followed with his eyes the pattern of debris stretching out from the small crater into the darkness beyond the floodlights. The soldiers were crawling all over on their hands and knees with scraping devices and carrying sacks or walking in straight lines waving metal detectors in front of them. They were sweeping the area clean, it seemed to him, so that any curiosity seekers who floated out here during the day would find nothing to reveal the identity of what had been here. Dwyer reached down to pick up a patch of a dull gray metallic clothlike material that seemed to shine up at him from the sand. He stuffed it into his fist and rolled it into a ball. Then he released it and the metallic fabric snapped back into shape without any creases or folds. He thought no one was looking at him, so he stuffed it into the pocket of his fire jacket to bring back to the firehouse.

He would later show it to his young daughter, who forty-five years later and long after the piece of metallic fabric itself had disappeared into history, would describe it on television documentaries to millions of people. But that night in July 1947, if Dwyer thought he was invisible, he was wrong.

"Hey you," a sergeant wearing an MP armband bawled. "What the hell are you doing out here?"

"I responded with the fire company," Dwyer said as innocently as possible.

"Well, you get your civilian ass back on that truck and get it the hell out of here," he ordered. "You take anything with you?"

"Not me, Sergeant," Dwyer said.

Then the MP grabbed him as if he were under arrest and hustled him off to a major, who was shouting orders near the generator that was powering the string of floodlights. He recognized him as Roswell resident Jesse Marcel.

"Caught this fireman wandering around in the debris, sir," the sergeant reported.

Marcel obviously recognized Dwyer, although the two weren't friends, and gave him what the fireman only remembered as an agonized look. "You got to get out of here," he said. "And never tell anyone where you were or what you saw."

Dwyer nodded.

"I mean it, this is top security here, the kind of thing that could get you put away," Marcel continued. "Whatever this is, don't talk about it, don't say anything until somebody tells you what to say. Now get your truck out of here before someone else sees you and tries to lock the whole bunch of you up. Move!" He faced the helmeted MP. "Sergeant, get him back on that fire truck and move it out."

Dwyer didn't need any more invitations. He let the sergeant hustle him along, put him back on the truck, and told his driver to bring it back to the station. The MP sergeant came up to the driver's-side window and looked up at the fireman behind the wheel.

"You've been ordered to evacuate this site," the MP told the driver. "At once!"

The Roswell police unit had already made a U-turn on the sand and was motioning for the truck to back up. The driver dropped the truck into reverse, gently fed it gas as its wheels dug into the sand, made his U-turn, and headed back for the firehouse in Roswell. The Ford flatbed had already passed through the sleeping town in the moments between darkness and light, the sound of its engines causing no alarm or stir, the sight of a large tarpaulin-covered object on the back of an army vehicle rolling along the main street of Roswell against the purple-gray sky raising nobody's eyebrows because it was nothing out of the ordinary. But later, by the time Dwyer backed his field truck into the station house, the sun was already up and the first of the GMC transport trucks was just reaching the main gate at the 509th.

Plumbing subcontractor Roy Danzer, who had worked through the night at the base fitting pipe, knew something was up from the way the trucks tore out of the compound through the darkness. He had just walked out of the base hospital to grab a cigarette before going back to work. That's when he heard the commotion over at the main gate. Danzer had cut his hand a few days earlier cutting pipe, and the infirmary nurse wanted to keep checking the stitches to make sure no infection was setting in. So Danzer took the opportunity to get away from the job for a few minutes while the nurse looked over her work and changed his bandage. Then, on his way back to the job, he would grab a cup of coffee and take an unscheduled cigarette break. But this morning, things would be very different.

The commotion he heard by the main gate had now turned into a swirling throng of soldiers and base workers shoved aside by what looked like a squad of MPs using their bodies as a wedge to force a pathway through the crowd. There didn't even seem to be an officer giving orders, just a crowd of soldiers. Strange. Then the throng headed right for the base hospital, right for the main entrance, right for the very spot where Roy was standing.

Nobody moved him out of the way or told him to vacate the area. In fact, no one even spoke to him. Roy just looked down as the line of soldiers passed him, and there it was, strapped tightly to a stretcher that two bearers were carrying into the base hospital right through the main door. Roy looked at it; it looked at Roy, and as their eyes met Roy knew in an instant that he was not looking down at a human being. It was a creature from somewhere else. The pleading look on its face, occupying only a small frontal portion of its huge watermelon-sized skull, and the emotion of pain and suffering that played itself behind Roy Danzer's eyes and across his brain while he stared down at the figure told Roy it was in its final moments of life. It didn't speak. It could barely move. But Roy actually saw, or believed he saw, an expression cross over its little circle of a face. And then the creature was gone, carried into the hospital by the stretcher bearers, who shot him an ugly glare as they passed. Roy took another drag on the cigarette butt still in his hand.

"What the hell was that?" he asked no one in particular. Then he felt like he'd been hit by the front four of the Notre Dame football team.

His head snapped back against the top of his spine as he went flying forward into the arms of a couple of MPs, who slammed him against an iron gate and kept him there until an officer—he thought it was a captain—walked up and stuck his finger directly into Danzer's face.

"Just who are you, mister?" the captain bellowed into Danzer's ear. Even before Danzer could answer, two other officers walked up and began demanding what authorization Danzer had to be on the base.

These guys weren't kidding, Danzer thought to himself; they looked ugly and were working themselves up into a serious lather. For a few tense minutes, Roy Danzer thought he would never see his family again; he was that scared. But then a major approached and broke into the shouting.

"I know this guy," the major said. "He works here with the other civilian contractors. He's OK."

"Sir," the captain sputtered, but the major—Danzer didn't know his name—took the captain by the arm right out of earshot. Danzer could see them talking and watched as the red-faced captain gradually calmed down. Then the two returned to where the MPs were holding Danzer against the wall.

"You saw nothing, you understand?" the captain said to Danzer, who just nodded. "You're not to tell anybody about this, not your family, not your friends—nobody. You got that?"

"Yes, sir," Danzer said. He was truly afraid now.

"We'll know if you talk; we'll know who you talk to and all of you will simply disappear."

"Captain," the major broke in.

"Sir, this guy has no business here and if he talks I can't guarantee anything." The captain complained as if he were trying to cover his ass to a superior who didn't know as much as he did.

"So forget everything you saw," the major said directly to Danzer. "And hightail it out of here before someone else sees you and wants to make sure you stay silent."

"Yes, SIR," Danzer just about shouted as he extricated himself from the grip of the MPs on either side of him and broke for his pickup truck on the other side of the base. He didn't even look back to see the team of soldiers carrying the body bags of the remaining creatures into the hospital where, before there were any other briefings, the creatures were prepared for autopsy like bagged game waiting to be dressed.

The rest of the story about that week has become the subject of history. First, 509th base commander Bull Blanchard authorized the release of the "flying saucer" story that was picked up by news services and carried around the country. Then General Roger Ramey at 8th Army Air Force headquarters in Texas ordered Maj. Jesse Marcel to go back before the press and retract the flying saucer story. This time, Marcel was ordered to say that he'd made a mistake and realized the debris had actually come from a weather balloon. Swallowing a story he himself never believed, Jesse Marcel posed with some faked debris from an actual balloon and confessed to an error he never could have made, even on a bad day. It was a confession that would haunt him the rest of his life until, decades later and shortly before he died, he would retract his public story and restate that he had actually retrieved an alien spacecraft that night in the Roswell desert.

Meanwhile, in the days and weeks after the crash and retrieval, Army Intelligence and CIC personnel fanned out through Roswell and neighboring communities to suppress whatever information they could. With ill-advised threats of violence, actual physical intimidation, and, according to some of the rumors, at least one homicide, army officers bludgeoned the community into silence. Mac Brazel, one of the civilians near whose property the crash took place and one of the visitors to the site, was allegedly bribed and threatened. He suddenly became silent about what he had seen in the desert even after he had told friends and newspeople that he'd retrieved pieces from a downed spacecraft. Officers from the Chavez County Sheriff's Department and other law-enforcement agencies were forced to comply with the army edict that the incident outside of Roswell was a matter of national security and was not to be discussed. "It never happened," the army decreed, and civilian authorities willingly complied. Even the local Roswell radio station news correspondents, John McBoyle from KSWS and Walt Whitmore Sr. from KGFL, who'd conducted interviews with witnesses to the debris field, were forced to submit to the official line that the army imposed and never broadcast their reports.

For some of the civilians who claimed to have experienced intimidation from the army officers who flooded into Roswell after the crash, the trauma remained with them for the rest of their lives. One was Dan Dwyer's daughter, who was a young child in July 1947, and who endured the sight of a huge, helmeted army officer, his expression obscured by sunglasses, looming over her in her mother's kitchen and telling her that if she didn't forget what she had been told by her father, she and the rest of her family would simply disappear in the desert. Sally who had played with the metallic fabric her father had brought back to the firehouse that morning and had heard his description of the little people carried away on stretchers, quaked in terror as the officer finally got her to admit that she had seen nothing, heard nothing, and handled nothing. "It never happened," he hissed at her. "And there's nothing you will ever say about it for the rest of your life because we will be there and we will know it," he repeated over and over again, slapping a police baton into his palm with a loud crack at every word. Even today, tears form at the corners of her eyes as she describes the scene and remembers the expression of her mother, who had been told to leave the kitchen while the officer spoke to Sally. It's tough for a kid to see her parents so terrorized into silence that they will deny the truth before their eyes.

Roy Danzer's daughter, too, was frightened at the sight of her father when he came home from the base that morning on July 5, 1947. He wouldn't talk about what had gone on there, of course, even though the town was abuzz with rumors that creatures from outer space had invaded Roswell. Wasn't it true that all the children in town knew about it and there'd been stories about flying saucers in newspapers for weeks? It was even on the radio. But Roy Danzer wouldn't say a word in front of his daughter. She heard her parents talking through the closed door of her bedroom at night and caught snippets of conversations about little creatures and "they'll kill us all." But she buried these in a part of her memory she never visited until her father, shortly before his death, told her what really happened at the base that day in July when the convoy arrived out of the desert.

Steve Arnold stayed in Roswell, finishing out his official reenlistment with the army and, without his direct knowledge, remaining a part of my own team right through the 1960s. Some say he works for the government still, carrying out a job that fell to him right out of the New Mexico skies, pumping out disinformation from the army or the CIA or whomever, perpetuating a camouflage story that, fifty years later, has taken on a life of its own and goes forward, like a tale out of a Dickens novel, simply on inertia. You can see Steve today walking around Roswell, visiting old friends from his army days, giving interviews on television to the news crews that periodically pay visits to the folks at Roswell who want to talk about those days in the summer of 1947.

As for the debris retrieved out of the desert that July, it had another destiny. Shipped to Fort Bliss, Texas, headquarters of the 8th Army Air Force, and summarily analyzed for what it was and what it might contain, all of it was transferred to the control of the military. As quickly as it arrived, some of the debris was flown to Ohio, where it was put under lock and key at Wright Airfield—later Wright-Patterson. The rest of it was loaded onto trucks and sent up to a rest stop at Fort Riley in Kansas. The 509th returned to its daily routine, Jesse Marcel went back to work as if he'd never held the wreckage from the strange craft in his own hands, and the contractors returned to their work on the pipes and doors and walls at the base just as if nothing had ever arrived there from the desert.

By the time the first week of July 1947 was over, the crash outside of Roswell might as well have never taken place. Like the night that engulfs you as you drive through the expanse of desert and chaparral toward Roswell, so the night of silence engulfed the story of Roswell itself for over thirty years.

These are the stories as I heard them, as people later told them to me. I wasn't there at Roswell that night. I didn't see these events for myself. I only heard them years later when the task fell to me to make something out of all this. But the debris from the crash of the object that was either caused by lightning or by our targeting radar, some say, and fell out of the sky that night was on its way to a collision course with my life. Our paths would cross officially at the Pentagon in the 1960s even though, for a very brief moment in 1947, when I was a young major at Fort Riley, fresh from the glory of victory in Europe, I would see something that I would tuck away in my memory and hope against hope I would never see again for the rest of my life.

CHAPTER 2

Convoy to Fort Riley

I CAN REMEMBER A TIME WHEN I WAS SO YOUNG AND FEELING SO invincible that there was nothing in the world I was afraid of. I had faced down fear in North Africa. With General Patton's army I stood toe-to-toe against the artillery in Rommel's Panzer Divisions and gave them better than they dished out to us. We were an army of young men from a country that hadn't started the war but found itself right in the midst of it before we even got out of church the Sunday Pearl Harbor was attacked. The next thing we knew Hitler declared war on us and we were fighting in Europe. But by 1942, we drove the Germans right out of Africa and jumped across the sea to Sicily. Then, while Mussolini was still reeling from the punches, we invaded Italy and fought our way up the peninsula until we came to Rome. We were the first invading army to conquer Rome since the Middle Ages, and obviously the first invading army from the New World to ever occupy Rome.

But there we were by early 1944, sitting in Rome after Mussolini fled and the German front collapsing all around us. And as a too-young captain in Army Intelligence, I was ordered to oversee the formation of a civilian government under Allied military rule in the magical city of my ancestors that I'd only read about in history books. Pope Pius himself offered me an audience to discuss our plans for the city government. You can't even dream this stuff up. It has to happen to you in real life, and then you pinch yourself to make sure you don't wake up in your own bed outside of Pittsburgh on a winter morning.

I stayed in Rome for three years from the months before the landing at Normandy in 1944, when the German front lines were still only a few miles south of Rome and our boys were slugging their way up the slopes of Monte Casino, to early 1947, when I was shipped back home and my wife and I threw everything we had into the trunk of a used Chevy convertible and drove across the farmland state routes of peacetime America from Pennsylvania to Kansas. I'd been away five years. But now I was home! Driving top-down across Missouri to an assignment that was considered a plum for any young officer on his way up the army ladder: Military Intelligence School, only one step away from Strategic Intelligence, the army's version of the Ivy League; I was moving up in the world. And what was I? Just a draftee out of Pennsylvania who was chosen for Officer Candidate School, and now fresh from a wartime intelligence command in Allied-occupied Europe and ready to begin my new career in Army Intelligence.

Having been in Africa and Europe for so many years, I was anxious to see America again. By this time its people were not stooping under the weight of the depression nor in factories nor in uniform sweating out a desperate war across two oceans. This was an America exultant in victory, and you could see it as you drove through the small towns of southern Ohio and Illinois and then across the Mississippi. We didn't stop overnight to see St. Louis or even to linger on the Kansas side of the river. I was so excited to be a career officer that we didn't stop driving until we pulled straight into Fort Riley and set up an apartment in nearby Junction City, where we'd live while they got our house ready on the base.

For most of the next few weeks, my wife and I got used to living in America again on a peacetime army base. We had lived in Rome after the war while I was still trying to help pacify the city and fend off the Communist attempts to take over the government. It was as if we were still fighting a war because each day had brought renewed challenges from either the Communists or the organized-crime families who had tried to infiltrate their way back into the civilian government. My life was also in danger each day from the different cadres of terrorists in the city, each group with its own agenda. So in contrast to Italy, Fort Riley was like the beginning of a vacation.

And I was back in school again. This time, however, I was taking courses in career training. I knew how to be an intelligence officer and, in fact, had been trained by the British MI19, the premier wartime intelligence network in the world. My training had been so thorough that even though we were up against crack Soviet NKVD units operating within Rome, we were able to outthink them and actually destroy them. Prior to the war, the United States really didn't have a peacetime intelligence service, which is why they quickly formed the OSS when war broke out. But the Army Intelligence units and the OSS didn't operate together for most of the war because communication lines were faulty and we never really trusted the OSS agenda. Now with the war over and Army Intelligence having come into its own, I was part of a whole new cadre of career intelligence officers who would keep watch on Soviet activities. The Soviets had become our new old enemies.

In intelligence school during those first months we reviewed not only the rudiments of good intelligence gathering—interrogation of enemy prisoners, analysis of raw intelligence data, and the like—but we learned the basics of administration and how to run a wartime intelligence unit called the aggressor force. None of us realized during those early days how quickly our newly acquired skills would be tested nor where our enemies would choose to fight. But those were confident days as the weather turned warmer on the plains and the days grew long with the coming of summer.

Before the war broke out and when I was in high school back in California, Pennsylvania, my hometown, I was something of a bowler. It was a sport I wanted to get back to when the war ended, so when I got to Fort Riley, one of the first places I looked up was the bowling alley on the base, which had been built in one of the former stables. Fort Riley was a former cavalry base, the home of Custer's 7th Cavalry, and still had a polo field after the war. I started practicing my bowling again and was soon rolling enough strikes that the enlisted men who bowled there began talking to me about my game. Before too many months had passed, M.Sgt. Bill Brown—the men called him "Brownie"—stopped me when I was changing out of my bowling shoes and said he wanted to talk.

"Major, sir," he began, more than a little embarrassed to address an officer out of uniform and not on any official army business. He couldn't possibly have realized that I was a draftee just like him and had spent the first few months in the service taking orders from corporals in boot camp.

"Sergeant?" I asked.

"The men at the post want to start up a bowling league, sir, have teams to bowl against and maybe come up with a team to represent the base," he began. "So we've been watching you bowl on Saturdays."

"So what am I doing wrong?" I asked. I figured at first maybe this sergeant was going to give me a tip or two and wanted to establish some authority. OK, I'll take a tip from anybody. But that's not what he asked.

"No, sir. Nothing at all," he stammered. "I'm saying something different. We, the guys, were wondering if you've bowled before—do you think maybe you'd like to become part of the team?" He had gotten more confidence the more he framed his request.

"You want me for your team?" I asked. I was pretty surprised because officers weren't supposed to fraternize with enlisted men at that time. Things are very different now, but then, fifty years ago, it was a different world, even for much of the officer corps that started out as draftees and went through officer training.

"We know it's out of the ordinary, sir, but there are no rules against it." I gave him a very surprised look. "We checked," he said. This was obviously not a spur-of-the-moment question.

"You think I can hold up my end of things?" I asked. "It's been a long time since I've bowled against anybody."

"Sir, we've been watching. We think you'll really help us out. Besides," he continued, "we do need an officer on the team."

Whether out of modesty or because he didn't want to put me off, he had completely understated the nature of the bowling team. These guys had been champions in their own hometowns and, years later, you could have found them on *Bowling for Dollars.* There was no reason in the world I should have been on that team except that they wanted an officer because it would give them prestige.

I told him I'd get back to him on it because I wanted to check on the rules, if there were any, for myself. In fact officers and enlisted personnel were allowed to compete on the same athletic teams, and, in very short order, I joined the team, along with Dave Bender, John Miller, Brownie, and Sal Federico. We became quite a remarkable team, winning most of our matches, more than a few trophies, and had lots of exciting moments when we made the impossible splits and bowled our way all the way to the state finals. We ultimately won the Army Bowling Championships, and the trophy sits on my desk to this very day. Magically, the barrier between officer and enlisted man seemed to drop. And that's the real point of this story.

Through the months I spent on the team, I became friends with Bender, Miller, Federico, and Brown. We didn't socialize much, except for the bowling, but we also didn't stand on ceremony with each other, and I liked it that way. I found that a lot of the career intelligence officers also liked to see some of the barriers drop because sometimes men will speak with more honesty to you if you don't throw what's on your shoulders into their faces every time you talk to them. So I became friends with these guys, and that's what got me into the veterinary building on Sunday night, July 6, 1947.

I remember how hot it had been that whole weekend of July 4th celebrations and fireworks. These were the days before everybody had to have air-conditioning, so we just sweltered inside the offices at the base and swatted away the fat lazy flies that buzzed around looking for hot dog crumbs or landing on chunks of pickle relish. By Sunday, the celebrations were over, guys who'd had too much beer had been dragged off to their barracks by members of their company before the MPs got hold of them, and the base was settling down to the business of the week. Nobody seemed to take much notice of the five deuce-and-a-halfs and side-by-side low-boy trailers that had pulled into the base that afternoon full of cargo from Fort Bliss in Texas on their way to Air Materiel Command at Wright Field in Ohio. If you had looked at the cargo manifests the drivers were carrying, you'd have seen lists itemizing landing-gear-assembly struts for B29s, wingtank pods for vintage P51s, piston rings for radial aircraft engines, ten crates of Motorola walkie-talkies, and you wouldn't think anything of the shipment except for the fact that it was going the wrong way. These spare parts were usually shipped *from* Wright Field *to* bases like Fort Bliss rather than the other way around, but, of course, I wouldn't know that until years later when the real cargo on those trucks fell straight onto my desk as if it had dropped out of the sky.

It got quiet that evening right after dark, and I remember that it was very humid. Off in the distance you could see lightning, and I wondered if the storms were going to reach the base before morning. I was the post duty officer on that night—similar to the chief duty officer of the watch on a naval vessel—and hoped, even more fervently, that if a storm were on its way, it would wait until morning to break so that I might be spared walking through the mud from sentry post to sentry post in the midst of a summer downpour. I looked over the sentry duty roster for that night and saw that Brownie was standing a post over at one of the old veterinarian buildings near the center of the compound.

The post duty officer spends his night at the main base headquarters, where he watches the phones and is the human firewall between an emergency and a disaster. Not much to do unless there's a war on or a company of roustabouts decides to tear up a local bar. And by late night, the base settles into a pattern. The sentries walk their posts, the various administrative offices close down, and whoever is on night watch takes over the communications system—which in 1947 consisted primarily of telephone and telex cable. I had to walk a beat as well, checking the different buildings and sentry posts to make sure everyone was on duty. I also had to close down the social clubs. After I made my obligatory stops at the enlisted men's and officers' clubs, shutting down the bars and tossing, with all due respect to the senior officers, the drunks back to their quarters, I footed it over to the old veterinary building where Brown was standing watch. But when I got there, where he was supposed to be, I didn't see him. Something was wrong.

"Major Corso," a voice hissed out of the darkness. It had an edge of terror and excitement to it.

"What the hell are you doing in there, Brownie?" I began cussing out the figure that peeked out at me from behind the door. "Have you gone off your rocker?" He was supposed to be outside the building, not hiding in a doorway. It was a breach of duty.

"You don't understand, Major," he whispered again. "You have to see this."

"Better be good," I said as I walked over to where he was standing and waited for him outside the door. "Now you get out here where I can see you," I ordered.

Brown popped his head out from behind the door.

"You know what's in here?" he asked.

Whatever was going on, I didn't want to play any games. The post duty sheet for that night read that the veterinary building was off-limits to everyone. Not even the sentries were allowed inside because whatever had been loaded in had been classified as "No Access." What was Brown doing on the inside?

"Brownie, you know you're not supposed to be in there," I said. "Get out here and tell me what's going on."

He stepped out from inside the door, and even through the shadow I could see that his face was a dead pale, just as if he'd seen a ghost. "You won't believe this," he said. "I don't believe it and I just saw it."

"What are you talking about?" I asked.

"The guys who off-loaded those deuce-and-a-halfs," he said. "They told us they brought these boxes up from Fort Bliss from some accident out in New Mexico?"

"Yeah, so what?" I was getting impatient with this.

"Well, they told us it was all top secret but they looked inside anyway. Everybody down there did when they were loading the trucks. MPs were walking around with sidearms and even the officers were standing guard," Brown said. "But the guys who loaded the trucks said they looked inside the boxes and didn't believe what they saw. You got security clearance, Major. You can come in here."

In fact, I was the post duty officer and could go anywhere I wanted during the watch. So I walked inside the old veterinary building, the medical dispensary for the cavalry horses before the First World War, and saw where the cargo from the convoy had been stacked up. There was no one in the building except for Bill Brown and myself.

"What is all this stuff?" I asked.

"That's just it, Major, nobody knows," he said. "The drivers told us it came from a plane crash out in the desert somewhere around the 509th. But when they looked inside, it was nothing like anything they'd seen before. Nothing from this planet."

It was the silliest thing I'd ever heard, enlisted men's tall stories that floated from base to base getting more inflated every lap around the track. Maybe I wasn't the world's smartest guy, but I had enough engineering and intelligence schooling to pick my way around pieces of wreckage and come up with two plus two. We walked over to the tarpaulin-shrouded boxes, and I threw back the edge of the canvas.

"You're not supposed to be in here," I told Brownie. "You better go."

"I'll watch outside for you, Major."

I almost wanted to tell him that that's what he was supposed to be doing all along instead of snooping into classified material, but I did what I used to do best and kept my mouth shut. I waited while he took up his position at the door to the building before I dug any further into the boxes.

There were about thirty-odd wooden crates nailed shut and stacked together against the far wall the building. The light switches were the push type and I didn't know which switch tripped which circuit, so I used my flashlight and stumbled around until my eyes got used to the darkness and shadows. I didn't want to start pulling apart the nails, so I set the flashlight off to one side where it could throw light on the stack and then searched for a box that could open easily.

Then I found an oblong box off to one side with a wide seam under the top that looked like it had been already opened. It looked like either the strangest weapons crate you'd ever see or the smallest shipping crate for a coffin. Maybe this was the box that Brownie had seen. I brought the flashlight over and set it up high on the wall so it would throw as broad a beam as possible. Then I set to work on the crate.

The top was already loose. I was right—this one had just been opened. I jimmied the top back and forth, continuing to loosen the nails that had been pried up with a nail claw, until I felt them come out of the wood. Then I worked along the sides of the five-or-so-foot box until the top was loose all the way around. Not knowing which end of the box was the front, I picked up the top and slid it off to the edge. Then I lowered the flashlight, looked inside, and my stomach rolled right up into my throat and I almost became sick right then and there.

Whatever they'd crated this way, it *was* a coffin, but not like any coffin I'd seen before. The contents, enclosed in a thick glass container, were submerged in a thick light blue liquid, almost as heavy as a gelling solution of diesel fuel. But the object was floating, actually suspended, and not sitting on the bottom with a fluid over top, and it was soft and shiny as the underbelly of a fish. At first I thought it was a dead child they were shipping somewhere. But this was no child. It was a four-foot human-shaped figure with arms, bizarre-looking six-fingered hands—I didn't see a thumb—thin legs and feet, and an oversized incandescent lightbulb-shaped head that looked like it was floating over a balloon gondola for a chin. I know I must have cringed at first, but then I had the urge to pull off the top of the liquid container and touch the pale gray skin. But I couldn't tell whether it was skin because it also looked like a very thin one-piece head-to-toe fabric covering the creature's flesh.

Its eyeballs must have been rolled way back in its head because I couldn't see any pupils or iris or anything that resembled a human eye. But the eye sockets themselves were oversized and almond shaped and pointed down to its tiny nose, which didn't really protrude from the skull. It was more like the tiny nose of a baby that never grew as the child grew, and it was mostly nostril.

The creature's skull was overgrown to the point where all of its facial features—such as they were—were arranged absolutely frontally, occupying only a small circle on the lower part of the head. The protruding ears of a human were nonexistent, its cheeks had no definition, and there were no eyebrows or any indications of facial hair. The creature had only a tiny flat slit for a mouth and it was completely closed, resembling more of a crease or indentation between the nose and the bottom of the chinless skull than a fully functioning orifice. I would find out years later how it communicated, but at that moment in Kansas, I could only stand there in shock over the clearly nonhuman face suspended in front of me in a semiliquid preservative.

I could see no damage to the creature's body and no indication that it had been involved in any accident. There was no blood, its limbs seemed intact, and I could find no lacerations on the skin or through the gray fabric. I looked through the crate encasing the container of liquid for any paperwork or shipping invoice or anything that would describe the nature or origin of this thing. What I found was an intriguing Army Intelligence document describing the creature as an inhabitant of a craft that had crash-landed in Roswell, New Mexico, earlier that week and a routing manifest for this creature to the log-in officer at the Air Materiel Command at Wright Field and from him to the Walter Reed Army Hospital morgue's pathology section where, I supposed, the creature would be autopsied and stored. It was not a document I was meant to see, for sure, so I tucked it back in the envelope against the inside wall of the crate.

I allowed myself more time to look at the creature than I should have, I suppose, because that night I missed the time checks on the rest of my rounds and believed I'd have to come up with a pretty good explanation for the lateness of my other stops to verify the sentry assignments. But what I was looking at was worth any trouble I'd get into the next day. This thing was truly fascinating and at the same time utterly horrible. It challenged every conception I had, and I hoped against hope that I was looking at some form of atomic human mutation. I knew I couldn't ask anybody about it, and because I hoped I would never see its like again, I came up with explanation after explanation for its existence, despite what I'd read on the enclosed document: It was shipped here from Hiroshima, it was the result of a Nazi genetic experiment, it was a dead circus freak, it was anything but what I knew it said it was—what it had to be: an extraterrestrial.

I slid the top of the crate back over the creature, knocked the nails loosely into their original holes with the butt end of my flashlight, and put the tarp back in position. Then I left the building and hoped I could close the door forever on what I'd seen. Just forget it, I told myself. You weren't supposed to see it and maybe you can live your whole life without ever having to think about it. Maybe.

Once outside the building I rejoined Brownie at his post.

"You know you never saw this," I said. "And you tell no one."

"Saw what, Major?" Brownie said, and I walked back to the base general headquarters, the image of the creature suspended in that liquid fading away with each and every step I took. By the time I slid back behind the desk, it was all a dream. No, not a dream, a nightmare—but it was over and, I hoped, it would never come back.

CHAPTER 3

The Roswell Artifacts

THE NIGHTMARE OF THE CREATURE I SAW AT FORT RILEY NEVER faded from my memory, although I was able to bury it during my years as a guided-missile commander in Europe. And I never saw its body again the rest of my life except for the autopsy photos and the medical-examiner sketches that would catch up to me, along with the rest of what happened at Roswell, when I returned to Washington from Germany for assignment at the Pentagon in 1961. I can remember my first day back when I was waiting outside my boss's door for entry into the inner sanctum. And, boy, was I ever nervous.

The last time I remembered being that nervous in Washington, I was standing in the little anteroom outside the Oval Office in the White House waiting for President Eisenhower to get off the phone. I had a big request to make and I wanted to do it face-to-face, not go through any aides or assistants or wait for special assistant C. D. Jackson to show up to make everything OK. I was almost a regular in the Oval Office those days, back in the 1950s, dropping off National Security Council staff papers for the President, making reports, and sometimes waiting while he read them just in case he wanted me to relay a message. But this time was different. I needed to speak to him myself, alone. But Ike was taking a longer time than he usually took on this phone call, and I shifted around and sneaked a glance at the switchboard lights on Mrs. Lehrer's desk off to the side. Still on the phone, and you could see at the bottom of the switch panel where the calls were backing up.

I was asking President Eisenhower for a personal favor: to let me out of my fifth year on the White House National Security staff so I could pick up the command of my own antiaircraft guided-missile battalion being formed up in Red Canyon, New Mexico. Ike had once promised me a command of my own when I returned from Korea and was posted to the White House. And in 1957 the opportunity came up, a juicy assignment at a high-security base with the coveted green tabs and all the trappings: train and command an antiaircraft battalion to use the army's most secret new surface-to-air missile and then take it to Germany for some front-line target practice right where the Russians could see us. In case of World War III, the order of battle read, Soviet bombers will drop an inferno of high explosives on our positions first and the East German tanks will roll straight into our barracks. We stand and fight, torching off every missile we have so as to take out as many attacking aircraft as we have missiles, and get the hell out of there. I could almost taste the thrill in my mouth as I waited for Ike to get off the phone that day back in 1957.

Those were my memories this afternoon as I stood outside the back door of General Trudeau's office on the third floor of the outer ring of the Pentagon. It was 1961, four years after I left the White House and put on my uniform again to stand guard across the electronic no-man's-land of radar sweeps and photo sensors just a few kilometers west of the Iron Curtain. Ike had retired to his farm in Pennsylvania, and my new boss was General Arthur Trudeau, one of the last fighting generals from the Korean War. Trudeau became an instant hero in my book when I heard about how his men were pinned down on the cratered slopes of Pork Chop Hill, dug into shallow foxholes with enemy mortars dropping round them like rain. You couldn't order anyone up that hell of an incline to walk those boys back down; just too damn many explosions. So Trudeau pulled off his stars, clapped a sergeant's helmet over his head, and fought back up the hill himself, leading a company of volunteers, and then fought his way back down. That was how he did things, with his own hands, and now I'd be working directly for him in the Army R&D Division.

I was a lieutenant colonel when I came to the Pentagon in 1961, and all I brought with me were my bowling trophy from Fort Riley and a nameplate for my desk cut out of the fin of a Nike missile from Germany. My men made it for me and said it would bring me luck. After I got to the Pentagon—it was still a couple of days before my assignment actually began—I found out right away I'd need a lot of it. In fact, as I opened the door and let myself directly into the general's inner office, I found out how much luck I'd need that very day.

"So what's the big secret, General?" I asked my new boss. It was strange talking to a general this way, but we'd become friends while I was on Eisenhower's staff. "Why not the front door?"

"Because they're already watching you, Phil," he said, knowing exactly what kind of cold chill that would send through me. "And I'd just as soon have this conversation in private before you show up officially."

He walked me over to a set of file cabinets. "Things haven't changed that much around here since you went to Germany," he said. "We still know who our friends are and who we can trust."

I knew his code. The Cold War was at its height and there were enemies all around us: in government, within the intelligence services, and within the White House itself. Those of us in military intelligence who knew the truth about how much danger the country was in were very circumspect about what we said, even to each other, and where we said it. Looking back on it now from the safe distance of forty years, it's hard to believe that even as big eight-cylinder American cars rolled off the assembly lines and into suburban driveways and television antennas sprung up on roofs of brand-new houses in thousands of subdivisions around the country, we were in the midst of a treacherous war of nerves.

Deep inside our intelligence services and even within the

President's own cabinet were cadres of career government officers working—some knowingly, some not—for the Soviet Union by carrying out policies devised inside the KGB. Some of the position papers that came out of these offices made no sense otherwise. We also knew the CIA had been penetrated by KGB moles, just as we knew that some of our own policy makers were advocating ideas that would only weaken the United States and lead us down the paths that served the best interests of our enemies.

A handful of us knew the awful truth about Korea. We lost it not because we were beaten on the battlefield but because we were compromised from within. The Russian advisers fighting alongside the North Koreans were given our plans even before they reached those of us on MacArthur's staff. And when we threw our best technology into the field and into the air, the Soviets had already formulated plans to capture it and take it back to Russia. When the time came to talk peace at Panmunjom and negotiate a POW exchange, I knew where those Americans were, ten miles north of the border, who wouldn't be coming home. And there were people right inside our own government who let them stay there, in prison camps, where some of them might be alive to this very day.

So General Trudeau gave me his very grim smile and said, as he walked me toward the locked dark olive military file cabinet on the wall of his private office, "I need you to cover my back, Colonel. I need you to watch because what I'm going to do, I can't cover it myself."

Whatever Trudeau was planning, I knew he'd tell me in his own time. And he'd tell me only what he thought I needed to know when I needed it. For the immediate present, I was to be his special assistant in R&D, one of the most sensitive divisions in the whole Pentagon bureaucracy because that was where the most classified plans of the scientists and weapons designers were translated into the reality of defense contracts. R&D was the interface between the gleam in someone's eye and a piece of hardware prototype rolling out of a factory to show its potential for the army brass. Only it was my job to keep it a secret while it was developed.

"But there's something else I want you to do for me,

Phil," General Trudeau continued as he put his hand on top of the cabinet. "I'm going to have this cabinet moved downstairs to your office."

The general had put me in an office on the second floor of the outer ring directly under him. That way, as I would soon find out, whenever he needed me in a hurry I could get upstairs and through the back door before anybody even knew where I was.

"This has some special files, war materiel you've never seen before, that I want to put under your Foreign Technology responsibilities," he continued.

My specific assignment was to the Research & Development Division's Foreign Technology desk, what I thought would be a pretty dry post because it mainly required me to keep up on the kinds of weapons and research our allies were doing. Read the intelligence reports, review films of weapons tests, debrief scientists and the research people at universities on what their colleagues overseas were doing, and write up proposals for weapons the army might need. It was important and it had its share of cloak and dagger, but after what I'd been through in Rome chasing down the Gestapo and SS officers the Nazis left behind and the Soviet NKVD units masquerading themselves as Italian Communist partisans, it seemed like a great opportunity to help General Trudeau keep some of the army's ideas out of the hands of the other military services. But then I didn't know what was inside that file cabinet.

The army generally categorized the types of weapons research it was doing into two basic groups, domestic and foreign. There was the research that sprang out of work going on in the United States and research by people overseas. I knew I'd be keeping track of what the French were doing with advanced helicopter design and whether the British would be able to build a practical vertical takeoff and landing fighter, something we'd given up on after World War II. Then there was the German big gun, the V3, granddaughter of Big Bertha that the Germans threatened Paris with during the First World War. We'd found the barrel assemblies of the German artillery pieces near Calais after we invaded Normandy and knew that the Nazis were working on something that, like their jet engine fighter and new Panzer tank, could have changed the outcome of the war if they'd held us off any longer at the Battle of the Bulge.

I was responsible for developing this technology, ideas we hadn't come up with ourselves, and work up recommendations for how we could incorporate this into our weapons planning. But I didn't know why the general kept on patting the top drawer of that file cabinet.

"I'll get to those files right away if you like, General," I said. "And write up some preliminary reports on what I think about it."

"It's going to take you a little longer than that, Phil," Trudeau said. Now he was almost laughing, something he didn't do very much in those days. In fact, the only time I remember him laughing that way was after he heard that his name had been put up to command the U.S. forces in Vietnam. He also heard that they wanted me to head up the intelligence section for the Army Special Forces command in Vietnam. We both knew that the army mission in Vietnam was headed for disaster because it was a think-tank war. And the people in the think tank were more worried about restraining the army than in wiping out the Vietcong. So Trudeau had a plan: "We'll either win the war or get court-martialed," he said. "But they'll know we were there." And he laughed when he said that the same way he was laughing as he told me to take my time with the contents of the file cabinet. "You'll want to think about this before you start writing any reports," he said.

I couldn't help but pick up the nervousness in his voice, forcing itself through his laughter, the same sound over the phone that got me nervous when I heard it the first time. There really was something here he wasn't telling me.

"Is there something else about this I should know, General?" I asked, trying not to show any hesitation in my voice. Business as usual, nothing out of the ordinary, nothing anybody can throw my way that I can't handle.

"Actually, Phil, the material in this cabinet is a little different from the run-of-the-mill foreign stuff we've seen up to now," he said. "I don't know if you've ever seen the intelligence on what we've got here when you were over at the White House, but before you write up any summaries maybe you should do a little research on the Roswell file."

Now I'd heard more about Roswell than I was ready to admit right on the spot my first day at the Pentagon. And there were more wild stories floating around about Roswell and what we were still doing there than anyone could have imagined. But I hadn't made the connection between the Roswell files and what was in the cabinet General Trudeau was talking about. Basically I had hoped after Fort Riley that it would all go away and I could simply stick my head in the sand and worry about things I could get my brain around like bureaucratic infighting inside Washington instead of little aliens inside sealed coffins.

The general didn't wait for me to answer him. He left me standing there in his office and walked out to the reception room, where I heard him giving orders into a speakerphone. He had barely clicked off the speaker and walked back to where I was standing when four enlisted men pulling a hand truck showed up, saluted, and stood there at attention while Trudeau kept looking at me. He didn't say anything. He turned to the enlisted men instead. "Load up this cabinet on that dolly and follow the colonel to his office on the second floor. Don't stop for anybody. Don't talk to anybody. If anyone stops you, you tell them to see me. That's an order."

Then he turned back to me. "Why don't you take some time with this, Phil." He paused. "But not too much time. Sergeant"—he turned his attention back to the enlisted man with the shortest haircut—"please see the colonel back to his own office below."

They loaded the file cabinet onto the dolly as if there were nothing inside, pulled it toward the back door, and stared at me until I followed them out. "Not too much time, Colonel," General Trudeau called after me as we went out the door and down the hall.

I remember I spent quite a while just looking at that cabinet after it was loaded off the dolly and set up in my inner office. There was an almost ominous quality to it that belied its quiet, official army presence. So I must confess that, given the reverse hype of the general's introduction, part of me wanted to tear it open right away as if it were a present on Christmas morning. But the part of me that won just let it sit there, protected, until I thought about what

General Trudeau had said about Roswell and the amount of paperwork that had circulated through the White House when I was on the National Security staff there. No, I wasn't going to review the Roswell files. Not just yet. Not until I took a long hard look at what was inside this file cabinet. But even that was going to wait until the rest of my office was set up. Whatever I was supposed to do, I wanted to do it right.

I spent a little time pacing around my new office while I thought some more about what the general said, why this file was waiting for me in his private office, and why he had wanted to talk to me specifically about it. It also wasn't lost on me that I had not seen one scrap of paper from the general covering his delivery of the material to me nor my receipt of it. It could have just as easily been that this file cabinet didn't even exist. As far as I knew, only his eyes and soon my eyes would review it. So whatever it was, it was serious and, only if by omission, very secret.

I remembered a hot July night fourteen years before at Fort Riley when I was the young intelligence officer after having just been shipped back from Rome. I remembered being hustled into a storage hangar by one of the sentries, a fellow member of the Fort Riley bowling team. What he pointed to under the thick olive tarp that night was also very, very secret, and I held my breath, hoping that what was inside this cabinet wasn't anything like what I saw that night in Kansas, July 6, 1947.

I opened the cabinet, and almost immediately my heart sank. I knew, from looking at the shoebox of tangled wires and the strange cloth, from the visorlike headpiece and the little wafers that looked like Ritz crackers only with broken edges and colored a dark gray, and from an assortment of other items that I couldn't even relate to the shapes and sizes of things I was familiar with, that my life was headed for a big change. Back in Kansas that night in July, I told myself that I was seeing an illusion, something that if I wished real hard, didn't have to exist for me. Then, after I went to the White House and saw all the National Security Council memos describing the "incident" and talking about the "package" and the "goods," I knew that the strange figure I'd seen floating in liquid in a casket within a casket at

Fort Riley wasn't just a bad dream I could forget about. Nor could I forget about the radar anomalies at the Red Canyon missile range or the strange alerts over Ramstein air base in West Germany. I only hoped all of it would never catch up with me again and I could go through the rest of my army career in some kind of peace. But it was not to be. There, mangled like somebody else's junk, were the trinkets I knew would involve me in something deeper than I had ever wanted. Whatever else I had to do in this life, here was a job that would change it all.

You know how in the movies when Bud Abbott would open a closet, see the dead body hanging there, close the closet door, open it up again, and find the body gone? That's what I actually did with the file cabinet. Nobody was there to see me, or so I believed, so I opened it, closed it, opened it again. But this was no movie and the stuff was still there.

So here it was, some of the material they'd recovered from Roswell. And now, just like a bad penny, it turned up again. I heard footsteps outside my door and caught my breath. There were always sounds in the Pentagon at night because the building was never empty. Somewhere, in some office, in parts of the building most people don't even know about, some group is planning for a war we hope we will never fight. Therefore, more than any other building except for the White House, the Pentagon is a place where someone is always walking around after something.

General Trudeau peeked his head around the door.

"Look inside?" he asked.

"What'd you do to me, General?" I said. "I thought we were friends."

"That's why I gave you this, Phil," he said, but he wasn't laughing, wasn't even smiling. "You know how valuable this property is? You know what any of the other agencies would do to get this into their hands?"

"They'd probably kill me," I said.

"They probably want to kill you anyway, but this makes them even more rabid. The air force wants it because they think it belongs to them. The navy wants it because they want anything the air force wants. The CIA wants it so they can give it to the Russians."

"What do you want me to do, General?" I asked. I

couldn't figure out what he was thinking unless he thought I should just bury the stuff and leave it at that.

"I need a plan from you," he said. "Not simply what this property is, but what we can do with it. Something that keeps it out of play until we know what we have and what use we can make of it."

This had all the makings of a plot, pure and simple.

"Look, who's our biggest problem?" I asked, but it was a pro forma question because I already knew the answer.

"The same people who lost Korea for us and who you had to fight over at the White House," he said. "You know exactly who I mean. We got to keep whatever's valuable here from falling into the wrong hands because as sure as we're standing in this Pentagon, it'll find its way right to the Kremlin."

There were people floating around Washington right at that very moment who, even out of the most well-meaning intentions they could muster, would have shipped this Roswell file over to Russia while patting President Kennedy on the back and congratulating him for contributing to world peace. Just as there were people who would have cut Trudeau's and my throat and left us right on the rug to bleed to death while they packed that file away. Either way, Trudeau didn't have to quote me chapter and verse to explain that he was handing me one of the most important assignments I would ever receive from him. He was giving me the keys to a whole new kingdom, but neither he nor I knew what in the world we could do with this stuff, short of keeping it out of the hands of the Russians. At the very least, that was a start.

"We have to know what we have first," I said.

"Then that's your job right away. What do we have? Anything usable here? Put together people you can trust from the specialists we have and go over the contacts at our defense contractor lists. And this is only part of the property we have. There's some more of it downstairs in the file basement that the other intelligence agencies don't know anything about. Came here from New Mexico instead of going out to Ohio. Don't ask me why. It's coming up to you right now in boxes. Just put everything together, take some time, and evaluate this for me."

"Anybody know I have this?" I asked.

"Everybody knows that if you're poking around something it's got to be important," he said. "So don't act like the cat that ate the canary. They're watching you as much as they're watching me." Then he walked to the doorway, looked down both ends of the hall, and turned back to me. "But move this thing along, because we could be out of this office in under a year and I don't want to have to worry about running out of time on this."

And he was gone in a heartbeat, as if we'd never had the conversation.

I didn't take the file apart that night, even after another nondescript wooden crate that looked like something you ship vegetables in was carted to my office by an equally nondescript army corporal. I didn't go through the material the next night, either. But over the following week, whenever I could be sure that no one was around who could pop in without warning, I moved the material from the box into the file and allowed myself time to look at it. It was just like falling through the looking glass into a different world, a puzzle of separate pieces that only vaguely captured what had been in the memos I'd read over at the White House. No wonder no one had really wanted anything to do with this junk, which held out the promise of a whole world we knew nothing about but that as far back as 1947, the government had decided to keep an absolute secret.

Career after career of anyone in government who even hinted at the big dark secret of Roswell was pulverized by whoever was behind this operation. And, although I knew far more than I had even admitted to myself, I would never be the one to shoot off my mouth. But now this file, what I would eventually call the "nut file" to General Trudeau, had come into my possession, and as the ensuing weeks turned into a month, I gradually figured out where some of the puzzle pieces fit.

First there were the tiny, clear, single-filament, flexible glasslike wires twisted together through a kind of gray harness as if they were cables going into a junction. They were narrow filaments, thinner than copper wire. As I held the harness of strands up to the light from my desk, I could see an eerie glow coming through them as if they were conducting the faint light and breaking it up into different colors. When the personnel at the retrieval site in the desert outside of Roswell pulled this piece out of the wreckage of the delta-shaped object, they thought it was some sort of wiring device—a harness is what they said—or maybe some of them thought it was a junction box or electrical relay. But whatever they thought it was, they believed there was nothing like it on this planet. As I turned the object over in my hand, I figured, from the way the individual filaments flexed back and forth but didn't break and the way they were able to conduct a light beam along their length, they were a wire of some sort. But for what purpose I didn't have a clue.

Then there were the thin two-inch-around matte gray oyster cracker–shaped wafers of a material that looked like plastic but had tiny road maps of wires barely raised/etched along the surface. They were the size of a twenty-five-cent piece, but the etchings on the surface reminded me of squashed insects with their hundred legs spread out at right angles from a flat body. Some were more rounded or elliptical. It was a circuit—anyone could figure that out by 1961, especially when you put it under a magnifying glass— but from the way these wafers were stacked on each other, this was a circuitry unlike any other I'd ever seen. I couldn't figure out how to plug it in and what kind of current it carried, but it was clearly a wire circuitry of a sort that came from a larger board of wafers on board the flying craft. My hand shook ever so slightly as I held these pieces, not because they themselves were scary but because I was awed, just for a few seconds, about the momentous nature of this find. It was like an architectural treasure trove, the discoveries of some long-departed culture, a Rosetta stone, even though whoever crashed onto the desert floor was still very active and roaming around our most secret army and air force bases.

I was most interested in the file descriptions accompanying a two-piece set of dark elliptical eyepieces as thin as skin. The Walter Reed pathologists said they adhered to the lenses of the extraterrestrial creatures' eyes and seemed to reflect existing light, even in what looked like complete darkness, so as to illuminate and intensify images in the darkness to allow their wearer to pick out shapes. The reports had said that the pathologists at Walter Reed hospital who autopsied one of these creatures tried to peer through them in the darkness to watch the one or two army sentries and medical orderlies walking down a corridor adjacent to the pathology lab. These figures were illuminated in a greenish orange, depending upon how they moved, but the pathologists could see only their outer shape. And when they got close to each other, their shapes blended into a single form. But they could also see the outlines of furniture and the wall and objects on desktops. Maybe, I thought as I read this report, soldiers could wear a visor that intensified images through the reflection and amplification of available light and navigate in the darkness of a battlefield with as much confidence as if they were walking their sentry posts in broad daylight. But these eyepieces didn't turn night into day, they only highlighted the exterior shapes of things.

There was a dull, grayish-silvery foil-like swatch of cloth among these artifacts that you could not fold, bend, tear, or wad up but that bounded right back into its original shape without any creases. It was a metallic fiber with physical characteristics that would later be called "supertenacity," but when I tried to cut it with scissors, the arms just slid right off without making even a nick in the fibers. If you tried to stretch it, it bounced back, but I noticed that all the threads seemed to be going in one direction. When I tried to stretch it widthwise instead of lengthwise, it looked like the fibers had reoriented themselves to the direction I was pulling in. This couldn't be cloth, but it obviously wasn't metal. It was a combination, to my unscientific eye, of a cloth woven with metal strands that had the drape and malleability of a fabric and the strength and resistance of a metal. I was on top of some of the most secret weapons projects at the Pentagon, and we had nothing like this, even under the wish-list category.

There was a written description and a sketch of another device, too, like a short, stubby flashlight almost with a self-contained power source that was nothing at all like a battery. The scientists at Wright Field who examined it said they couldn't see the beam of light shoot out of it, but when they pointed the pencil-like flashlight at a wall, they could see a tiny circle of red light, but there was no actual beam from the end of what seemed like a lens to the wall as there would have been if you were playing a flashlight off on a distant object. When they passed an object in front of the source of the light, it interrupted it, but the beam was so intense the object began smoking. They played with this device a lot before they realized that it was an alien cutting device like a blowtorch. One time they floated some smoke across the light and suddenly the whole beam took shape. What had been invisible suddenly had a round, microthin, tunnel-like shape to it. Why did the inhabitants of this craft have a cutting device like this aboard their ship? It wasn't until later, when I read military reports of cattle mutilations in which entire organs were removed without any visible trauma to the surrounding cell tissue, that I realized that the light-beam cutting torch I thought was in the Roswell file was actually a surgical implement, just like a scalpel, that was being used by the aliens in medical experiments on our livestock.

Then there was the strangest device of all, a headband, almost, with electrical-signal pickup devices on either side. I could figure out no use for this thing whatsoever unless whoever used it did so as a fancy hair band. It seemed to be a one-size-fits-all headpiece that did nothing, at least not for humans. Maybe it picked up brain waves like an electroencephalogram and projected a chart. But no private experiment conducted on it seemed to do anything at all. The scientists didn't even determine how to plug it in or what its source of power was because it came with no batteries or diagrams.

There were nights I'd spread these articles all around me as if they were indeed Christmas presents. There were nights when I'd just take one thing out and turn it around until I almost memorized what it looked like from different angles before putting it back. The days were passing and, without having been told directly by Trudeau, I knew that he was getting anxious. We'd sit at meetings together when other people were around and he couldn't say anything, and I could almost hear his insides burst. There were times when we were alone and Trudeau almost didn't want to broach our shared secret.

Outside the Pentagon there was a battle starting up all over again set to rage just as it had during the Truman and Eisenhower presidencies. Whose intelligence was accurate? Whose was truthful? Who was trying to manipulate the White House and who believed that by coloring or twisting fact that he could change the course of history? John Kennedy was leading a young administration capable of making extraordinary mistakes. And there were people at the heart of his administration whose own views of how the world should work were inspiring them to distort facts, misstate intentions, and disregard obvious realities in the hope that their views would prevail. Worse, there were those, deep within a secret government within the government, who had been placed there by the spymasters at the Kremlin. And it was those individuals we had the greatest reason to fear. Right now, Army R&D had stewardship over these bits and pieces of foreign technology from Roswell. How long we would have them I did not know. So, over a late-night pot of coffee in General Trudeau's office, he decided that we would move this material out, out to defense contractors, out to where scientists would see it and where, under the guise of top secrecy, it would be in the system before the CIA could stow it where no one would find it except the very people we were trying to hide it from.

"This is the devil's plan, General," I said to Trudeau that night. "What makes you think we can get away with it?"

"Not we, Phil," he said. "You. You're the one who's going to get away with it. I'll just keep them off your back long enough until you do."

Now, all I could think about was what I'd seen that night in 1947 and, worse, what in the world I was going to do with all this stuff next. I'd asked myself "why me?" hundreds of times since that night in the Pentagon. And asked why after fourteen years and my experience at Fort Riley I had become the inheritor of the Roswell file. But I had no answers then and no answers now. If General Trudeau had meant for this to happen when he took over R&D three years before I got there, I'll never know. He never gave me any reasons, only orders. But since he was the master strategizer, I sometimes think he believed I must have had some experience with alien encounters and wouldn't be spooked by working with the technology from the Roswell file.

I never asked him about it, as strange as that seems, because the military being what it is, you don't ask. You simply do. So, now as then, I don't question. I only remember that I went forward from that night to put into development as much of the Roswell file as I could and believed that whatever happened, I was doing the right thing.

CHAPTER 4

Inside the Pentagon at the Foreign Technology Desk

THE PENTAGON NEVER SLEEPS.

And neither did I in those first few weeks at the R&D Foreign Technology desk as I racked my brain to come up with a strategy I could recommend to my boss. Amidst the constant twenty-four-hour motion of an office building where someone is always working, I spent more time at my desk than I did at home. Evenings, weekends, early mornings before the sunrise set the windows across the river in Washington an orange blaze, you could find me staring at the four-drawer file cabinet against my corner wall. I'd fiddle with the combination lock, sometimes so absorbed in coming up with a strategy for these strange artifacts that I'd forget the sequence of numbers and have to wait until my brain reset itself. And always, just outside my office was the pent-up urgency of crisis, the cocked trigger of a military machine always poised to attack anywhere, anytime, at the sound of a voice on the other end of a scrambled phone behind the soft-colored walls of an inner office along the miles of corridors on the inner or outer ring.

You think of the Pentagon as something of an amorphous entity with a single mind-set and a single purpose. It's probably the same way most people see the structure of the American military: one army, one goal, everybody marches together. But that's almost totally false. The American military—and its home office, the Pentagon—is just like any other big business with hundreds of different bureaus, many in direct and explicit competition with each other for the same resources and with different agendas and tactical goals. The separate military branches have different goals when it comes to how America should be defended and wars fought, and it's not uncommon for differences to emerge even within the same branch of the service.

I was plunged right into this in my first weeks back in D.C. Debates were still going on from World War II, sixteen years before, and all of this formed the backdrop of Roswell. There was a huge wrangling within the navy between the aircraft carrier advocates from World War II and the submariners under Adm. Hyman Rickover, who saw the big flattops as herds of elephants, slow and vulnerable. Subs, on the other hand, running almost forever on nuclear fuel, could slip deep beneath the sea, lay a thousand or so miles off enemy territory, and blast away at his most vulnerable targets with multiple-warhead ICBMs. No way our enemies would escape destruction as long as we had our submarine fleet. So who needs another aircraft carrier with its screen of destroyers and other escorts when just one sub can deliver a knockout punch anywhere, anytime, without enemy orbiting intel satellites snapping pictures of its every move? Look what our subs did to the Japanese in the Pacific; look what the German U-boats did to us in the Atlantic. But you couldn't convince the navy brass of all that in the 1960s.

Like the navy, the air force had different advocates for different goals, and so did the army. And when there are competing agendas and strategies articulated by some of the best and brightest people ever to graduate from universities, war colleges, and the ranks of officers, you have hard-nosed people playing high-stakes games against one other for the big prizes: the lion's share of the military budget. And, at the very center of it all, the place where the dollars get spent, are the weapons-development people who work for their respective branches of the military.

And that's right where I was in the early days of 1961 shortly after John F. Kennedy came to town to begin his new administration. I had only just returned to Washington from the front lines of a war that nobody thought of as a real war except for us, the guys who were there. It was easier during a real war, like Korea. Your objective is to push the other guy back as far as you can, kill as many of his people as you can, and force him to surrender. You have a very pragmatic strategy: You try it and if it works you keep on doing it until it stops working. But on the front lines in Germany, where the battles were only fought with electron beams, threats, and feints, you had to assess how many soldiers *might* be killed or how many planes you *could* bring down if the shooting were to start for real. For Americans this was the Cold War, the combined military machines of two massive superpowers each capable of obliterating each other the moment either one perceived a material weakness in the other's ability to retaliate.

So you had a chess game played and replayed every day around the world in scores of different war rooms where different scenarios were formulated to see who would win. It was all a game of numbers and strategies with different armed services around the world winning and losing battles on computers—very elegant and precise. But what very few people outside of government knew was that the Cold War was really a Hot War, fought with real bullets and real casualties, only no one could step forward to admit it because the front lines were within the very government capitals of the countries that were fighting it. I saw this with my own eyes right here in Washington, where the war had been going on since 1947.

So with the sides drawn and tensions between the various bureaus and services within the Pentagon, it didn't take me long in those first few weeks to learn the politics of my new job. With the field reports, scientific analyses, medical autopsies, and technological debris from the Roswell crash I had under lock and key, my first rule was to be as circumspect as possible, draw no attention to myself. I'd learned this skill when I served on MacArthur's staff in Korea ten years earlier: I had to be the little man who wasn't there. If people don't think you're there, they talk. That's when you learn things.

And within those first few weeks I saw and learned a lot about how the politics of the Roswell discovery had matured over the fourteen years since the crash and since the intense discussions at the White House after Eisenhower became president. Each of the different branches of the military had been protecting its own cache of Roswell-related files and had been actively seeking to gather as much new Roswell material as possible. Certainly all the services had their own reports from examiners at Walter Reed and Bethesda concerning the nature of the alien physiology. Mine were in my nut file along with the drawings. It was pretty clear, also, from the way the navy and air force were formulating their respective plans for advanced military-technology hardware, that many of the same pieces of technology in my files were probably shared by the other services. But nobody was bragging because everybody wanted to know what the other guy had. But since, officially, Roswell had never happened in the first place, there was no technology to develop.

On the other hand, the curiosity among weapons and intelligence people within the services was rabid. Nobody wanted to come in second place in the silent, unacknowledged alien-technology-development race going on at the Pentagon as each service quietly pursued its version of a secret Roswell weapon. I didn't know what the air force or navy had or what they might have been developing from their respective files on Roswell, but I assumed each service had something and was trying to find out what I had. That would have been a good intelligence procedure. If you were in the know about what was retrieved from Roswell, you kept your ears open for snippets of information about what was being developed by another branch of the military, what was going before the budget committees for funding, or what defense contractors were developing a specific technology for the services. If you weren't in the Roswell loop, but were too curious for your own good, you could be spun around by the swirling rumor mill that the Roswell race had kicked up among competing weapons-development people in the services and wind up chasing nothing more than dust devils that vanished down the halls as soon as you turned the corner on them.

There were real stories, however, that wouldn't go away

no matter how many times somebody official stepped up to say the story was false. For example, I picked up the rumors pretty quickly concerning the UFO the air force was supposed to be keeping at Edwards Air Force Base in California and the research they were conducting on the spacecraft's technology, especially its electromagnetic-wave propulsion system. There were also rumors circling around the air force about the early harvesting of Roswell technology in the design of the all-wing bombers, but I didn't know how much stock to put in them. The army had been developing an all-wing design since right after World War I, and within a year after the Roswell crash Jack Northrop's company began test flights of their YB49 flying wing recon/bomber models. The YB49's quadruple vertical tail fins were so uncannily reminiscent of the head-on Roswell craft sketches in our files that it was hard not to make a connection between the spacecraft and the bomber. But the flying wing's development took place over ten years before I got to the Foreign Technology desk, so I had no direct evidence relating the bomber to the spacecraft.

General Trudeau was right, though, when he said that people at the Pentagon were watching Army R&D because they thought we were onto something. People wanted to know what Foreign Technology was working on, especially the more exotic things in our portfolio just to make sure, the memos read, that we weren't duplicating budgetary resources by spending twice or three times for the same thing. There was a lot of talk and pressure from the Joint Chiefs of Staff about technology sharing and joint weapons development, but my boss wanted us to keep what we had to ourselves, especially what he jokingly kept calling "the alien harvest."

As if the eyes of the other military services weren't enough, we also had to contend with the analysts from the Central Intelligence Agency. Under the guise of coordination and cooperation, the CIA was amalgamating as much power as it could. Information is power, and the more the CIA tried to learn about the army weapons-development program, the more nervous it made all of us at the center of R&D.

Acquaintances of mine in the agency had dropped hints, shortly after I took over the Foreign Technology desk, that if I needed any intelligence about what other countries were developing, they could help me out. But one hand washes the other, and they dropped hints that if I had any clues about where any stray pieces of "the cargo," or "the package" as the Roswell artifacts were commonly referred to within the military, might be found, they would surely appreciate it if I let them know. After the third time my CIA contacts bumped into me and whispered this proposal for exchanges of information into my ear, I told my boss that our friends might be anxious about what we had.

"You really put me on the hot seat, General," I said to Trudeau over one of our morning briefings at the end of my first month on the job. I was still working on the strategy for the nut file and, thankfully, my boss hadn't pressured me yet to come up with recommendations for the plan. But it was coming. "How does the CIA know what we have?"

"They're guessing, I suppose," he said. "And figuring it out by the process of elimination. Look, everybody suspects what the air force has."

Trudeau was right. In the rumor bank from which everybody in the Pentagon made deposits and withdrawals, the air force was sitting on the Holy Grail—a spaceship itself and maybe even a live extraterrestrial. Nobody knew for sure. We knew that after it became a separate branch of the military in 1948, the air force kept some of the Roswell artifacts at Wright Field outside of Dayton, Ohio, because that's where "the cargo" was shipped, stopping off in Fort Riley along the way. But the air force was primarily interested in how things fly, so whatever R&D they worked on was focused on how their planes could evade radar and outfly the Soviets no matter where we got the technology from.

"And," he continued, "I'm sure the agency fellows would love to get into the Naval Intelligence files on Roswell if they've not done so already."

With its advanced submarine technology and missile-launching nuclear subs, the navy was struggling with its own problem in figuring out what to do about UUOs or USOs— Unidentified Submerged Objects, as they came to be called. It was a worry in naval circles, particularly as war planners advanced strategies for protracted submarine warfare in the event of a first strike. Whatever was flying circles around our jets since the 1950s, evading radar at our top-secret missile bases like Red Canyon, which I saw with my own eyes, could plunge right into the ocean, navigate down there just as easy as you please, and surface halfway around the world without so much as leaving an underwater signature we could pick up. Were these USOs building bases at the bottom of oceanic basins beyond the dive capacity of our best submarines, even the Los Angeles–class jobbies that were only on the drawing boards? That's what the chief of Naval Operations had to find out, so the navy was occupied with fighting its own war with extraterrestrial craft in the air and under the sea.

That left the army.

"But they don't know for sure what we have, Phil," Trudeau continued. He'd been talking the whole time. "And they're busting a gut to find out."

"So we have to keep on doing what we do without letting them know what we have, General," I said. "And that's what I'm working on." And I was. Even though I wasn't sure how we'd do it, I knew the business of R&D couldn't change just because we had Roswell crash artifacts in our possession.

However we were going to camouflage our development of the Roswell technology, it had to be within the existing way we did business so no one would recognize any difference. We operated on a normal defense development projects budget of well into the billions in 1960, most of it allocated to the analysis of new weapons systems. Just within our own bureau we had contracts with the nation's biggest defense companies with whom we maintained almost daily communication. A lot of the research we conducted was in the improvement of existing weapons based on the intelligence we received about what our enemies were pointing at us: faster tanks, heavier artillery, improved helicopters, better-tasting MREs.

At the Foreign Technologies desk, we kept an eye on what other countries were doing, ally or adversary, and how we could adapt it to our use. The French, the Italians, the West Germans, all of them had their own weapons systems and streams of development that seemed exotic by our standards yet had certain advantages. The Russians had gotten ahead of us in liquid rocket-propulsion systems and were using simpler, more efficient designs. My job was to evaluate the potential of the foreign technology and implement whatever we could. I'd get photos, designs, and specs of foreign weapons systems, like the French helicopter technology, for example, and bring it to American defense companies like Bell, Sikorski, or Hughes to see whether we could develop aspects of it for our own use. And it was the perfect cover for protecting the Roswell technology, but we still had to figure out what we wanted to do with it. It couldn't simply stay in file cabinets or on shelves forever.

What we had retrieved from the Roswell crash and had managed to hold on to was probably the most closely guarded secret the army had. Yet it was nothing more than an orphan. Up until 1961, the army had come up with no plan to use the technology without revealing its nature or its source and in so doing blow the cover on the single biggest secret the government was keeping. There was no one bureau within the army charged with managing Roswell and other aspects of UFO encounters, as there was in the air force, and therefore nobody was keeping any public records of how the army got its hands on its Roswell technology in the first place and, consequently, no oversight mechanism. Everything up until 1961 was catch-as-catch-can, but now it had to change. General Trudeau was looking for the grand endgame development scheme. It began with researching the history of how the whole file—the field reports, autopsy information, descriptions of the items found in the wreckage, and the bits and pieces of Roswell technology themselves—came into the possession of Army R&D.

Luckily enough for me, the whole Roswell story was still unknown outside the highest military circles in 1961. Retired major Jesse Marcel, the intelligence officer at the 509th who had been at the crash site in July 1947 and who had given the initial reports of a spacecraft, would not yet tell his story in public for at least another ten years. Everyone else connected to the incident was either dead or sworn to silence.

The air force, which moved quickly to take over management of the Roswell affair and ongoing UFO contacts and sightings, still kept everything they learned highly classified under the Air Force Intelligence Command and waged a push-and-pull war with the CIA for information about sightings and ongoing contacts with anything extraterrestrial. These really weren't my concerns yet, but they would be.

My research was not concerned with the crash at Roswell itself, nor at Corona or at San Agustin—if those crashes did, in fact, occur in early July 1947—but on the day after Roswell, the day Bill Blanchard from the 509th crated up the alien debris and shipped it to Fort Bliss, where Gen. Roger Ramey's staff determined its final disposition and the official government history of the event began to unfold.

In the early hours after the cargo arrived in Texas, there was so much confusion about what was found and what wasn't found that army officers, who were in charge of the entire retrieval operation, quickly scraped together both a cover story and a plan to silence all the military and civilian witnesses to the recovery. The cover story was easy. General Ramey ordered Maj. Jesse Marcel to recant his "flying saucer" story and pose for a news photo with debris from a weather balloon, which he described as the wreckage the retrieval team recovered from outside Roswell. Marcel followed orders and the flying saucer officially became a weather balloon.

The silencing of military witnesses was also accomplished easily enough through top-down orders from General Ramey to everyone at the 509th and at Fort Bliss to deny that they were a part of any operation to recover anything other than a balloon. Once the material left Ramey's command and arrived at Lt. Gen. Nathan P. Twining's Air Materiel Command at Wright Field, all General Ramey had to do was keep denying what he was already denying and it was no longer his responsibility. Now it belonged to General Twining, from whose desk a whole new era of army involvement with the Roswell material began.

General Ramey treated the incident as a threat to national security and deployed whatever forces he could to bring the material back for evaluation and to suppress any rumors that might light a brushfire of panic. Therefore, Ramey used the counterintelligence personnel already posted to the 509th and ordered them deployed into the civilian community as well as the military to use any means necessary to suppress the story of the crash and retrieval. No news should be allowed to get out, no speculation was to be tolerated, and the story already circulating about a crashed flying saucer had to be quashed.

By the next morning, July 8, the suppression of the crash story was in full operation. The army had already issued a new cover story to the press by the time CIC officers had gotten to the witnesses and, using threats and outright promises of cash, forced them to recant their statements about what they saw. Rancher Mac Brazel, who first said he had been at the site during the recovery and had described the strange debris, disappeared for two days and then showed up in town driving a new pickup truck and denying he'd ever seen anything. CIC officers turned up at people's houses and spoke quietly to parents about what their children had learned. Whatever people thought was happening, army personnel said, wasn't, and it would have to stay that way.

"You didn't see a thing," they ordered. "Nothing happened here. Let me hear you repeat that."

The silencing worked so well that for the next thirty years the story seemed to have been swallowed up by the quiet emptiness of desert where all things are worn down to a fine grade of sameness. But belying the quiet that settled over Roswell, a thousand miles away, part of the U.S. military went on wartime alert as bits and pieces of the craft reached their destinations. One of those destinations, Lt. Gen. Nathan Twining's desk at Wright Field, was the focal point from which the Roswell artifacts would reach the Foreign Technology desk at the Pentagon.

Among the first of the army's top commands notified of the events unfolding in Roswell in early July would have had to have been Lieutenant General Twining's Air Materiel Command at Wright Field, where the Roswell debris was shipped. Nathan Twining has become important to UFO researchers because of his association with a number of highly secret meetings at the Eisenhower White House having to do with the national security issues posed by the discovery of UFOs and his relationship to National Security Special Assistant Robert Cutler, who was the liaison between the NSC and President Eisenhower when I was on the NSC staff in the 1950s. The silver-haired General Twining was the point man for initial research and dissemination of Roswell-related materials and, partly because of the capability with which he administered the vital AMC at Wright, he became part of an ad hoc group of top military and civilian officials assembled by President Truman to advise him about the Roswell discovery and its national security implications.

General Twining had been scheduled to travel to the West Coast in early July 1947, but he canceled the trip, remaining in New Mexico at the army's air base at Alamogordo until at least July 10. Alamogordo was important not just because it was the nation's nuclear-weapons test site in the 1940s and 1950s but because it was also a field office of the AMC itself, where rocket scientists Wernher von Braun and others were primarily based. Close by was the White Sands guided-missile base, where some of our military's most advanced tracking and embryonic targeting radars were deployed. These were sensitive installations, especially during the UFO activity that week, and it made perfect sense that immediately after the recovery of the UFO the army general whose responsibility it would have been to manage the retrieval was almost directly on-site conferring with his top scientists.

Although I never saw the actual memos from President Truman to General Twining regarding his trip to New Mexico, I had heard stories about secret orders that Truman had issued to General Twining directing him to New Mexico to investigate the reports of the crash and to report directly to the White House on what he'd found. I believe that it was General Twining's initial report to the President that confirmed that the army had retrieved something from the desert and might have suggested the need for the formation of an advisory group to develop policy about whatever was discovered. And, remember, in those first forty-eight hours, nobody really knew what this was.

By the time the Roswell debris had been shipped out of Fort Bliss and had arrived at Wright Field, General Twining had flown back from New Mexico to Wright to oversee the analysis and evaluation of the Roswell treasure trove. Twining moved quickly once back at his office. The alien bodies had to be autopsied in utmost secrecy and the spacecraft and its contents analyzed, cataloged, and prepared for dissemination to various facilities within the military. Inasmuch as everything about the crash was given the highest security classification, stories had to be prepared for those with lower security classifications but whose contributions could be important to the creation of a credible cover story.

The official camouflage was almost as important to the military in 1947 as it was in 1961 when I took over. It was important because as far as the army was concerned, 1947 was still wartime, a Cold War, perhaps, but war nevertheless, and stories about military hardware as valuable as the material retrieved from Roswell could not be disclosed for fear that the Soviets would exploit it. Thus, from day 1, the army treated its retrieval of the debris as if it were an operation conducted in a wartime theater under battle conditions. Roswell became military intelligence.

General Twining had seen the material for himself, and even before he returned to Wright Field, he'd conferred with the rocket scientists who were part of his brain trust at Alamogordo. Now, during the remainder of the summer months, he quietly compiled a report that he would deliver to President Truman and an ad hoc group of military, government, and civilian officials, who would ultimately become the chief policy makers for what would become an ongoing contact with extraterrestrials over the ensuing fifty years. And as stories of the Roswell crash and other UFO sightings around U.S. military bases began to filter in through the command chain of the armed services, General Twining also needed to establish a lower security channel along which he could exchange information with other commands that were not cleared all the way to the top.

General Twining still reported to higher-ups who, though they may not have had the security clearance he had with regard to extraterrestrial contact, nevertheless were his commanding officers and routinely sought information from the AMC. Accordingly, General Twining needed to maintain a quasi cover-up even within the military.

The first of these reports was transmitted from General Twining to the commanding general of Army Air Forces in Washington, dated September 23, 1947. Written to the attention of Brig. Gen. George Schulgen, Twining's memo addressed, in the most general of terms, the official Air Materiel Command's intelligence regarding "flying discs." He drew a remarkable number of conclusions, most of which, I had to surmise when I was on Eisenhower's

National Security Council and then again when I got to the Pentagon, were based on Twining's own firsthand experience with the sighting reports from Roswell and other sighting reports as well as the materials themselves, which were in the military's possession.

Flying saucers or UFOs are not illusions, Twining says, referring to the sighting of strange objects in the sky as "something real and not visionary or fictitious." Even though he cites the possibility that some of the sightings are only meteors or other natural occurrences, he says that the reports are based upon real sightings of actual objects "approximating the shape of a disc, of such appreciable size as to be as large as man-made aircraft." Considering that this report was never intended for public scrutiny, especially in 1947, Twining marveled at the aircrafts' operating characteristics and went on record, drawing major conclusions about the material he had and the reports he'd heard or read. But, when he wrote that the extreme maneuverability of the aircraft and their "evasive" actions when sighted "or contacted" by friendly aircraft and radar led him to believe that they were either "manually, automatically, or remotely" flown, he not only suggested a guided flight but imparted a hostile intent to their evasive maneuvers to avoid contact. His characterization of the aircrafts' behavior revealed, even weeks after the physical encounter, that those officers in the military who were now running the yet-to-be-code-named extraterrestrial contact project already considered these objects and those entities who controlled them a military threat.

He described the aircraft as it had been reported in the sightings: a "light reflective or metallic surface," "absence of a trail except in those few instances when the object was operating under high performance conditions," "circular or elliptical in shape, flat on bottom and domed on top," flights in formation consisting of from "three to nine objects," and no sound except for those instances when "a substantial rumbling roar was noted." The objects moved quickly for aircraft at that time, he noted to General Schulgen, at level flight speeds above three hundred knots.

Were the United States to build such an aircraft, especially one with a range of over seven thousand miles, the cost, commitment, administrative and development overhead, and drain on existing high-technology projects required that the entire project should be independent or outside of the normal weapons-development bureaucracy. In other words, as I interpreted the memo, Twining was suggesting to the commander of the Army Air Force that were the air force, which would become a separate branch of the military by the following year, to attempt to exploit the technology that had quite literally dropped into its lap, it had to do so separately and independently from any normal weapons-development program. The descriptions of the supersecret projects at Nellis Air Force Base or Area 51 in the Nevada desert seem to fit the profile of the kind of recommendation that General Twining was making, especially the employment of the "skunk works" group at Lockheed in the development of the Stealth fighter and B2 bomber.

Not revealing to the Army Air Forces command that Twining himself had been ordered to visit bases in New Mexico in the hours after the crash, the general advised his bosses that the military should consider whether the flying disks were of domestic origin, "the product of some high-security project" already developed by the United States outside of normal channels, or developed by a foreign power that "has a form of propulsion possibly nuclear, which is outside of our domestic knowledge." At the same time, weaving a cover story that takes him out of the loop of reporting any of these flying disks as a firsthand observer, Twining writes that there is a "lack of physical evidence in the shape of crash recovered exhibits which would undeniably prove the existence of these objects."

But, even though General Twining has just written that there is no evidence, he nevertheless recommends to his superiors that:

Headquarters, Army Air Forces issue a directive assigning a priority, security classification and Code Name for a detailed study of this matter to include the preparation of complete sets of all available and pertinent data which will then be made available to the Army, Navy, Atomic Energy Commission, JRDB, the Air Force Scientific Advisory Group, NACA, and the RAND and NEPA projects for comments and recommendations, with a preliminary report to be forwarded within 15 days of receipt of the data and a detailed report thereafter every 30 days as the investigation develops. A complete interchange of data should be effected.

This was an important part of the memo, at least for me and my research into how the army got the Roswell file, because it accounted for the army's dissemination of the Roswell materials and accompanying reports within only a couple of months after the material's arrival at Wright Field. When General Twining suggested to his commanding officers at AAF that all the military branches as well as existing government and civilian commissions needed to share this information, the dispersal of the materials was already under way. This is how the technology came into the possession of Army R&D.

Finally, the general promised the Army Air Forces command that the Air Materiel Command would continue to investigate the phenomenon within its own resources in order to define its nature further and it would route any more information it developed through channels. Three days after the memo, on September 26, 1947, General Twining gave his report on the Roswell crash and its implications for the United States to President Truman and a short list of officials he convened to begin the management of this top-secret combination of inquiry, police development, and "ops." This working group, which included Adm. Roscoe H. Hillenkoetter, Dr. Vannevar Bush, Secretary James Forrestal, Gen. Hoyt Vandenberg, Dr. Detlev Bronk, Dr. Jerome Hunsaker, Sidney W. Souers, Gordon Gray, Dr. Donald Menzel, Gen. Robert M. Montague, Dr. Lloyd V. Berkner, and Gen. Nathan Twining himself, became the nucleus for an ongoing fifty-year operation that some people have called "Majestic-12."

At the Eisenhower White House, it was simply referred to as "the group," and in the days after Roswell it went into operation just as smoothly as slipping your new 1949 Buick with its "Dynaflow" automatic transmission into drive and pulling away from the curb. In this way General Twining had carefully orchestrated a complete cover-up of what had happened at Roswell as well as a full-scale, top-secret military R&D operation to identify the nature of the phenomenon and assess its military threat to the United States. It was as elegant as it was effective.

But the plan didn't stop with the creation of the working group—in fact, the operation very quickly developed into something far more sophisticated because General Twining's "flying discs" simply wouldn't go away. As more information on sightings and encounters came rolling in through every imaginable channel, from police officers taking reports from frightened civilians to airline pilots tracking strange objects in the sky, the group realized that they needed policies on how to handle what was turning into a mass-media phenomenon. They needed a mechanism for processing the thousands of flying saucer reports that could be anything from a real crash or close encounter to a couple of bohunks tossing a pie tin into the air and snapping its picture with their Aunt Harriet's Kodak Brownie. The group also had to assess the threat from the Soviet Union and Iron Curtain countries, assuming of course that flying saucers weren't restricted to North America, and gather intelligence on what kinds of information our allies had on flying saucers as well. And it still had to process the Roswell technology and figure out how it could be used. So from the original group there developed a whole tree structure of loosely confederated committees and subgroups, sometimes complete organizations like the air force Project Blue Book, all kept separate by administrative firewalls so that there would be no information leakage, but all controlled from the top.

With the initial and ongoing stories safely covered up, the plans for the long-term reverse-engineering work on the Roswell technology could begin. But who would do it? Where would the material reside? And how could the camouflage of what the military was doing be maintained amidst the push for new weapons, competition with the Soviets, and the flying saucer mania that was sweeping the country in the late 1940s? General Twining had a plan for that, too.

Just a little over a year after the initial group meetings at the White House, Air Force Intelligence, now that the air force had become a separate service, issued a December 1948 report—100-203-79—called "Analysis of Flying Object Incidents in the U.S." in which UFOs are never referred to as extraterrestrial objects but as elements of "foreign technology," which is actually the subject of the report. The report, innocuous to most people because it doesn't say that flying saucers came from outer space, is actually one of the first indications showing how the camouflage plan was supposed to work over the ensuing years.

The writers of the report had located within the existing military administrative structure the precise place where all research and development into the flying disk phenomenon could be pursued not only under a veil of secrecy but in the very place were no one could be expected to look: the Foreign Technology desk. Here, the materials could be deposited for safekeeping within the military while army and air force brass decided what our existing industrial and research technology allowed them to do. There could be fiascoes as weapons failed, secret experiments without fear of exposure, and, most importantly, an ongoing discussion of how the United States could develop this treasure trove of engineering information, all within the very structure where it was supposed to take place. Just don't call it extraterrestrial; call it "foreign technology" and throw it into the hopper with the rest of the mundane stuff the foreign technology officers were supposed to do.

And that's how, twelve years later, the Roswell technology turned up in an old combination-locked military file cabinet carted into my new Pentagon office by two of the biggest enlisted men I'd ever seen.

CHAPTER 5

The Cover-up

WHILE GENERAL TWINING WAS FLYING BACK AND FORTH FROM Ohio to New Mexico, on the other side of the world in Moscow, Chairman Josef Stalin was furious. Red-faced and not even trying to hide the rage that erupted like an exploding volcano, Stalin held up a copy of the *Roswell Daily Record* for Tuesday, July 8, 1947, and threw it out onto the center of the table for any of the scientists in the room who could read English. Stalin didn't need an American newspaper to tell him what his NKVD agents on the ground at Alamogordo reported weeks before: that a U.S. Army retrieval team had pulled a crashed alien spacecraft out of the New Mexico desert and was already evaluating the valuable technology they'd recovered.

At first, when the Soviet intelligence bosses got the reports from their agents at the American bases, they were more than skeptical. They figured the stories were plants, false information to flush out the Soviet spies the Americans suspected had infiltrated their most secret bases. If the Soviet government reacted to the disinformation, the American counterintelligence agents would be able to determine the path of the story and isolate the spies. But when newspapers began reporting the crash, then covered it up with stories about weather balloons, the Soviets knew they had stumbled onto the real thing. So it was true, Stalin told the group, the Americans had actually gotten their own flying saucer. Now, he asked, what would they do with it?

One of the chief designers of the Soviet's embryonic liquid-fuel-rocket program was at the meeting. He, like many of the Soviet engineers who'd read the German secret weapons files at the end of the war, knew exactly where the Americans should have been in their guided-missile-development program. What information his bosses in the Kremlin thought he still needed to know, they gave him from the reports they received from agents in the field. But nothing, nothing about the V2 launches at White Sands, nothing about the new tracking radars at Alamogordo gave the scientists in the Soviet rocket program any indications the Americans were even an iota ahead of them in guided missiles until he heard the news of the Roswell crash.

Both the Russian and American missile programs were based almost entirely upon the German weapons research spoils that the Allies were dividing up even before the end of the war. I was a firsthand participant in this, secreting out German weapons scientists through Italy after we occupied Rome as part of a secret operation code-named "Paper Clip" that began in 1944. With V2 designers Wernher von Braun, Willy Ley, and others running experiments on the German missiles we brought back to the United States, the army had successfully appropriated much of the German advanced weapons research and was carrying on experiments in New Mexico. The Soviets also got their own share of German technology through their own intelligence agents and local Communist Party cells in occupied countries.

And what a technology it was. The Germans had developed a crescent-shaped jet-powered flying wing, jet-powered Messerschmitts that blazed by our P51s as if they were standing still, and a U-boat-launched V1/V2 that, had the Germans been able to hide even a small flotilla off the American East Coast, could have bombed out much of heavily concentrated downtown Washington in a matter of hours. All they needed to buy was enough time to deploy their weapons and get their U-boats in position. And that was their strategy toward the end of 1944 when they turned around and counterattacked through Belgium in the dead of winter and pinned us down at the Battle of the Bulge. Break our advance on the ground, blast us out of the air with their new jets, bomb North American cities, and knock Britain out of the war. With their new weapons they could have fought us to a standstill and won a bitter truce. Both the Americans and the Soviets wanted to get their hands on those German weapons, especially the V2s.

Stalin didn't have to worry much about who held the advantage in German weaponry after the war. Both sides were about equal. But this flying saucer crash, that was a different matter, and it meant that in an instant the United States could have gained an enormous advantage in the Cold War weapons race that had begun only moments after the Germans surrendered. What might that advantage be? the Russian liquid-fuel engineer wondered aloud. What could the Americans have retrieved from that crash?

Soviet agents reported that the townspeople in Roswell had talked about little creatures at the crash site and a crescent-shaped aircraft that the army hauled away on trucks, but the stories had been quickly silenced by military counterintelligence. So any real intelligence on what the Americans might be developing would have to come from Soviet agents deep inside the U.S. government. Stalin would order it. And, as if they were activated by an invisible switch, spies from one of the most efficient and ruthless intelligence machines in the world began homing in on the American military bases associated with the Roswell retrieval and the key American military and civilian personnel the Russians knew would have to be involved.

The Americans might not have been the most efficient spy catchers in 1947, but Army Counterintelligence had been put on alert even before the Soviets knew that a flying saucer had been retrieved. Starting from the central point at the nexus of sensitive New Mexico bases during the summer of 1947, CIC agents questioned anybody who seemed interested in learning about what happened in Roswell. Ask too many questions and knocking at your door would be a couple of plainclothes investigators who didn't need a search warrant to rummage through your things. So maybe the army was a little overzealous about their interrogation procedures, but by early August it began producing results. By the time General Twining was writing his report to Army Air Forces command in Washington, both Army and Navy Intelligence commanders knew that the Soviets had a high-priority operation in place at military bases around the country.

Soviet agents were everywhere, Central Intelligence group director Adm. Roscoe Hillenkoetter, a member of President Truman's advisory group on UFOs, informed the president. A top-down counterintelligence operation had to be put in place immediately, he recommended, or every plan the military had to evaluate what they'd retrieved from Roswell would be compromised. There were a million questions. Were these flying objects the prelude to something much bigger? Were they communicating with the Soviets? Were they allied with the Soviets? Were they probing our defenses for a planetary invasion? We had already assumed that the behavior of these aircraft was hostile, but what did they want? Meanwhile, other reports of civilian flying saucer sightings were turning up in newspapers and coming in through local police. Even airline pilots were seeing strange lights. There wasn't much time to act. A secret this big about flying saucers was bound to get out and cause untold panic among the civilian population unless an elaborate camouflage was established. And worse, we had to keep the Soviets away from this until we knew what we had. We needed a plan, and right away.

Some have said it was Secretary of Defense James Forrestal's idea. Others said the whole scheme belonged to Central Intelligence director Hillenkoetter. I, frankly, don't know firsthand because when the plan was hatched I was sweating out the end of the summer at Fort Riley, still trying to shake out of my mind the image of that ghoulishly unearthly thing I'd seen floating in its container. But whoever said it first was saying the obvious, according to the people on Eisenhower's National Security staff whom I worked with six years later. Maybe it was Forrestal after all who was the only person in the cabinet who could have spoken to Truman that bluntly just a little over two years after the man had inherited the office from FDR and was already a very unpopular president.

"It's like this," I had heard President Truman was told. "We're in a real pickle here. Nate Twining says he doesn't know what the hell this thing is except that if the Soviets get ahold of it, it'll change the shape of things to come for sure."

"You fellas going to write up some report for me?" the President asked.

"General Twining says he'd rather do it as a briefing, sir, for the time being," Admiral Hillenkoetter suggested. "For your ears only. Then we have to have a working task group to manage this whole issue."

Maybe the working group, whatever it was going to be called, would come up with a report analyzing the situation as soon as they reviewed what General Twining was putting under lock and key at Wright Field, but nobody wanted to speculate until they knew what was there.

"Maybe you should sit down with General Twining first," both Forrestal and Hillenkoetter suggested. They knew that Harry Truman liked to get firsthand reports from people who had seen the situation with their own eyes. FDR was corporate and knew how to digest reports. He trusted his subordinates. But Truman was different. He knew how to run a haberdashery store; if a hat didn't fit he'd have to go back to the factory to find out why. It was the same with General Twining, who'd been at the crash sites himself. If Truman wanted answers, he'd have to see it through the eyes of someone who'd been there.

"Does he know what these SOBs are after?" Truman asked, referring to the aliens in the crashed saucer.

"That's one of the questions we want to address," they said.

"How do you plan to do it?"

Forrestal and Hillenkoetter explained that they wanted the President to hear what General Twining had to say and then convene a group of military, civilian, and intelligence personnel with strong old-school ties of trust for one another. In this way whatever decisions they made wouldn't have to be memoed all over the place, thus risking the possibilities of leaks and tip-offs to the Soviets. "We don't want the newspapers or radio people getting their hands on any of this either," they told the President.

"Winchell would crucify me with this if he found out what we were doing," Truman was reported to have said at that meeting. Nobody in the know liked President Truman very much, and he could appreciate it.

"It's just like the Manhattan Project, Mr. President," Admiral Hillenkoetter reminded him. "It was war. We couldn't tell anyone. This is war. Same thing."

Then they explained that after they had convened a working group, they would task out the research of the technology while keeping it from the Soviet spy machine already operating at full bore within the government.

"We hide it from the government itself," the secretary explained.

"Create a whole new level of security classification just for this," the Central Intelligence director said. "Any information we decide to release, even internally, we downgrade so the people getting the information never have the security clearance that allows them all the way to the top. The only way to hide it from the Russians is to hide it from ourselves."

But the President was still thinking about the difficulties of keeping an operation this far-reaching out of the news, especially when flying saucers had become one of the hottest new items to talk about. What was he supposed to say when people ask the government about the flying disk stories? he asked, pressing for details that still had to be established. How could they research these strange creatures without the news getting out? And how could they analyze the wealth of physical material Hillenkoetter had described to him without bringing people from outside government? President Truman simply didn't see how this government-within-a-government camouflage idea could work without the whole thing spinning out of control. Despite Forrestal's assurances, the President remained skeptical.

"And there's one final point," Truman was said to have brought up to his Central Intelligence group director and secretary of defense. It was a question so basic that its apparent naïveté belied an ominous threat that it suggested was just over the horizon. "Do we ever tell the American people what really happened?"

There was silence.

Don't ask me how I know. My old friend and enemy from the KGB wouldn't tell me how he knew, and I didn't press him. But, accept it as fact from the only source that could know, just as I did back when I was told, that neither the secretary of defense nor the director of intelligence had considered a disclosure like this as even a remote possibility.

"Well," President Truman said. "Do we?"

On November 7, 1944, the day FDR was elected to his fourth and final term, his chief adviser, Harry Hopkins, had described the new vice president Harry Truman as a man who couldn't block a hat but who shouldn't be underestimated. And James Forrestal, the man to whom he was speaking at the time, now understood what he meant as the secretary sat across from the now President Harry Truman.

This was a basic yes/no question, and although Forrestal and Hillenkoetter had a knee-jerk reflex answer, "no," Forrestal quickly saw that it wasn't that easy. As wartime administrators their first response was naturally to disclose nothing, abiding by the old saw that what the people don't know, they don't need to know. But President Truman, who had not come from a military background, had seen something neither Forrestal nor Hillenkoetter had seen. If these ships could evade our radar and land anywhere at will, what would stop them from landing in front of the White House or, for that matter, the Kremlin? Certainly not the U.S. Army Air Force.

"So what do we say when they land," I'm told that Truman continued, "and create more panic in the streets than if we'd disclosed what we think we know now?"

"But we really don't know anything," the director of intelligence said. "Not a thing until we analyze what we've retrieved."

But both the secretary of defense and director of intelligence agreed with President Truman that he was right to be skeptical, especially on his final point about disclosure.

"So can we postpone coming to any conclusions at least until after you've meet with General Twining?" Admiral

Hillenkoetter asked. "I think he'll provide some of the answers we're all looking for."

While Adm. Roscoe Hillenkoetter and James Forrestal were briefing President Truman on their plan for the working group, Gen. Nathan P. Twining was completing his preliminary analysis of the reports and material sent to Wright Field. Almost immediately, he dispatched the remains of the aliens to the Bethesda Naval Hospital and the Walter Reed Army Hospital for further analysis by the two military services. The aircraft itself remained at Wright Field but, as he would promise in his memo to the Army Air Forces command, General Twining was preparing to distribute the material from the wreckage among the different military and civilian bureaus for further evaluation. He'd already been cautioned by Admiral Hillenkoetter that new security classifications had been put in place regarding the Roswell intelligence package. No one within the military other than names he would receive from the President himself had the full security clearance to learn the complete story about Roswell that Twining would deliver to the President and other members of a working group.

Within three months after he'd been dispatched to New Mexico to learn what had happened at Roswell, General Twining met with President Truman, as Hillenkoetter and Forrestal had suggested, and explained exactly what he believed the army had pulled out of the desert. It was almost beyond comprehension, he described to the President, nothing that could have come from this planet. If the Russians were working on something like this, it was so secret that not even their own military commanders knew anything about it, and the United States would have to establish a crash program just to prepare a defense. So it was Twining's assessment that what they found outside of Roswell was, in his words, "not of this earth."

Now President Truman had heard it, he told Forrestal after Twining had left for Ohio, "directly from the horse's mouth," and he was convinced. This was bigger than the Manhattan Project and required that it be managed on a larger scale and obviously for a longer period. The group proposed by Forrestal and Hillenkoetter had to consider what they were really managing and for how long. Were they only trying to keep one secret—that an extraterrestrial alien spaceship crashed at Roswell—or were they hiding what would quickly become the largest military R&D undertaking in history, the management of what would become America's relationship with extraterrestrials?

General Twining had made it clear in his preliminary analysis that they were investigating the whole phenomenon of flying disks, including Roswell and any other encounter that happened to take place. These were hostile entities, the general said, who, if they were on a peaceful mission, would have not avoided contact by taking evasive maneuvers even as they penetrated our airspace and observed our most secret military installations. They had a technology vastly superior to ours, which we had to study and exploit in case they turned more aggressive. If we were forced to fight a war in outer space, we would have to understand the nature of the enemy better, especially if it came to preparing the American people for an enemy they had to face. So investigate first, he suggested, but prepare for the day when the whole undertaking would have to be disclosed.

This, Truman could understand. He had trusted Twining to manage this potential crisis from the moment Forrestal had alerted him that the crash had taken place. And Twining had done a brilliant job. He kept the lid on the story and brought back everything that he could under one roof. He understood as Twining described to him the strangeness of the spacecraft that seemed to have no engines, no fuel, nor any apparent methods of propulsion, yet outflew our fastest fighters; the odd childlike creatures who were inside and how one of them was killed by a gunshot; the way you could see daylight through the inside of the craft even though the sun had not yet risen; the swatches of metallic fabric that they couldn't burn or melt; thin beams of light that you couldn't see until they hit an object and then burned right through it, and on and on; more questions than answers. It would take years to find these answers, Twining had said, and it was beyond the immediate capacity of our military to do anything about it. This will take a lot of manpower, the general said, and most of the work will have to be done in secret.

General Twining showed photographs of these alien beings and autopsy reports that suggested they were too human; they had to be related to our species in some way. They were obviously intelligent and able to communicate, witnesses at the scene had reported, by some sort of thought projection unlike any mental telepathy you'd see at a carnival show. We didn't know whether they came from a planet like Mars in our own solar system or from some galaxy we could barely see with our strongest telescopes. But they possessed a military technology whose edges we could understand and exploit, even if only for self-defense against the Soviets. But by studying what these extraterrestrials had we might be able to build a defense system against them as well.

At the very least, Twining had suggested, the crescent-shaped craft looked so uncomfortably like the German Horten wings our flyers had seen at the end of the war that he had to suspect the Germans had bumped into something we didn't know about. And his conversations with Wernher von Braun and Willy Ley at Alamogordo in the days after the crash confirmed this. They didn't want to be thought of as *verrückt* but intimated that there was a deeper story about what the Germans had engineered. No, the similarity between the Horten wing and the craft they had pulled out of the arroyo was no accident. We always wondered how the Germans were able to incorporate such advanced technology into their weapons development in so short a time and during the Great Depression. Did they have help? Maybe we were now as lucky as the Germans and broke off a piece of this technology for ourselves. With an acceleration capability and maneuverability we'd never seen before, this craft would keep American aircraft engineers busy for years just incorporating what they could see into immediate designs.

The issue of security was paramount, but so were questions of disclosure, the President reminded him. This thing was too big to hide and getting bigger all the time while reporters were just like dogs on a scent. So just putting a higher security classification on it and threatening anybody who came too close wasn't enough to hide a secret this big. You couldn't prevent leaks, and eventually it would all have to come out anyway. General Twining should think about that before the group made any final decisions, the President advised.

By the middle of September it was obvious to every member of President Truman's working group, which included the following:

> Central Intelligence Director Adm. Roscoe Hillenkoetter
>
> Secretary of Defense James Forrestal
>
> Lt. Gen. Nathan Twining of the AAF and then USAF Air Materiel Command
>
> Professor Donald Menzel, Harvard astronomer and Naval Intelligence cryptography expert
>
> Vannevar Bush, Joint Research and Development Board Chairman
>
> Detlev Bronk, Chairman of the National Research Council and biologist who would ultimately be named to the National Advisory Committee on Aeronautics
>
> Gen. Robert Montague, who was General Twining's classmate at West Point, Commandant of Fort Bliss with operational control over the command at White Sands
>
> Gordon Gray, President Truman's Secretary of the Army and chairman of the CIA's Psychological Strategy Board
>
> Sidney Souers, Director of the National Security Council
>
> Gen. Hoyt Vandenberg, Central Intelligence Group Director prior to Roscoe Hillenkoetter and then USAF Chief of Staff in 1948
>
> Jerome Hunsaker, aircraft engineer and Director of the National Advisory Committee on Aeronautics
>
> Lloyd Berkner, member of the Joint Research and Development Board

Unless this group established a long-term plan for protecting and developing the Roswell project, the secrets would soon leak out. I understand that it was General Twining who pointed out to the group that, in fact, the story had already leaked out. It was leaked, he said, hours after the crash and then retracted. In fact, people were still talking about it in New Mexico, but after the army's weather balloon story, the national newspapers were treating the flying disk reports as the delusions of people who had seen too many Buck Rogers movies. The national press was already doing the committee's work.

What was really needed, Twining suggested, was a method for gathering the information about continuing UFO activity—especially crashes, high-probability sightings by pilots or the military, or actual physical encounters with individuals—and surreptitiously filtering that information to the group while coming up with practical explanations that would turn unidentified flying disks into completely identifiable and explainable phenomena. Under the cover of explaining away all the flying disk activity, the appropriate agencies represented by members of the working group would be free to research the real flying disk phenomenon as they deemed appropriate. But through it all, Twining stressed, there had to be a way of maintaining full deniability of the flying disk phenomenon while actually preparing the public for a disclosure by gradually desensitizing them to the potential terror of confronting a more powerful biological entity from a different world. It would have to be, General Twining suggested, at the same time both the greatest cover-up and greatest public relations program ever undertaken.

The group agreed that these were the requirements of the endeavor they would undertake. They would form nothing less than a government within the government, sustaining itself from presidential administration to presidential administration regardless of whatever political party took power, and ruthlessly guarding their secrets while evaluating every new bit of information on flying saucers they received. But at the same time, they would allow disclosure of some of the most far-fetched information, whether true or not, because it would help create a climate of public attitude that would be able to accept the existence of extraterrestrial life without a general sense of panic.

"It will be," General Twining said, "a case where the cover-up is the disclosure and the disclosure is the cover-up.

Deny everything, but let the public sentiment take its course. Let skepticism do our work for us until the truth becomes common acceptance."

Meanwhile, the group agreed to establish an information-gathering project, ultimately named Blue Book and managed explicitly by the air force, which would serve public relations purposes by allowing individuals to file reports on flying disk sightings. While the Blue Book field officers attributed commonplace explanations to the reported sightings, the entire project was a mechanism to acquire photographic records of flying saucer activity for evaluation and research. The most intriguing sightings that had the highest probability of being truly unidentified objects would be bumped upstairs to the working group for dissemination to the authorized agencies carrying on the research. For my purposes, when I entered the Pentagon, the general category of all flying disk phenomena research and evaluation was referred to simply as "foreign technology."

CHAPTER 6

The Strategy

THERE IS AN OLD STORY I ONCE HEARD ABOUT KEEPING SECRETS. A group of men were trying to protect their deepest secrets from the rest of the world. They took their secrets and hid them in a shack whose very location was a secret. But the secret location was soon discovered and in it was discovered the secrets that the group was hiding. But before every secret could be revealed, the men quickly built a second shack where they stored those secrets they still kept to themselves. Soon, the second shack was discovered and the group realized they would have to give up some secrets to protect the rest. So they again moved quickly to build a third shack and protect whatever secrets they could. This process repeated itself over and over until anyone wanting to find out what the secrets were had to start at the first shack and work their way from shack to shack until they came to where they could go no further because they didn't know the location of the next shack. For fifty years this was the very process by which the secrets of Roswell were protected by various serial incarnations of an ad hoc confederation of top-secret working groups throughout different branches of the government, and it is still going on today.

Were you to search through every government document to find the declassified secrets of Roswell and the contact we maintained with the aliens who were visiting us before and have been doing so ever since, you would find code-named project after code-named project, each with its own file, security classification, military or government administration, oversight mechanism, some form of budget, and even reports of highly classified documents. All of these projects were started to accomplish part of the same task: manage our ongoing relationship with the alien visitors we discovered at Roswell. However, at each level, once the security had been breached for whatever reason—even by design— part of the secret was disclosed through declassification while the rest was dragged into a new classified project or moved to an existing one that had not been compromised.

It makes perfect sense, especially to those of us who understand that the government is not some monolithic piece of granite that never moves or reacts. To those of us inside the military/government machine the government is dynamic, highly reactive, and even proactive when it comes to devising ways to protect its most closely held secrets. For all the years after Roswell we weren't just one step ahead of people wanting to know what really happened, we were a hundred steps ahead, a thousand, or even more. In fact, we never hid the truth from anybody, we just camouflaged it. It was always there, people just didn't know what to look for or recognize it for what it was when they found it. And they found it over and over again.

Project "Blue Book" was created to make the general public happy that they had a mechanism for reporting what they saw. Projects "Grudge" and "Sign" were of a higher security to allow the military to process sightings and encounter reports that couldn't easily be explained away as balloons, geese, or the planet Venus. Blue Fly and Twinkle had other purposes, as did scores of other camouflage projects like Horizon, HARP, Rainbow, and even the Space Defense Initiative, all of which had something to do with alien technology. But no one ever knew it. And when reporters were actually given truthful descriptions of alien encounters, they either fell on the floor laughing or sold the story to the tabloids, who'd print a drawing of a large-headed, almond-eyed, six-fingered alien. Again, everybody laughed. But that's what these things really look like because I saw the one they trucked up to Wright Field.

Meanwhile, as each new project was created and administered, another bread crumb for anyone pursuing the secrets to find, we were gradually releasing bits and pieces of information to those we knew would make something out of it. Flying saucers did truly buzz over Washington, D.C., in 1952, and there are plenty of photographs and radar reports to substantiate it. But we denied it while encouraging science fiction writers to make movies like *The Man from Planet X* to blow off some of the pressure concerning the truth about flying disks. This was called camouflage through limited disclosure, and it worked. If people could enjoy it as entertainment, get duly frightened, and follow trails to nowhere that the working group had planted, then they'd be less likely to stumble over what we were really doing. And what were we really doing?

As General Twining had suggested in his report to the Army Air Forces, "foreign technology" was the category to which research on the alien artifacts from Roswell was to be delegated. Foreign technology was one of the great catch-all terms, encompassing everything from researching French air force engineering advances on helicopter blades to captured Russian MiGs flown in from Cuba by savvy pilots who could negotiate our southern radar perimeter better than our own pilots. So what if a few pieces of technological debris from a strange crescent-shaped hovering wing turned up in an old file somewhere in the army's foreign technology files? If nobody asked about it—and nobody did because foreign technology was just too damned dull for most reporters to hang around—we didn't have to say anything about it. Besides, most foreign-technology stuff was classified anyway because it dealt with weapons development we were hiding from the Soviets and most reporters knew it. Foreign technology was the absolute perfect cover. All I had to do was figure out what to do with the stuff I had. And General Trudeau wasn't in the mood to wait any longer.

"Come on, Phil, let's go." The general's voice suddenly

filled the room over the blown-speaker hum of my desk intercom. I put down my coffee and headed up the stairway to the back door of his inner office. This was a routine that repeated itself three, sometimes four times a day. The general always liked to get briefed in person because even in the most secure areas of the Pentagon, the walls tended to listen and remember our conversations.

Our sessions were always private, and from the way our conversation bounced back and forth among different topics, if it weren't for his three stars and my pair of leaves, you wouldn't even think you were listening to a pair of army officers. It was cordial and friendly, but my boss was my boss and, even after we both retired like two old warhorses put out to pasture, our meetings were never informal.

"So now you figured out how the package arrived?" he asked me after I sat down. I had figured it out by going through all of the files I could get my hands on and tracing the path of the Roswell information from the 509th to Fort Bliss and from there to Wright Field, the dissemination point.

General Trudeau motioned for me to sit down and I settled into a chair. It was already ten-thirty in the morning so I knew there'd be at least two other sit-down briefings that day.

"I know it didn't come by the parcel service," I said. "I don't think they have a truck that big."

"Does that help you figure out what we should do?" he asked.

Actually, knowing how the material got into the Foreign Technology files was critically important because it meant that it was dispatched there originally. Even if it had been neglected over the years, it was clear that the Foreign Technology desk of the R&D system was its intended destination, part of the original plan. And I even had the documents from General Twining's own files to substantiate this. Not that I would have ever revealed them at that time. General Twining, more than anyone else during those years after the war, understood the sensitive and protected nature of the R&D budget. And now that I understood how the camouflage was to take place, I also saw how brilliant the general's plan was. R&D, although important and turning over records like topsoil from the Nazi weapons-development files captured after the war, was kind of a backwater railroad junction.

Unnoticed by most officers on their way to the top and not called upon in the late 1940s to do much more than record keeping, it turned out to be the perfect hideaway when the CIA hirelings came sniffing through the Pentagon in the early 1950s looking for anything they could find on the Roswell technology. Unless they were part of the working group from the start, not even members of the Eisenhower White House National Security staff knew that R&D was the repository of Roswell artifacts. I was there. I can vouch for that. In fact, it wasn't until I saw the files for myself and reverse-traced their path to my doorstep that I realized what General Twining and the working group had accomplished. By the time I had arrived at the White House, though, it was all ancient history. People were more worried about the sighting information deluging Project Blue Book every day than they were about the all-but-forgotten story of Roswell.

But my mind was drifting and the general was still speaking. He wanted to know what my research had uncovered and what I had learned about Roswell during my years at the White House, what I'd seen, how far the concentric circles of the group and the people who worked for them went.

"Phil, we both know that the package you have is no surprise," he said very flatly.

I didn't respond substantively, and he didn't expect me to, because to do so would have meant breaching security confidentiality that I'd sworn to maintain when I was assigned to the NSC staff at the White House.

"You don't have to say anything officially," he continued. "And I don't expect you to. But can you give me your impressions of how people working for the group talked about the package?"

"I wasn't working for the group, General," I said. "And whatever I saw or heard was only because it happened to pass by, not because I was supposed to do anything about it."

But he pushed me to remember whether the NSC staff

had any direct dealings with the group and how much the Central Intelligence staffers at the White House pressed to get any information they could about what the group was doing. Of course I remembered the questions going back and forth about what might have happened at Roswell, about what was really behind Blue Book, and about all those lights buzzing the Washington Monument back in 1952. I didn't have anything substantive to tell my boss about my involvement, but his questions helped me put together a bigger picture than I thought I knew. From my perspective in 1961, especially after reviewing everything I could about what happened in the days after the Roswell crash, I could see very clearly the things that I didn't understand back in 1955. I didn't know why the CIA was so aggressively agitated about the repeated stories of flying saucer sightings or why they kept searching for any information about the technology from Roswell. I certainly didn't volunteer any information, mainly because nobody asked me, about having seen parts of "the cargo" as it passed through Fort Riley. I just played position, representing the army as the military member of the National Security Staff, but I listened to everything I heard like a fly on the wall.

General Trudeau's questions forced me to ask myself what the big picture was that he saw. He was obviously looking for something in my descriptions of the architecture of the group, as I had learned it from my review of the history, and of the staffers on the lower security classification periphery as I understood it from my experience at the White House. He really wanted to know how the bureaucracy worked, how much activity the group itself generated, what kinds of policy questions came up in my presence, and whether I was asked to comment informally on anything having to do with the issues of the group.

Did Admiral Hillenkoetter host many briefings for President Eisenhower where Generals Twining, Smith, Montague, and Vandenburg were present? Gen. W. B. Smith had replaced Secretary Forrestal after he committed suicide during the second year of the Truman administration. Were Professor Menzel and Drs. Bush and Berkner visitors to the White House on regular occasions? Did they meet at the White House with Admiral Hillenkoetter or the generals?

What was the level of presence of the CIA staffers at the White House through all of this? And did I recognize anyone from the Joint Research and Development Board or the Atomic Energy Commission at any briefings chaired by Admiral Hillenkoetter?

Through General Trudeau's questions I could see not only that the general knew his history almost as well as I did about how the original group was formed and how it must have operated, but he also had a sense of what kind of problem was facing the military R&D and how much leeway he had to solve it. Like most ad hoc creations of government, the group must have at some point become as self-serving as every other joint committee eventually became the longer it functioned and the more its job increased. As the camouflage about flying disks grew, so did the role of the group. Only the group didn't have the one thing most government committees had: the ability to draw upon other areas of the government for more resources. This group was above top secret and, officially, had no right to exist. Therefore, as its functions grew over the next ten years to encompass the investigations of more flying saucer sightings and the research into more encounters with alien aircraft or with the extraterrestrials themselves, its resources became stretched so thin that it had to create reasons for drawing upon other areas of the government.

Accordingly, task-defined subgroups were formed to handle specific areas of investigation or research. These had to have had lower security classifications even if only because the number of personnel involved couldn't have been cleared that quickly to respond to the additional work the group was taking on. In fact, the work of the group must have become unmanageable. Bits and pieces of information slipped out, and the group had to determine what it could let go into the public record and what had to be protected at all costs. As in the story about the shacks, the group members retreated to create new protected structures for the information they had to preserve.

The official camouflage was sagging under the weight of the information the group had to investigate and the pressure of time they were allotted. Soon the military representatives found, just as we did in Korea, that they really couldn't trust the career intelligence people, especially the CIA, because they seemed to have a different agenda. Maybe the military became resistant to giving up all the information it was collecting independently to the central group? Maybe, in the absence of any actual legislation establishing how the group's work was to be paid for, the military saw valuable and fundable weapons opportunities slip through its fingers to the CIA's budget? Maybe— and I know this *is* what happened—a power struggle developed within the group itself.

The whole structure of the working group had changed, too, since the late 1940s when it was formed. What started out as a close-knit group of old friends from prep school had become an unmanageable mess within five years. Many pieces of the pie were floating around, and the different military branches wanted to break off chunks of the black budget so that you needed an entire administration just to manage the managers of the cover-up. Therefore, at some point near the middle of the Eisenhower administration, seams opened up in the grand camouflage scheme where nobody knew what anybody else was doing. Because of the cover-up, nobody really had a need to know, so nobody knew anything. The only people who wanted to get their hands on information and hardware belonged to the CIA, but nobody, even those who vaguely understood what had happened fourteen years earlier, trusted the CIA. Officially, then, nobody knew anything and nothing happened.

Through the 1950s a cascade effect developed. What had started out as a single-purpose camouflage operation was breaking up into smaller units. Command-and-control functions started to weaken and, just like a submarine that breaks up on the bottom of the ocean, debris in the form of information bubbled to the surface. Army CIC, once a powerful force to keep the Roswell story itself suppressed, had weakened under the combined encroachments of the CIA and the FBI. It was during this period that my old friend J. Edgar Hoover, never happy at being kept out of any loop, jumped into the circle and very quietly began investigating the Roswell incident. This shook things up, and very soon afterward, other government agencies—the ones with official reporting responsibilities—began poking around as well.

For all intents and purposes, the original scheme to perpetrate a camouflage was defunct by the late 1950s. Its functions were now being managed by series of individual groups within the military and civilian intelligence agencies, all still sharing limited information with each other, each pursuing its own individual research and investigation, and each—astonishingly—still acting as if some super intelligence group was still in command. But, like the Wizard of Oz, there was no super intelligence group. Its functions had been absorbed by the groups beneath it. But nobody bothered to tell anyone because a super group was never supposed to exist officially in the first place. That which did not exist officially could not go out of existence officially. Hence, right through the next forty years, the remnants of what once was a super group went through the motions, but the real activities were carried out by individual agencies that believed on blind faith that they were being managed by higher-ups. Remember the lines of cars at gas pumps during the fuel shortage of 1973 when one driver, thinking a gas station was open, would wait at a pump and within fifteen minutes scores of other cars pulled up behind him? Lines a mile long formed behind pumps that were never open because there was no gas. That's what the great flying saucer camouflage was like by the time President Kennedy was inaugurated.

"There's nobody home, Phil," General Trudeau told me as we compared our notes at that morning's briefing. "Nobody home except us. We have to make our own policy."

I was a soldier and followed orders, but Trudeau was a general, the product of a political process, stamped with congressional approval, and reporting to a civilian executive. Generals are made by the government, not by the army. They sit between the government and the vast military machine and from the Army Chief of Staff all the way down to the brigadiers at bases around the world, generals create the way military policy is supposed to work. And on the morning of this briefing over cups of coffee in his inner office of the third floor of the Pentagon, Lieutenant General Trudeau was going to make policy and do the very thing that over ten years of secret work groups and committees and research planning had failed to do: exploit the Roswell technology.

"I need you to tell me you found a way to make something out of this mess," General Trudeau told me. "There must be some piece of technology in your file that'll make a weapon, that we can use for one of our helicopters. What do we have in there, Phil?" Then he said. "Time is now of the essence. We have to do something because nobody else will."

In the great cloud of unknowing that had descended upon the Pentagon with respect to the Roswell package, the five or six of us in the navy, air force, and army who actually knew what we had didn't confide in anyone outside his own branch of the military and certainly didn't talk to the CIA. So, in a way that could only happen inside the military bureaucracy, the cover-up became covered up from the cover-up, leaving the few of us in the know free to do whatever we wanted.

General Trudeau and I were all alone out there insofar as the package went. Whatever vestige of the group remained had simply lost track of the material delivered to Foreign Technology fourteen years earlier. And the general was right, nobody was home and our enemies inside government were capitalizing on whatever information they could find. The Roswell package was one of the prizes, and if we didn't do anything with it, the Russians would. And they were onto us.

Our own military intelligence personnel told us that the Soviets were trafficking so heavily in our military secrets that they knew things about us in the Kremlin before we knew them in Congress. The army at least knew the KGB had penetrated the CIA, and the leadership of the CIA had been an integral part of the working group on flying disks since the early 1950s. Thus, whatever secrets the group thought they had, they certainly weren't secrets to the KGB.

But here's what kept the roof from falling in on all of us. The KGB and the CIA weren't really the adversaries everybody thought them to be. They spied on each other, but for all practical purposes, and also because each agency had thoroughly penetrated the other, they behaved just like the same organization. They were all professional spies in a single extended agency playing the same intelligence game and trafficking in information. Information is power to be used. You don't simply give it away to your government's political leadership, whether it's the Republicans, the Tories, or the Communists, just because they tell you to. You can't trust the politicians, but you can trust other spies. At least that's what spies believe, so their primary loyalty is to their own group and the other groups playing the same game. The CIA, KGB, British Secret Service, and a whole host of other foreign intelligence agencies were loyal to themselves and to the profession first and to their respective governments last.

That's one of the reasons we in the military knew that the *professional* KGB leadership, not the Communist Party officers who were only inside for political reasons, were keeping as much information from the Soviet government as the CIA was keeping from our government. Professional spy organizations like the CIA and the KGB tend to exist only to preserve themselves, and that's why neither the U.S. military nor the Russian military trusted them. If you look at how the great spy wars of the Cold War played out you'll see how the KGB and CIA acted like one organization: lots of professional courtesy, lots of shared information to make sure nobody got fired, and a few human sacrifices now and then just to keep everybody honest. But when it came down to loyalty, the CIA was loyal to the KGB and vice versa.

I believe they had a rationale for what they did. I know they thought the rest of us were too stupid to keep the world safe and that by sharing information they kept us out of a nuclear war. I believe this because I knew enough KGB agents during my time and got enough bits and pieces of information off the record to give me a picture of the Soviet Union during the 1950s and 1960s that's very different from what you'd read on the front page of the *New York Times.*

CIA penetration by the KGB and what amounted to their joint spying on the military was a fact we accepted during the 1950s and 1960s, even though most of us in the

Pentagon played spy versus spy as much as we could; those of us, like me, who'd gone to intelligence school during the war and knew some of the counterespionage tricks that kept the people watching you guessing. We would change our routes to work, always used false information stories as bait to test phones we weren't sure about, swept our offices for listening devices, always used a code when talking with one another about sensitive subjects. We had a counterintelligence agent in the military attaché's office over at the Russian consulate in Washington whose friends in the Soviet army trusted the KGB less than I did. If my name came up associated with a story, he'd let me know it. But he'd never tell the CIA. Believe it or not, in the capital of my very own country, that kind of information helped me stay alive.

It was very disconcerting that the CIA had a tail on me all throughout my four-year tenure at the White House. I was mad about it, but there was nothing much I chose to do. Then, when I came back to Washington in 1961 to work for General Trudeau, they put the tail back on and I led him down every back alley and rough neighborhood in D.C. that I could. He wouldn't shake. So the next day, after I told my boss what I was going to do, I led my faceless pursuer right to Langley, Virginia, past a sputtering secretary, and straight into the office of my old adversary, the director of covert operations Frank Wiesner, one of the best friends the KGB ever had. I told Wiesner to his face that yesterday was the last day I would walk around Washington without a handgun. And I put my .45 automatic on his desk. I said if I saw his tail on me tomorrow, they'd find him in the Potomac the next day with two bloody holes for eyes; that is, if they bothered to look for him. Wiesner said, "You won't do that, Colonel." But I reminded him very pointedly that I knew where all his bodies were buried, the people he'd gotten killed through his own ineptitude and, worse, his cooperation with the Russians. I'd tell his story to everyone I knew in Congress. Wiesner backed down. Subsequently, on a trip to London, Wiesner committed suicide and was found hanging in his hotel room. I never did tell his story. Two years later in 1963, one of Wiesner's friends at the agency told me that it was "all in good fun, Phil." Part of an elaborate recruitment process to get me into the CIA after I retired from the army. But I went to work for Senator Strom Thurmond on the Foreign Relations Committee and then Senator Richard Russell on the Warren Commission instead.

Our collective experience dodging the CIA and the KGB only meant that when General Trudeau wanted the CIA kept out of our deliberations at all cost, it was because he knew that everything we discussed would be a topic of conversation at the KGB within twenty-four hours, faster if it were serious enough for the KGB to get their counterparts in the CIA to throw a monkey wrench into things.

How do I know all this? The same way I knew how the KGB stayed one step ahead of us during the Korean War and were able to advise their friends, the North Koreans, how to hold POWs back during the exchange. We had leaks inside the Kremlin just like they had leaks inside the White House. What General Trudeau and I knew in Army R&D, our counterparts in the navy and air force also believed. The CIA was the enemy. You trust no one. So when it became clear to the general even before 1961 that no one remembered what the army had appropriated at Roswell, whatever we had was ours to develop according to our own strategy. But we had to do it so as not to allow the CIA, and ultimately our government's enemies, to appropriate it from us. So when General Trudeau said we have to run radio silent on the Roswell package, I knew exactly what he was talking about.

Logic, and clearly not my military genius, dictated the obvious course. If nobody knows what you have, don't announce it. But if you think you can make something out of what you have, make it. Use any resources at your disposal, but don't say anything to anyone about what you're doing. The only people in the room when we came up with our plan were the general and myself, and he promised, "I won't say anything if you don't, Phil."

"There's nobody in here but us brooms, General," I answered.

So we began to devise a strategy.

"Hypothetically, Phil," Trudeau laid the question out. "What's the best way to exploit what we have without anybody knowing we're doing anything special?"

"Simple, General," I answered. "We don't do anything special."

"You have a plan?" he asked.

"More of an idea than a plan," I began. "But it starts like this. It's what you asked: If we don't want anybody to think we're doing anything out of the ordinary, we don't do anything out of the ordinary. When General Twining made his original recommendations to President Truman and the army, he didn't suggest they do anything with this nut file other than what they ordinarily do. Business as usual. That's how this whole secret group operated. Nobody did anything special. What they did was organize according to a business plan even though the operation was something that hadn't been done before. That's the camouflage: don't change a thing but use your same procedures to handle this alien technology."

"So how do you recommend we operate?" he asked. I think he already figured out what I was saying but wanted me to spell it out so we could start moving my nut file out of the Pentagon and out of the encroaching shadow of the CIA.

"We start the same way this desk has always started: with reports," I said. "I'll write up reports on the alien technology just like it's an intelligence report on any piece of foreign technology. What I see, what I think the potential may be, where we might be able to develop, what company we should take it to, and what kind of contract we should draw up."

"Where will you start?" the general asked.

"I'll line up everything in the nut file," I began. "Everything from what's obvious to what I can't make heads or tails out of. And I'll go to scientists with clearance who we can trust, Oberth and von Braun, for advice."

"I see what you mean," Trudeau acknowledged. "Sure. We'll line up our defense contractors, too. See which ones have ongoing development contracts that allow us to feed your development projects right into them."

"Exactly. That way the existing defense contract becomes

the cover for what we're developing," I said. "Nothing is ever out of the ordinary because we're never starting up anything that hasn't already been started up in a previous contract."

"It's just like a big mix and match," Trudeau described it.

"Only what we're doing, General, is mixing technology we're developing in with technology not of this earth," I said. "And we'll let the companies we're contracting with apply for the patents themselves."

"Of course," Trudeau realized. "If they own the patent we will have completely reverse-engineered the technology."

"Yes, sir, that's right. Nobody will ever know. We won't even tell the companies we're working with where this technology comes from. As far as the world will know the history of the patent is the history of the invention."

"It's the perfect cover, Phil," the general said. "Where will you start?"

"I'll write up my first analysis and recommendation tonight," I promised. "There's not a moment to lose."

"The photographs in my file," I began my report that night over the autopsy reports, which I attached,

show a being of about 4 feet tall. The body seemed decomposed and the photos themselves aren't of much use except to the curious. It's the medical reports that are of interest. The organs, bones, and skin composition are different from ours. The being's heart and lungs are bigger than a human's. The bones are thinner but seem stronger as if the atoms are aligned differently for a greater tensile strength. The skin also shows a different atomic alignment in a way that appears the skin is supposed to protect the vital organs from cosmic ray or wave action or gravitational forces that we don't yet understand. The overall medical report suggests that the medical examiners are more surprised at the similarities between the being found in the spacecraft (note: NSC reports refer to this creature as an Extraterrestrial Biological Entity [EBE]) and human beings than they are at the differences, especially the brain which is bigger in the EBE but not at all unlike ours.

I wrote on into the first of many nights that year, drafting rough notes that I would later type into formal reports that no one would ever see except General Trudeau, reaching conclusions that seemed more science fiction than real. I was most happy not because I was finally working on these files but, oddly enough, because when I sat down to write, I believed these reports would never see the light of day. In the harsh reality of the everyday world, they sound, even now as I remember them, fantastic. Even more fantastic, I remember, were the startling conclusions I allowed myself to come to. Was this really me writing, or was it somebody else? Where did these ideas come from?

If we consider similar biological factors that affect human beings, like long distance runners whose hearts and lungs are larger than average, hill and mountain dwellers whose lung capacity is greater than those who live closer to sea level, and even natural athletes whose long striated muscle alignment is different from those who are not athletes, can we not assume that the EBEs who have fallen into our possession represent the end process of genetic engineering designed to adapt them to long space voyages within an electromagnetic wave environment at speeds which create the physical conditions described by Einstein's General Theory of Relativity? (Note for the record: Dr. Hermann Oberth suggests we consider the Roswell craft from the New Mexico desert not a spacecraft but a time machine. His technical report on propulsion will follow.)

CHAPTER 7

The EBE

Therefore, perhaps we should consider the EBEs as described in the medical autopsy reports humanoid robots rather then life forms, specifically engineered for long-distance travel through space or time.

A HOT WASHINGTON SUMMER MORNING HAD ALREADY SETTLED over the Potomac like a wet towel on the day I finished the first of my reports for General Trudeau. And what a report it was. It set the tone for all of the other reports and recommendations I was to make for the general over the next two years. It began with the biggest find we had: the alien extraterrestrial itself.

Had I not read the medical examiner's report of the alien from Walter Reed with my own eyes and reviewed the 1947 army photographs and sketches, I would have called any description of this creature pure science fiction; that is, had I not seen either this or its twin suspended in a transparent crypt at Fort Riley. But here it was again, just a yellowing sheaf of papers and a few cracked glossy prints in a brown folder sitting among scores of odds and ends, bits of debris, and strange devices in my nut file.

Even stranger to me than the medical examiner's report was my reaction: What could we exploit from this entity? I wrote the general that "whether we found an 'extraterrestrial biological entity' is not as important in the R&D arena as are the ways we can develop what we learn from it so that man can travel in space." This quickly became the overriding concern with all of the Roswell artifacts and the general format for all of my reports. Once I swallowed back the "oh wow" aspect to all of this life-altering information—and sometimes it took a very big swallow—I was still left with the job of sorting out what looked promising for R&D to develop from what seemed beyond our realistic grasp for the present. I began with the EBE.

The medical report and supporting photographs in front of me suggested that the creature was remarkably well adapted for long-distance space travel. For example, biological time, the Walter Reed medical examiners hypothesized, must have passed very slowly for the entity because it possessed a very slow metabolism, evidenced, they said, by the enormous capacities of the huge heart and lungs. The physiology of this thing indicated that this was not a creature whose body had to work hard to sustain it. A larger heart, my ME's report read, meant that it took fewer beats than an average human heart to drive the thin, milky, almost lymphatic-like fluid through a limited, more primitive-looking, and apparently reduced-capacity circulatory system. As a result, the biological clock beat more slowly than a human's and probably allowed the creature to travel great distances in a shorter biological time than humans.

The heart was very decomposed by the time the Walter Reed pathologists got their hands on it. It seemed to them that our atmosphere was quite toxic to the creature's organs. Given the time that passed between the crash of the vehicle and the creature's arrival at Walter Reed, it decomposed all of the organs far more rapidly than it would have decomposed human organs. This fact particularly impressed me because I had seen one of these things, if not the very one described in the report, suspended in a gel-like substance at Fort Riley. So whatever exposure it must have had was very minimal by human standards because the medical personnel at the 509th's Walker Field got it into a liquid preservation state very quickly. Nevertheless, the Walter Reed pathologists were unable to determine with any certainty the structure of the creature's heart except to guess that because it functioned as a passive blood-storage facility as well as a pumping muscle that it didn't work the same way as did a four-chambered human heart. They said the alien heart seemed to have had internal diaphragm-like muscles that worked less hard than human heart muscle did because the creatures were meant to survive within a reduced gravity field as we understand gravity.

As camels store water, so did this creature store whatever atmosphere it breathed in the large capacity of its lungs. The lungs functioned in ways similar to a camel's humps or to our scuba tanks and released atmosphere very slowly into the creature's system. Because of the large heart and the storage function we believed it had, we also surmised that it took far less breathable atmosphere to sustain the creature, thereby reducing the need for carrying large volumes of atmosphere along on the voyage. Perhaps the aircraft had a means of recirculating its atmosphere, recycling spent or waste air back into the craft. Moreover, because the creatures were only four or so feet tall, the large lungs occupied a far greater percentage of the chest cavity than human lungs did, further impressing the pathologists who examined the creatures' remains. This also indicated to us that perhaps we were dealing with an entity specifically engineered for long-distance travel.

If we believed the heart and lungs seemed bioengineered for long-distance travel so, too, was the creature's skeletal tissue. Although it was in a state of advanced decomposition, the creature's bones looked to the army medical examiners to be fibrous, actually thinner than comparable human bones such as the ribs, sternum, clavicle, and pelvis. Pathologists speculated that the bones were more flexible than human bones and had a resiliency that might be related to the function of shock absorbers. More brittle human bones might more easily shatter under the stresses these alien entities must have been routinely subjected to. However, with a flexible skeletal frame, these entities appeared well suited for potential shocks and physical traumas of extreme forces and could withstand the fractures that would cripple human space travelers in a similar environment.

The military recovery team at the Roswell site had reported that the two creatures still alive after the crash had difficulty breathing our atmosphere. Whether that was because they were suddenly tossed out of their craft, unprotected, into our gravity envelope or whether our atmosphere itself was toxic to them, we don't know. We also don't know whether the one creature who died very shortly after the crash was struggling to breathe because he was fatally wounded by gunshots or because of other reasons. Military witnesses recounted different stories about the creature that survived and tried to run. Some said it was struggling to breathe from the moment the military had secured the area; others said that it was gasping only after it had been shot by one of the sentries. My guess was that it was the alien's sudden exposure to the earth's strong gravity that caused the creature to panic at first. That could have been one reason his breathing seemed labored. Then, after he fled and was shot, he was struggling to breathe because of his wounds. The medical examiner's report mentioned nothing about toxic gases or the kind of atmosphere he believed the creatures naturally breathed.

If the Roswell craft were a scout or surveillance ship, as the military analysts back at Wright believed, then it was also more than likely that the creatures never intended to exit the craft. This was a craft equipped with a device that was capable of penetrating our nighttime or utilizing the temperature differentials of different objects to create a visual image, enabling the occupants to navigate and observe in darkness. And because it could elude our interceptors and appear and disappear on our radar screens at will, we believed that the occupants simply stayed inside and observed rather than roamed about. Perhaps other types of craft deployed from this same culture were equipped to land and carry out missions and therefore had breathing and antigravity apparatus on board for its crew that permitted them to exit the craft without suffering any consequences. The medical examiner didn't speculate on this.

What did intrigue those who inspected the aircraft once it

was shipped to Wright Field was the complete absence of any food-preparation facilities. Nor were there any stored foodstuffs on board. At a time when space travel was a science fiction writer's fantasy, military analysts were already at work formulating ideas for how just such a technology could be practically implemented. It was not for travel to other planets, but for navigation around the earth because that's the technology that military planners believed the Germans were developing as an extension of their V2 rocket program. If you're going to put airmen into earth orbit, how do you process their waste products, provide adequate oxygen, and sustain them during prolonged periods? Clearly, after you've developed a launch vehicle with enough thrust to put a craft into earth orbit, keeping it there long enough for it to accomplish a mission is the next problem to tackle. The Roswell craft seemed to have tackled it because somehow it got here from somewhere else. But there was no indication of how such household problems as food preparation and the disposal of waste were solved.

There was much speculation from the different medical analysts about what these beings were composed of and what could have sustained them. First of all, doctors were more tantalized by the similarities the creatures shared with us than they were concerned about the differences. Rather than hideous-looking insects or the reptilian man-eaters that attacked Earth in *War of the Worlds,* these beings looked like little versions of us, only different. It was eerie.

While doctors couldn't figure out how the entities' essential body chemistry worked, they determined that they contained no new basic elements. However, the reports that I had suggested new combinations of organic compounds that required much more evaluation before doctors could form any opinions. Of specific interest was the fluid that served as blood but also seemed to regulate bodily functions in much the same way glandular secretions do for the human body. In these biological entities, the blood system and lymphatic systems seem to have been combined. And if an exchange of nutrients and waste occurred within their systems, that exchange could have only taken place through the creature's skin or the outer protective covering they wore because there were no digestive or waste systems.

The medical report revealed that the creatures were enclosed within a one-piece protective covering like a jumpsuit or outer skin in which the atoms were aligned so as to provide a great tensile strength and flexibility. One examiner wrote that it reminded him of a spider's web, which appears very fragile but is, in fact, very strong. The unique qualities of a spiderweb result from the alignment of fibers that provide great tenacity because they're able to stretch under great pressure, yet display a resiliency that allows them to snap back into shape even after the shock of an impact. Similarly, the creature's spacesuit or outer skin appeared to be stretched around it as if it were literally spun over the creature and seized up around it, providing a perfect skin-tight protective fit. The doctors had never seen anything like it before.

I think I finally understood it years later, after I had left the Pentagon and I was buying a Christmas tree. As I stood there in the frosty air, I watched as the young man who prepared the tree for transport inserted it, top first, into a stubby barrel-like device that automatically spun a twine mesh covering around the branches to keep them in place for the trip home. After I got home I had to cut through the mesh with a knife to remove the tree and separate the branches. This tree setup reminded me specifically of the medical report on the creature from the Roswell crash, and I imagined that maybe the spinning process of the creature's outer garment resembled something like this.

The lengthwise alignment of the fibers in the suit also prompted the medical analysts to suggest that the suit might have been capable of protecting the wearer against the low-energy cosmic rays that would routinely bombard any craft during a space journey. The interior organs of the creature seemed so fragile and oversized that the Walter Reed medical analysts imagined that without the suit the entity would have been vulnerable to the cumulative physical trauma from a constant energy particle bombardment. Space travel without protection from subatomic particle bombardment might subject the traveler to the same kind of effects he'd experience if he were cooked in a microwave oven. The particle bombardment inside the craft, if heavy enough to constitute a shower, would so excite and accelerate the creature's atomic structure that the resulting heat energy would literally cook the entity up.

The Walter Reed doctors were also fascinated by the nature of the creature's inner skin. It resembled, although their preliminary reports didn't go into any chemical analysis, a thin layer of fatty tissue unlike any they'd ever seen before. And it was completely permeable, as if it were constantly exchanging chemicals back and forth with the combination blood/lymphatic system. Was this the way the creatures nourished themselves during their journeys and was this how waste was processed? The very small mouths and the lack of a human digestive system troubled the doctors at first because they didn't know how these things were sustained. But their hypothesis that they processed chemicals released from their skin and maybe even recirculated waste chemicals would have explained the lack of any food-preparation or waste-processing facilities on the craft. I speculated, however, that they didn't require food or facilities for waste disposal because they weren't actual lifeforms, only a kind of robot or android.

Another explanation, of course, suggested by the engineers at Wright Field, is that there would have been no need for food-preparation facilities had this craft been only a small scout ship that didn't venture far from a larger craft. The creatures' low metabolism meant that they could survive extended periods away from the main craft by subsisting on some form of military prepackaged foods until they returned to base. Neither the Wright Field engineers nor the Walter Reed medical examiners had an explanation for the lack of waste disposal on board the craft, nor could they explain how the creatures' waste was processed. Maybe I was speculating too far about robots or androids when I was writing my report for General Trudeau, but I kept thinking, also, that the skin analysis that I was reading sounded more akin to the skin of a houseplant than the skin of a human being. That, too, could have been another explanation for the lack of food or waste facilities.

Much of the attention during the preliminary and later autopsies of the creatures focused on the size, nature, and anatomy of their brains. Much credence also was given to the firsthand descriptions of on-scene witnesses who said they received impressions from the dying creature that it was suffering and in great pain. No one heard the creature make any sounds, so any impressions, Army Intelligence personnel assumed, would have to have been created through some type of empathic projection or outright mental telepathy. But witnesses said they heard no "words" in their mind, only the resonance of a shared or projected impression much simpler than a sentence but far more complex because they were able to share with the creature a sense not only of suffering but of profound sadness, as if it were in mourning for the others who perished on board the craft. These witness reports intrigued me more than any other information we took from the crash site.

The medical examiners believed that the alien brain, way oversized in comparison with the human brain and in proportion to the creature's tiny stature, had four distinct sections. The creatures were dead and the brains had begun to decompose by the time they were removed from the soft spongy skulls that felt to the doctors more like palatal cartilage than the hard bone of a human cranium. Even had the creatures been alive when they were examined, 1947 medical technology didn't have ultrasound scanning or the high-resonance tomography of today's radiology labs. Accordingly, there was no way for the doctors to evaluate the nature of the cranial lobes, or "spheres," as they called them in the report. Thus, despite the rampant speculation about the nature of the creatures' brains—thought projection, psychokinetic powers, and the like—no hard evidence existed of anything, and the reports were very light on real scientific data.

Where the possibility of some evidence about the workings of the alien brains did exist was in what I referred to in my reports as the "headbands." Among the artifacts we retrieved were devices that looked something like headbands but had neither adornment nor decoration of any kind. Embedded by some very advanced kind of vulcanizing process into a form of flexible plastic were what we now know to have been electrical conductors or sensors, similar to the conductors on an electroencephalograph or polygraph. This band was fitted around the part of the alien cranium just above the ears where the skull began to expand to accommodate the large brain. At the time, the field reports from the crash and the subsequent analysis at Wright Field indicated that the engineers at the Air Materiel Command thought these might be communication devices, like the throat mikes our pilots wore during World War II. But, as I would find out when I evaluated the device and sent it into the market for reverse-engineering, this was a throat mike only in a way that a primitive stylus can be considered the forerunner of the color laser-imaging printer.

Suffice it to say that in the few hours the material was at Walker Field in Roswell, more than one officer at the 509th gingerly slipped this thing over his head and tried to figure out what it did. At first it did nothing. There were no buttons, no switches, no wires, nothing that could even be considered to have been a control panel. So no one knew how to turn it on or off. Moreover, the band was not really adjustable, though it had enough elasticity to have been one-size-fits-all for the creatures whose skulls were large enough to accommodate them. However, the reports I read stated, the few officers whose heads were just large enough to have made contact with the full array of conductors got the shocks of their lives. In their descriptions of the headband, these officers reported everything from a low tingling sensation inside their heads to a searing headache and a brief array of either dancing or exploding colors on the insides of their eyelids as they rotated the device around their head and brought the sensors into contact with different parts of their skull.

These eyewitness reports suggested to me that the sensors stimulated different parts of the brain while at the same time exchanged information with the brain. Again, using the analogy of an EEG, these devices were a very sophisticated mechanism for translating the electrical impulses inside the creatures' brains into specific commands. Perhaps these headband devices comprised the pilot interface of the ship's navigational and propulsion system combined with a long-range communications device. At first I didn't know, but it was only when we began development of the long brain-wave research project toward the end of my tenure at the Pentagon that I realized just what we had and how it might be developed. It took a long time to harvest this technology, but fifty years after Roswell, versions of these devices eventually became a component of the navigational control system for some of the army's most sophisticated helicopters and will soon be on the American consumer electronics market as user-input devices for personal computer games.

The first Army Air Force analysts and engineers both at the 509th and at Wright Field were also bedeviled by the lack of any traditional controls and propulsion system in the crashed vehicle. Looking at their reports and the artifacts from the perspective of 1961, however, I imagined that the keys to understanding what made the craft go and directed its flight lay not only within the craft itself but in the relationship between the pilots and the craft. If we hypothesized a brain-wave guidance system that was as specific to the pilots' electronic signature as it was to the spacecraft's, then we were looking at an entirely revolutionary concept of guided flight in which the pilot *was* the system. Imagine transportation devices in which the key to the ignition is a digitized code derived from your electroencephalographic signature and is read automatically upon your donning some sort of sensorized headband. That's the way I believed the spacecraft was navigated, by direct interaction between the electronic waves generated within the minds of the pilots and the craft's directional controls. The electronic brain signals were interpreted and transmitted by the headband devices, which served as interfaces.

I never managed to obtain a copy of the Bethesda autopsy of the alien body the navy received from General Twining. I only had the army report. The remaining bodies were kept in storage at Wright Field initially. Then they were split up among the services. When the air force became a separate branch of the service, the remaining bodies, stored at Wright, along with the spacecraft, were sent to Norton Air Force Base in California, where the air force began experiments to replicate the technology of the vehicle. This made sense. The air force cared about the flight capabilities of the craft and how to build defenses against it.

Experiments were carried out at Norton and ultimately at Nellis Air Force Base in Nevada, at the famous Groom Lake site where the Stealth technology was developed. The army cared only for the weapons systems aboard the craft and how they could be reengineered for our own use. The original Roswell spacecraft remained at Norton, however, where the air force and CIA maintained a kind of alien technology museum, the final resting place of the Roswell spacecraft. But experiments in replicated alien craft continued to be carried on through the years as engineers tried to adapt the propulsion and navigation systems to our level of technology. This continues to this very day, almost in plain sight for people with security clearance who are taken to where the vehicles are kept. Over the years, the replicated vehicles have become an ongoing, inner-circle saga among top-ranking military officers and members of the government, especially the favored senators and members of the House who vote along military lines. Those who are shown the secrets are immediately bound by national secrecy legislation and cannot reveal what they saw. Thus, the official camouflage is maintained despite the large number of people who really know the truth. I admit I've never seen the craft at Norton with my own eyes, but enough reports passed across my desk during my years at Foreign Technology so that I knew what the secret was and how it was maintained.

There were no conventional technological explanations for the way the Roswell craft's propulsion system operated. There were no atomic engines, no rockets, no jets, nor any propeller-driven form of thrust. Those of us in R&D from all three branches of the service tried for years to adapt the craft's drive system to our own technology, but, through the 1960s and 1970s, fell short of getting it operational. The craft was able to displace gravity through the propagation of magnetic waves controlled by shifting the magnetic poles around the craft so as to control, or vector, not a propulsion system but the repulsion force of like charges. Once they realized this, engineers at our country's primary defense contractors raced among themselves to figure out how the craft could retain its electric capacity and how the pilots who navigated it could live within the energy field of a wave. At issue was not only a great discovery, but the nuts-and-bolts chance to land multibillion-dollar development contracts for a whole generation of military air and undersea craft.

The initial revelations into the nature of the spacecraft and its pilot interface came very quickly during the first few years of testing at Norton. The air force discovered that the entire vehicle functioned just like a giant capacitor. In other words, the craft itself stored the energy necessary to propagate the magnetic wave that elevated it, allowed it to achieve escape velocity from the earth's gravity, and enabled it to achieve speeds of over seven thousand miles per hour. The pilots weren't affected by the tremendous g-forces that build up in the acceleration of conventional aircraft because to aliens inside, it was as if gravity was being folded around the outside of the wave that enveloped the craft. Maybe it was like traveling inside the eye of a hurricane. But how did the pilots interface with the wave form they were generating?

I reported to General Trudeau that the secret to this system could be found in the single-piece skin-tight coveralls spun around the creatures. The lengthwise atomic alignment of the strange fabric was a clue to me that somehow the pilots became part of the electrical storage and generation of the craft itself. They didn't just pilot or navigate the vehicle; they *became* part of the electrical circuitry of the vehicle, vectoring it in a way similar to the way you order a voluntary muscle to move. The vehicle was simply an extension of their own bodies because it was tied into their neurological systems in ways that even today we are just beginning to utilize.

So the creatures were able to survive extended periods living inside a high-energy wave by becoming the primary circuit in the control of the wave. They were protected by their suits, which enclosed them head to feet, but their suits enabled them to become one with the vehicle, literally part of the wave. In 1947 this was a technology so new to us that it was as frightening as it was frustrating. If we could only develop the power source necessary to generate a consistently well-defined magnetic wave around a vehicle, we could harness a technology which would have surpassed all forms of rocket and jet propulsion. It's a process we're still trying to master today, fifty years after the craft fell into our possession.

I pushed myself through the night to complete the report for the general. At least I wanted him to see that our strategy held out the probability that even in a basic evaluation of the material we recovered, the seeds were there for specific products we could develop. I wanted to start the entire process by writing him a background report about the nature of the beings we'd autopsied and what we could understand of the technology from an analysis of their spacecraft.

By the time I finished, it was already just before sunup, and I looked like hell. This was the day I was going to drop my report on the general's desk, first thing. I'd snap right to attention in front of him and say, "Here's that report you were waiting for, General," confident it contained more than he ever thought it would because the subject was that new and complicated. But I wanted to be clean-shaven and in a clean, crisp shirt. That's what I wanted. I didn't even need any sleep because my optimism and confidence at that moment were more powerful than anything a few hours of sleep could give me. I knew I was onto something here, something that could change the world. Here in the basement of the Pentagon, lying close to dormancy for over a decade, were secrets my predecessors had just begun to discover before they were stopped. Maybe it had been the Korean War, maybe the CIA or other intelligence agencies had cast a pall over R&D's operation, but those days were over now. I was at the Foreign Technology desk and the responsibility for this material was mine, just like General Twining had said it should be fourteen years ago.

In those drawers I had found the puzzle pieces for a whole new age of technology. Things that were only twinkles in the minds of engineers and scientists were right here in front of me as hard, cold artifacts of an advanced culture. Craft that navigated by brain waves and floated on a wave of electromagnetic energy, creatures who look through devices that helped them turn night into day, and beams of light so narrow and focused you couldn't see them until they bounced off an object far away.

For years scientists had thought about what it would have been like to travel in space, especially since the Russians first put up their Sputnik. Plans for a military-operated moon base had been developed by the army in the 1950s under the leadership of Gen. Arthur Trudeau at R&D but were ultimately shelved because of the formation of NASA. Those plans had tried to confront the issues of space travel for prolonged periods of time and adjusting to a low-gravity state on the moon. But here, right in front of us, was the evidence of how an alien culture had adapted itself to long-range space travel, different gravities, and the exposure to energy particles and waves crashing into a spacecraft by the billions. All we had to do was marshal the vast array of resources in the military and industry at R&D's disposal and harvest that technology. It was all laid out for us, if we knew how to use it. This was the beginning and I was right there on the cusp of it.

So in the first few minutes of glimmering light just on the edge of the horizon, a promise of the day to come, I took off for home, for a shower, a shave, a pot of coffee, and the crispest new uniform I could find. I was driving east into the dawn of a brand-new age, my report right alongside me in my briefcase on the front seat. There would be other reports and the details of long-term complicated projects to confront me in the future, I knew, but this was the first, the foundation, the beam of light into a hidden past and an uncertain future. But it was a light, and that's what was important. No time for sleep now. There was too much to do.

CHAPTER 8

The Project Gets Under Way

"THIS IS A HELLUVA REPORT, PHIL," GENERAL TRUDEAU SAID, looking up from the paper-clipped sheaf of typewritten sheets I'd handed him first thing that morning. I'd been waiting at my desk since before six when I got back to the Pentagon, taking looks outside the building every once in a while as the bright orange reflection of the rising sun that exploded in a distant window and looked as if it had caught fire. "What'd you do, stay up all night writing it?"

"I put in some work after hours," I said. "I don't want to spend too much time in the nut file when people are supposed to be working."

The general laughed as he fingered through the paperwork, but you could see he was impressed. As much as I wanted to denigrate the Roswell file in front of him as a bunch of drawers full of stuff that people would put me away for, we both knew that it contained much of the future of our R&D.

Military research and development agencies were under growing pressure from the Congress to put some success points on the scoreboard or get out of the rocket-launching business for good. Early failures to lift off the navy's WAC

Corporal and the army Redstone had made laughingstocks out of the American rocket program while the Soviets were showing off their success like basketball players on fancy layups right across the court. The army's Project Horizon moon-base project was sitting in its own file cabinet gathering dust. And there was also a growing concern among the military that we'd be pushed into taking over the failed French mission in Indochina to keep the Vietcong, Pathet Lao, and Khmer Rouge from making the whole area Communist. It was a war we could not win but that would drain our resources from the real battlefront in Eastern Europe.

So, even more than scoring some field goals, General Trudeau needed projects going into development to keep the civilian agencies from cutting us back and diverting our resources. Now my boss held my first report in his hands and knew that our strategic plan had some rational grounding. He pushed for a tactical plan.

"We know what we want to do," he said. "Now, how do we do it?"

"I've been thinking about that, too, General," I said. "And here's how I'd like to start."

I explained that I wanted to compile a list of all our technical human resources, like the rocket scientists from Germany then still working at Alamogordo and White Sands. I'd met more than my share of our rocket-fuel and guidance specialists in the guided-missile program during my years at Red Canyon in command of the Nike battalion. But we were working with theoretical scientists as well, men with experience who could combine the cold precision of an engineer with the speculative vision of a free thinker. These were the people I wanted to assemble into a brain trust, people I could talk to about strange artifacts and devices that had no basis in earthly reality. They were the scientists who could tell me what the potential was in items like wafer-shaped plywood-thin pieces of silicon with mysterious silver etchings on them.

"And once you have this brain trust," General Trudeau asked, "then what?"

"Match them up with technologies," I said. I admitted that we were flying blind on much of the material that we had. We couldn't go out to the general scientific and academic communities to ask them what we had because we would very quickly lose control of our own secrets. Besides, a lot of it had to do with weaponry, and there were very strict rules on what we could and could not disclose without the appropriate clearances. But our brain trust would be invaluable. And, with the proper orientation and security checks, they would keep our secrets, too, just as they had since the end of World War II.

"Which of the scientists do you have in mind?" Trudeau asked, taking out the little black leather-covered notepad he kept in his inside pocket.

"I was thinking of Robert Sarbacher," I said. "Wernher von Braun, of course. Hans Kohler. Hermann Oberth. John von Neumann."

"How much do they know about Roswell?" Trudeau wanted to know. If they'd been consulted on the Roswell material back in 1947, as I knew Wernher von Braun had been by General Twining, then we weren't revealing any secrets. If they had never been informed about the crash, then we were going out on a limb by sharing information that was still classified above top secret. General Trudeau needed to know how dangerous it was to bring these scientists into the loop. But I assured him that all of them knew something about Roswell because of their connection with the Research and Development Board. During the Eisenhower administration information about the classified research and data collection projects into extraterrestrials was routinely filtered to the Office of Research and Development because the head of the Research and Development Board had been one of the original members of the group.

"I was at the White House when Sarbacher was on the board, General," I told my boss. "So I can be pretty sure he was in the know. And Hermann Oberth," I admitted to Trudeau. "He already told me that he believed that the objects we saw popping up on our radar screens at Red Canyon and then disappearing as if they were never there were probably the same kinds of extraterrestrial aircraft that we picked up at Roswell. So he knew, but I don't know how."

"Well, that's good news, at least," the general said. "I'd

rather not be the one authorizing the release of classified information to anyone who didn't know it beforehand. And I don't want to put you in the position, Phil, of having to explain to any higher-ups why you decided to release top-secret information to people without clearances, even in the interest of national security."

I appreciated that, but for our plan to work, we needed the technical and scientific expertise people like von Braun, Oberth, and Sarbacher could bring to any reverse-engineering and product-development strategies.

"How will you approach them?" Trudeau asked.

"We'll have to begin by taking an inventory of all of the defense industry contracts we're currently managing, General," I said. "Line up the contracts and systems we're developing with the materials in the nut file to see where they fit in. Then bring in the scientists to consult on making sure we know what we think we have, that is, if they can figure out what we have."

"Let's go through a potential product list first," the general suggested. "Then see where our contracts line up and where the scientists can help. And you know what happens then," Trudeau asked.

I wasn't sure where he was going to take this.

"We're sticking you back in civilian clothes and sending you on the road to visit our friends in these defense contractors."

"I don't even get to keep my battle ribbons," I joked.

"I don't want anyone to know," General Trudeau explained, "that some lieutenant colonel on the CIA's Most Wanted list is traveling to our biggest defense contractors with a mysterious briefcase full of nobody knows what. You might as well wear a sign," he laughed. "We have to get to work on that list."

That same afternoon I went back to my report on the EBE and his craft and began to list the riddles it contained and the opportunities for the discovery of product it presented to us. The entire event was like an enigma to us because every conventional requirement one would expect to have found at the crash site, in the craft, or even in the EBEs themselves was missing.

Where was the engine or the power supply for the craft? It

had neither jet engines nor propellers. It had no rocket propulsion like the V2 missiles, nor did it carry any fuel. At Norton Air Force Base, where the craft eventually was hangared, engineers marveled at the thin amalgam of the most refined copper and purest silver they had ever seen that covered the ship's underside. The metal was remarkable for its conductivity, as if the entire craft was an electrical circuit offering no resistance to the flow of current. Yet it was something our military engineers could not replicate. By the 1950s at Norton Air Force Base, at least two prototypes of the alien craft had been fabricated, but neither had the power source of the craft that had crashed. In its stead were crude attempts at nuclear fission generators, but they were ineffective and dangerous. Even the portable nuclear generators that would power the primitive Soviet and American satellites in the 1960s were insufficient for the needs of the replicated spacecraft. So the question remained, what powered the Roswell spacecraft?

I reviewed all of my discoveries in a checklist:

- The crescent-shaped space vehicle also had no traditional navigational controls as we understood them. There were no control sticks, wheels, throttles, pedals, cables, flaps, or rudders. How did the creatures pilot this ship and how did they control the speed, accelerating from a near stationary hover above a given spot, like a helicopter, to speeds in excess of seven thousand miles per hour in a matter of seconds?
- What protected the creatures from the tremendous g-forces they would have had to have pulled in any conventional aircraft? Our own pilots in World War II had to wear special devices as they pulled up out of dives that kept the oxygen from flowing out of their brains and causing them to black out. But we found nothing in the flight suits of the creatures that indicated that they faced the same problem. Yet their craft should have pulled ten times the g-forces our own pilots did, so we couldn't figure out how they managed this.

No controls, no protection, no power supply, no fuel: these were the riddles I listed.

Alongside them I listed that:

- The craft itself was an electrical circuit.
- That the flight suits—"flight skins" is a better description—the creatures wore were made of a substance whose atomic structure was elongated, strengthened lengthwise, so as to provide a directional flow to any current applied to it.

The engineers who first discovered this were amazed at the pure conductivity of these skins, functionally like the skin of the craft itself, and their obvious ability to protect the wearer while at the same time vectoring some kind of electronic field. Where was the physical junction of the circuit between the pilot and the ship? Was it turned on and off somehow by the pilot himself through a switch we didn't know about?

Alongside the riddle of the apparent absence of navigational controls I listed the sensorized headband that so intrigued the officers at Roswell's Walker Field and fascinated me as well. If, as we all suspected, this device picked up the electronic signatures from the creatures' oversized brains, what did it do with them? I believed—and our industrial product development from the 1960s through today as the brain-wave-control helmets finally came into service ultimately confirmed—that these headbands translated the brain's electronic signals into system commands that controlled speed, direction, and elevation. Maybe the headbands had to be calibrated or tuned to each individual pilot, or maybe the pilots—since I believed they were genetically engineered beings biologically manufactured especially for flight or long-term exploration—had to be calibrated to the headband. Either way, the headbands were the interface between the pilot and the ship. But that still didn't resolve the question of the lack of cables, gears, or wires.

Maybe the answer lay not in the lack of structural controls but in the way the suit, the headband, the creatures' brains, and the entire craft worked together. In other words, when I looked at the possible function of the entire system, the synchronicity between the brain interface in the headband, the pure conductivity of the spacecraft, and the elongated structure of the space skins, which also acted like a circuit, I could see how directional instructions could have been translated by the headbands into some form of current flowing through the skins and into the series of raised deck panels where there were indentations for the creatures' hands. The indentations on these panels, as the Roswell field reports described them, looked like the handprints pressed into the concrete at the old Grauman's Chinese Theater in Hollywood. Were the directional commands a series of electronic instructions transmitted directly from the creatures' brains along their bodies and through the panels into the ship itself as if the ship were only an extension of the creature's body? For that to have been the case, something was still missing. The engine.

Again, I settled on the idea of function over structure. The debris and the spacecraft indicated that an engine didn't somehow fall out of the craft when it crashed. A conventional engine was never there in the first place. What we found was that the craft seemed to have had the ability to store as well as conduct a vast amount of current. What if the craft itself were the engine, imparted with a steady current from another source that it stored as if it were a giant capacitor? This would be like charging the battery in an electric car and running it until the battery was drained. Sound far-fetched? It's not much different from filling up a car with gas at the pump and driving until the tank's dry, or fueling a plane and making sure you land before the fuel's gone. I suspected the Roswell craft was simply a capacitor that stored current that was controlled or vectored by the pilot and was able to be recharged in some way or could recharge itself with some form of built-in generator.

That would have explained the power supply, I noted alongside the riddle of the missing engine, but what was the means of propulsion and direction? If there was a force that functioned the same way thrust does, it wasn't immediately obvious how it was created and vectored. As early as September 1947, scientists who had gone to the Air Materiel Command at Wright Field to see the debris were speculating that the electronic potential of the Roswell craft reminded them of the German and British antigravity experiments of the 1920s and 1930s. General Twining was reported to have said more than once that the name of the Serbian electrical engineer and inventor of alternating current, Nikola Tesla, kept bubbling up in the conversation because the scientists examining the damaged craft described the way it must have converted an electromagnetic field into an antigravity field. And, of course, the craft itself reminded them of the German experimental fighter aircraft that made their appearance near the end of the war but that had been in development ever since the 1930s.

Tesla and a number of other European scientists had been pioneers in the conversion of circumscribed small-area antigravity fields out of electromagnetic fields. However, the effort to develop true antigravity aircraft never came to fruition among conventional aircraft manufacturers because gasoline, jet, and rocket engines provided a perfectly good weapons technology. But the theory of electromagnetic antigravity propulsion was not unknown even if it was not well understood and, without a power source like a small portable nuclear fission generator, not at all feasible. But, what if the flying craft already carried enough electric potential and storage capacity to retain its power, just like a very advanced flying battery? Then it might have all the power it needed to propagate and vector a wave directionally by shifting its magnetic poles. If the magnetic field theory experiments carried out by engineers and electrical energy pioneers Paul Biefeld and Townsend Brown in the 1920s at the California Institute for Advanced Studies were accurately reported—and the U.S. military as well as scientific record keepers at Hoover's young Bureau of Investigation kept very close tabs on what these engineers were doing—then the technological theory for antigravity flight existed before World War II.

In fact, prototypes for vertical takeoff and landing disk-shaped aircraft had been on the drawing boards at the California Institute since before the war. It was just that in the United States nobody paid them much attention. The Germans did develop and had flown flying disks, or so the intelligence reports read, even though they had no impact on the outcome of the war other than stimulating a race between the United States and the USSR to gather as much of the German technology as possible. Thus, even though engineers had attempted to build vertical takeoff and flying-wing aircraft before and had succeeded, the Roswell space-craft, because it was so truly functional and outflew any-thing we had—as well as traveled in space—represented a practical technological challenge to the scientists visiting the Air Materiel Command. We knew what the EBEs did, we just couldn't duplicate how. My reports for Army R&D were analyses of the types of technology that we had to develop to either challenge this spacecraft militarily with a credible defense or build one ourselves.

In my notes to General Trudeau, I reviewed for him all the technological implications that I believed were relevant in any discussion about what could be harvested from the Roswell craft. I also wrote up what I understood about the magnetic field technology and how unconventional design-ers and engineers had drafted prototypes for these "anti-gravs" earlier in the century. All of this pointed in one direction, I suggested: that we now had a craft and could farm out to industry the components that comprised this electromagnetic antigravity drive and brain-wave-directed navigational controls. We had to dole them out piecemeal once we broke them down into developable units, each of which could have its own engineering track. For that we'd need the advice of the scientists who would eventually comprise our brain trust, individuals we could rely on and whom we could talk to about the Roswell debris. These were scientists who routinely worked with our prime defense contractors and could tell us whom to approach in their R&D divisions for secure and private consultations.

I was hoping that the evaluation of the kinds of things we were able to learn from the EBE and his craft that I was preparing for General Trudeau would lead me toward the solution of some of the physiological problems we knew our astronauts would encounter in spaceflight. In the early 1960s, astronauts from both the United States and the USSR had made their first orbital flights and had experi-enced more than a few negative physical symptoms from the weightless environment during the mission. Despite our official claims that humans could travel safely in space, our doctors knew that even short periods of weightlessness were extremely disorienting to some of our astronauts, and the longer the flight, the more uncomfortable the symptoms could become. We were worried about loss of physical strength, reduced muscle capability in the heart and diaphragm, reduction of lung capacity, and loss of tensile strength in the bones.

Yet, scattered across the desert floor outside of Roswell were creatures who seemed completely adapted to spaceflight. Just to be able to examine these entities was an enormous opportunity, but I knew we had the ability to harvest what we could observe about aliens. So, again, alongside the speculations I had made about the EBEs and their craft I listed what I thought were the major possibilities of developing product to enable us to travel in space for extended periods of time.

Renewable oxygen and food supplies were obvious directions to take, and by the 1960s, NASA engineers were already designing ways to recharge the atmosphere inside a capsule and provide for food storage. We helped. It was Army R&D and our plan for developing an irradiation process for food that even today provides the basis for nonrefrigerated food supplies on board spacecraft. But beyond that were real issues of health and survival. Merely getting human beings into earth orbit or even launching them into lunar orbit and bringing them back safely were straightforward engineering projects. But the readaptation of the human body to earth gravity after an extended period of weightlessness or reduced gravity was a far more intractable problem to solve. The physiology of the EBEs provided an important clue. Besides the development of supertenacity fibers that would protect the astronauts and the skin of the spacecraft and the development of a food-preservation process that would neutralize all the bacteria that cause spoilage, we needed to examine the ways we trained our astronauts physically so that they would be more adaptable to periods of weightlessness and spatial disorientation. At the same time we needed to develop nutritional packages that would not place undue stress on a digestive system that needed to compensate for deprivation of gravity.

Since there were no food-preparation facilities on board the spacecraft, we didn't know how they stored or processed food or even what they ate, if anything at all. However, my concern over a process to preserve food for space travel was prompted by the obvious challenge posed by the spacecraft itself. If we were going to travel in space, and it was clear from what the army found at Roswell that at least one culture had developed the technology to do so, then R&D had to find a way to feed our pilots in space. Therefore, we needed to develop a process to preserve food for space missions that didn't require refrigeration facilities and the consumption of excessive amounts of energy.

The problem of long-term space travel still hasn't been solved, in part because we continue to rely upon conventional means of propulsion that subject our astronauts to great periods of physical stress, especially during takeoff. We also have no magic way for astronauts to readjust to earth gravity after a long ride in an orbiting space station like the Russian *Mir* or our own planned station early in the next century. Manned trips to Mars, also on the drawing boards for early in the twenty-first century, will also be a problem because they will last for months and subject our astronauts to a great deal of stress.

I suggested to General Trudeau in my report that although this wasn't explicitly an Army R&D mission, NASA should begin the preparation of astronaut candidates from the time they're still in school. "If we train our astronauts from the time they're children the same way we do with potential athletes at sports camps and provide the most promising candidates with flight training and military or government scholarships to ROTC colleges, we will create a cadre of officers physically adaptable and scholastically trained to enter the next generation of space travel," I wrote. I know that General Trudeau passed this recommendation along because NASA itself opened a space-training camp for future astronauts within a few years after my retirement from the service.

Beyond the issues concerning the training potential of astronauts for conventionally powered spaceflight, the examination of the EBE bodies and the ship's possible propulsion system raised other intriguing questions. What if, in

addition to having been bioengineered for interstellar travel, the EBEs weren't subjected to the kinds of forces human
pilots would routinely face? If the EBEs utilized a wave-
propagation technology as an antigravity drive and navigation system, then they traveled inside some form of adjustable electromagnetic wave. I suggested to General Trudeau
that we should study the potential physiological effects on
humans of long-term exposure to the kinds of energy
spillage generated by the propagation of an electromagnetic
field. Biologists needed to determine how feasible such a
form of space travel would be based upon whether energy
radiation would disrupt the cellular activity of the human
body. Perhaps the external one-piece skins worn by the
EBEs afforded them protection against the effects of being
enclosed in a portable electromagnetic field.

Although Army R&D never conducted these studies
because the medical issues surrounding space travel were
subsumed by NASA under contracts with the military,
indirect medical research was conducted years later. Studies
surrounding the physiological effects on persons living near
high-voltage power-transmission lines and persons using
extendable-antenna handheld cellular telephones both
proved inconclusive. While some people argued that there
were higher incidences of cancer among both groups, other
studies argued just the opposite or found other reasons for
any incidences of cancer. I believe that a definitive piece of
research on the effects of low-energy or ELM wave exposure
still needs to be done because, ultimately, even more than
atomic energy or ion drives, magnetic field generation will
be the system that will propel our near planetary voyages
from 2050 through the early twenty-second century. Beyond that, for humans to reach destinations beyond the
solar system technology will require a radically different
form of propulsion that will enable them to reach velocities
at or beyond the speed of light.

Thus did my second report cover the opportunities for
research presented to us by the autopsies of the EBEs and
from the crash of their vehicle. To my mind, it was nothing
less than a confirmation that the research into electromag-
netics in the 1920s and the highly experimental saucer- and
crescent-shaped development of aircraft by the Allies and

Axis powers would have led to an entirely new generation of airships. I know that my reports were read by the higher-ups in the military because top-secret research has continued right through to the present on a whole range of designs and propulsion systems from the Stealth fighter and bomber to prototypes for a very high altitude suborbital interceptor aircraft, developed at Nellis and Edwards, now on the drawing board, which can hover in place and fly at speeds over seven thousand miles per hour.

Once I finished my report on the opportunities we could possibly derive from the EBEs and the craft, I turned my attention to compiling a short list of immediate opportunities I believed achievable by the Army R&D's Foreign Technology Division from a reverse-engineering of items retrieved from the crash. These were specific things, not as theoretical as questions about the physiology of the EBE or the description of its craft. But, while some might call them purely mundane, each of these artifacts, as a direct result of Army R&D's intervention, helped spawn an entire technological industry from which came new products and military weapons.

Among the Roswell artifacts and the questions and issues that arose from the Roswell crash, on my preliminary list that needed resolution for development scheduling or simple inquiries to our military scientific community were:

Image intensifiers, which ultimately became "night vision"
Fiber optics
Supertenacity fibers
Lasers
Molecular alignment metallic alloys
Integrated circuits and microminiaturization of logic boards
HARP (High Altitude Research Project)
Project Horizon (moon base)
Portable atomic generators (ion propulsion drive)
Irradiated food
"Third brain" guidance systems (EBE headbands)
Particle beams ("Star Wars" antimissile energy weapons)

Electromagnetic propulsion systems
Depleted uranium projectiles

For each of the items on my list, General Trudeau went into his human resources file and found the names of scientists working on government defense projects or in allied research projects at universities where I could turn for advice and some consultation. I wasn't surprised to see Wernher von Braun turn up under every rocket-propulsion issue. Von Braun had gone on record in 1959 by announcing that the U.S. military had acquired a new technology as a result of top-secret research in unidentified flying objects. Nor was I surprised to see John von Neumann's name next to the mention of the strange-looking silver-imprinted silicon wafers that I thought looked like elliptical-shaped crackers. "If these are what I think they might be," General Trudeau said, "printed circuitry, there's only one person we can talk to."

Dr. Robert Sarbacher was an especially important contact person on our list of scientists because he had worked on the Research and Development Board during the Eisenhower administration. Not only had Sarbacher been consulted by members of Admiral Hillenkoetter's and General Vandenberg's working group on UFOs during the 1950s, he was part of the original decision General Twining made to bring all of the Roswell debris back to Wright Field for preliminary examination before farming it out to the military research community. As early as 1950, Sarbacher, commenting on the nature of the debris, said that he was sure the light and tough materials were being analyzed very carefully by government laboratories that had taken possession of the debris after the crash. Because he was already knowledgeable about the Roswell debris, Dr. Sarbacher was another obvious candidate for an Army R&D brain trust.

We also listed Dr. Wilbert Smith, who, in a memo to the controller of telecommunications in November 1950, had urged the government of Canada to investigate the nature of alien technology the United States had retrieved from crashed extraterrestrial vehicles and that was at that time being studied by Vannevar Bush. Dr. Smith, who had learned of the U.S. investigation from Sarbacher, said that regardless whether UFOs fit into our belief system or not, the fact was we had acquired them and it was important for us to harvest the technology they contained. He implored the government to make a substantial effort to utilize alien technology. General Trudeau joked that although Dr. Smith knew that we had acquired technology at Roswell, he didn't really know what it was. "I can't wait to see his face when you open your briefcase in front of him, Phil," the general said, thinking about how his old friend had always wanted to know the specifics of what he had secreted away in 1947.

Each of these scientists had maintained existing relationships with any number of defense contractors during the 1950s. General Trudeau also had relationships with the army contractors who were developing new weapons systems for the military within one part of the company while another part was harvesting some of the same technology for consumer products development. These were companies—Bell Labs, IBM, Monsanto, Dow, General Electric, and Hughes—that General Trudeau wanted to talk to about the list of technological products that we'd compiled from our R&D Roswell nut file.

"You begin calling our scientist friends," General Trudeau announced. "And make whatever appointments you want."

"Where are you going to be, General?" I asked.

"I'm going to be taking some trips, too," he said. "First to the chief of staff to make sure we have the discretionary budget we're going to need. Then to some of the people I want you to talk to once you have the backing from the scientific community for the projects on your list."

"Where to first?" I asked.

"What do you like?" the general shot right back to me.

"We've been working with image intensifiers for some time," I said. "We even got our hands on devices the Germans were working on at the end of the war."

"Well then, why don't you make a very preliminary trip over to Fort Belvoir," General Trudeau said. "They've had a night-vision project in the works for the past ten years, but it's got nothing over what you have in your file."

"I'll get over there first thing," I said.

"Yes, Phil, but you get out of that uniform and into a real

lawyer suit," the general ordered. "And don't take your staff car." He saw me raise my eyebrows. "All you're going to do is feed a project," Trudeau continued, "that's been under way since right after the war. They've got stuff, but you're going to give them a giant leap. Once you've fed them, you'll disappear and I'll assign a night-vision project manager here to see the development through." I prepared to leave his office. "No one will know, Phil," he said. "Just like you thought, the Roswell night viewer will put a seed of an idea in someone's mind over at Fort Belvoir and it will become part of a long project history. It will disappear just like you into the history of the product development."

"Yes, sir," I said. I was beginning to realize just how lonely this job could be.

"You still have a suit that fits?" the general asked.

"I think so," I answered. "Maybe what I wore over at the White House is a little out of style, but it'll pass."

"Good luck, Phil," General Trudeau said. "Make sure no one knows where you're going and I'll make sure you have all the budget you need."

This was the beginning. I saluted, but the general just stuck out his hand and I shook it. We both realized in that moment, as we were striking out on our own, just how momentous this was about to become. A lieutenant general allocating money for his development budget and a lieutenant colonel looking for someone to develop an innocuous-looking eye shield an unknown GI had picked up out of the sand near a UFO crashed into a rock in the lonely desert outside of Roswell in a lightning storm fourteen years ago.

What a pair we must have made.

CHAPTER 9

Hostile Intentions and the Other Cold War

THE PROJECT HAD OFFICIALLY BEGUN.

General Trudeau marched down the hall to his boss at the Pentagon to begin the process of funding the new items we'd identified in our Foreign Technology budget, and I went home that evening and tried on my official White House three-piece suit. President Eisenhower once told me that he always trusted a man who wore a vest, and I never forgot it. Although there were times when the President asked me to wear my uniform for special meetings when I had to look military, I usually wore suits every day to work. But after my years at the Red Canyon missile base and in combat uniform in Germany, I lost the knack of wearing civilian clothes. Nevertheless, here I was again, after all those years, wearing a suit just like any other nine-to-five commuting Joe as I headed toward Fort Belvoir, perhaps the army's most important base in the entire Washington Military District.

Fort Belvoir was one of those military posts where the mundane activity of training and weapons testing was an effective cover for what came to be known as the secret life of Fort Belvoir. It sat comfortably within thirty minutes of the Pentagon, and it was where some of the army's most top-secret research into UFO technology was also taking place. Belvoir housed the Army Engineering School and, for former artillery and missile officers like myself, maintained a vital information database about ballistics testing and the development of new weapons. But on the secret side of the ledger, Fort Belvoir was home to the Signal School where officers for the National Security Council who had top-secret crypto clearance were trained.

Even years after I retired from active duty, stories lingered about the records of UFOs that were stored at Fort Belvoir, including photos and even motion pictures of military retrievals of downed extraterrestrial craft. What very few people knew was that an elite secret air force unit operated out of Fort Belvoir—ostensibly an army base—that was responsible for retrievals of downed UFOs. That was how Fort Belvoir became a repository of classified UFO footage. Those secrets remained at Fort Belvoir over the years and were closely guarded while the installation remained shrouded in mystery. For those who suspect what information was kept at the base, Fort Belvoir remains a central part of the legends surrounding the official military cover-up of UFOs.

Me, I was on my way there to talk about the night-vision project to see what German World War II files they were keeping on the infrared viewfinders the Nazis were trying to deploy for their night-fighting troops. These were cumbersome, unwieldy devices that left infantry hampered and weighed down. They were never effective in the war but held out the enormous promise of opening up the night as a battlefield where an army could maneuver around its blind and helpless enemy. That was the promise that tantalized both the Soviets and American forces as we closed in on Germany's most secret weapons facilities during the final months of the war.

Our forces secured all of the German records on mountable weapons night viewers and headpieces, but it wasn't until we looked inside the crashed Roswell vehicle and saw a hazy daylight through the view ports that we realized just what the potential of night viewing could be. We understood in those few moments after the vehicle was brought back to Wright Field and General Twining made his initial report that *we* were the blind and helpless enemy through the eyes of the EBEs. These creatures controlled our night skies, observing us with an ease that we didn't enjoy until we had deployed our own night-viewing goggles years later and leveled the playing field against them and the Soviet client forces arrayed against us.

My very proper-looking deep blue Oldsmobile might not have been a secret weapon in America's arsenal, but it was carrying a description of one of the tiny components of what would be one of our most effective Cold War weapons. Guerrilla armies used the night itself on their familiar home territory as a tactical weapon that allowed them to move right past enemy positions without being spotted. They could secure a battlefield advantage as if they were invisible. But equip a patrol with night viewers, mount night viewers on tanks and observation vehicles, hover over a battlefield at night in helicopter gunships equipped for night vision, and suddenly the night becomes day and the invisible enemy appears in your gunsights like prey for the hunter.

To the EBEs, we were that prey, and we knew they were monitoring our defenses, surveilling the aircraft we scrambled to chase them, and hovering above the experimental satellites we launched. We could see them with our radar, I had seen them on our scopes with my own eyes, and we knew their presence wasn't benign. But they had an advantage over us that we couldn't overcome unless we acquired the technological ability to put up enough of a defense to make their cost too high to engage in any large-scale warfare. Not only was it an advantage that forced us to scrape whatever technology we could off the edge of our encounters with them; it was one of the many factors that forced us into a silence about the alien presence. If there was no public enemy, there would be no pressure from the public to do anything about it. So we simply denied all extraterrestrial activity because no aliens meant no military responsibility to counter their threat. But all the while we were still planning, measuring their hostile intentions, and pushing through weapons development that might reduce their advantage.

It would have been next to impossible to stage a military buildup that would help us fight extraterrestrial enemies had we not had a lot of help from our old adversaries, the Soviets and the Chinese. The Soviets made no bones about their intentions to dominate the world through Communist revolutionary coups and set about immediately to challenge us even before World War II ended. By 1948, the Iron Curtain had dropped over Eastern Europe and the Soviets were trying to back us into a position of appeasement. In 1949, Mao Tse-tung drove Chiang Kai-shek out of mainland China to the island of Taiwan, and the United States had another major Communist adversary trying to impose its will upon its Asian neighbors. We first tasted their blood in Korea and would soon almost choke on it in Vietnam, Laos, Thailand, and Cambodia.

Those were hard times, made even harder because the U.S. military also knew that not just the free world but the whole world was under a military threat from a power far greater than the combined forces of the Soviet Union and the Republic of China. We didn't know what the EBEs wanted at first, but we knew that between the cattle mutilations, surveillance of our secret weapons installations, reports of strange abductions of human beings, and their consistent buzzing of our unmanned and manned space launches, the EBEs weren't just friendly visitors looking for a polite way to say "Hello, we mean you no harm." They meant us harm, and we knew it. The problem was we couldn't do anything about it at first, and anything we did try to do had to be done in complete secrecy or it would set off a worldwide panic, we believed.

This was where the Cold War turned out to be a tremendous opportunity for us, because it allowed us to upgrade our military preparedness in public to fight the Communists while secretly creating an arsenal and strategy to defend ourselves against the extraterrestrials. In short, the Cold War, while real enough and dangerous enough, was also a cover for us to develop a planetary tracking and defense system that looked into space as well as into the Soviets' backyard. And the Soviets were doing the exact same thing we were, looking up at the same time they were looking down.

In an only tacitly acknowledged cooperative endeavor, the Soviets and the Americans, while each one was explicitly using the Cold War to gain an advantage over the other, both sought to develop a military capability to defend ourselves against extraterrestrials. There were very subtle indications of this policy in the types of weapons both countries developed as well as in our behavior toward one another every time one side came close to pushing the button. I can tell you definitively because I was there when we avoided nuclear war because both military commands were able to pull back when they stared over the cliff into the flaming volcano of war that threatened to engulf all of us at least four times between 1945 and 1975—the Berlin airlift, the Chinese invasion of Korea, the Cuban missile crisis, and the Yom Kippur War—and probably many more.

By the time President Nixon returned from China, having agreed to turn over Vietnam to the Communists, he had effectively turned the Soviets' flank in the Cold War. For the next decade, the Soviets felt caught between the Chinese, with whom they'd fought border wars in the past, and the United States. When President Ronald Reagan demonstrated to Mikhail Gorbachev that the United States was capable of deploying an effective antimissile missile defense and sought Soviet cooperation in turning it against the extraterrestrials, all pretext of the Cold War ended and the great Soviet monolith in Eastern Europe began to crumble.

But the Cold War worked its magic for both superpowers by allowing them to prepare defenses against the extraterrestrials without ever having to disclose to the public what they were really doing. When you examine it, the record itself should have showed that another agenda was present throughout the Cold War. After all, why did each side really have ten or more times the number of warheads needed to completely destroy the other side's nuclear missile arsenal as well as their major population centers? The real story behind the vast missile arsenals, the huge fleets of bombers, and the ICBM submarine platforms that both sides deployed was the threat to the aliens that if they occupied a portion of our planet, we had the firepower to obliterate them. If they attacked either the United States or the Soviet Union so as to render one of the arsenals inoperable, we had enough missiles to spare to make them pay so heavy a price for starting a war, it wasn't even worth trying. That was part of our secret agenda behind the huge military buildups of the 1950s and 1960s: sacrifice a portion of the planet so that the rest of us could live. It enabled the United States and USSR to intimidate one another, but it also worked for the heads of the military intelligence agencies as a way to intimidate any extraterrestrial cultures. Nobody wrote any memos about this because weapons deployment during the Cold War was the cover for the secret agenda against the extraterrestrials.

Sure, there was a gamesmanship going on during those forty years from 1948 through 1989, when the Berlin Wall came down. Each side tried to get the other to spend more money than they really had to so as to weaken the economy. Our CIA consistently gave us false estimates because they were feeding us KGB information while, I know, we tried to do the same thing to the Soviets. And if the Soviets could have won the Cold War as bloodlessly as possible, they would have done so. But in the end, as the futility of mutual destruction made World War III unfightable, our real attention became more focused on the common enemy: the extraterrestrials who refused to go away.

There were subtle and not-so-subtle hints during the entire Cold War that a hidden agenda was in play. Most people just didn't know where to look. For those who did, and there were and are plenty of them, the answers were in plain view. Although there was heavy censorship and the threat of ruined careers, plenty of military and civilian sources reported flying saucer sightings. Stories of abductions—while most were either fantasies, nightmares, or memory screens for other events in the so-called abductee's childhood—continued to abound. Some were true, and this caused great consternation among members of the UFO working group. If the government couldn't protect private citizens from abductions by extraterrestrials, then would that not signify a breakdown in governmental authority? That was a worry, but it didn't come to pass.

Similarly, if too many flying saucers were seen by too many people at the same time, wouldn't it become obvious that the military forces of the superpowers couldn't protect their populations? For a time it was true, but the public never realized it. Soon we were able to upgrade our ability to defend our airspace so that we could amass large numbers of interceptors against the EBEs' limited resources and pose a real threat to them. They backed off and probed our defenses only when it seemed safe. Thus, the race among the superpowers to spend billions of dollars to build the fastest and best interceptors had a true double purpose. We needed all these planes because they gave the superpowers a flexible response alternative to simply obliterating themselves with guided missiles, but at the same time both superpowers were developing the air-defense technology to defend the planet against the extraterrestrials.

Everybody wants the best and fastest plane, of course, so that we can outfly and outshoot the enemy we know about. But we were also defending our skies against an enemy we didn't admit to having. The second agenda was always there and the Cold War provided the budgetary impetus the military needed: We were building aircraft to protect against flying saucers. And in a very real measure, we succeeded.

Both the United States and USSR were sensitive to another area where the extraterrestrials were aggressing upon our military personnel: our respective space-exploration programs. From the very beginning of our endeavors to put satellites in orbit, the extraterrestrials have been surveilling and then actively interfering with our launch vehicles and in some cases the manned and unmanned payloads themselves by buzzing them, jamming radio transmissions, causing electrical problems with the spacecrafts' systems, or causing mechanical malfunctions. American astronauts and Soviet cosmonauts have separately reported sightings of UFOs so routinely that it's become commonplace. The audio/video transmission downlink between space capsules and NASA, however, is a secure scrambled signal so that commentary about UFOs shadowing the spacecraft can't be picked up by private listeners. Even then, the astronauts are specifically instructed not to report UFO sightings until they are debriefed once they've landed.

Astronaut Gordon Cooper, for example, reported that when he was a fighter pilot over Germany in the 1950s, he scrambled with other Sabre Jet fighter pilots to intercept a formation of UFOs flying over his base, but when his fighter group got too close, the formation of UFOs flew away. Cooper also described film that he saw at Edwards Air Force base in

California in 1957 of a UFO landing. He said that he sent the film to Washington and followed up on it with the officers at Project Blue Book, but they never responded to his queries.

Similarly, X-15 pilot Joe Walker revealed that his 1961 mission in setting a new world airspeed record was also to hunt for UFOs during his high-altitude flights. He also said that he filmed UFOs during an X-15 flight a year later in 1962. Other reports persisted about *Mercury 7* astronauts being shadowed by UFOs and about Neil Armstrong's having seen an alien base on the moon during the *Apollo 11* flyover and landing. NASA has, of course, not admitted to any of this, and, very correctly, it's been treated as a matter of high national security.

An extraterrestrial presence on the moon, whether it was true or not in the 1950s, was an issue of such military importance that it was about to become a subject for National Security Council debate before Admiral Hillenkoetter and Generals Twining and Vandenberg pulled it back under their working group's security classification. The issue never formally reached the National Security Council, although Army R&D under the new command of General Trudeau in 1958 quickly developed preliminary plans for Horizon, a moon base construction project designed to provide the United States with a military observation presence on the lunar surface. Started in the late 1950s and set for completion between 1965 and 1967, Horizon was supposed to establish defensive fortifications on the moon against a Soviet attempt to use it as a military base, an early-warning surveillance system against a Soviet missile attack, and, most importantly, a surveillance and defense against UFOs. It was, to be blunt, a plan to establish a skirmish line in space to protect the earth against a surprise attack. But Horizon was sidetracked when the National Space and Aeronautics Act gave control over space exploration to the civilian NASA, effectively eliminating the military branches from pursuing their own projects until much later in the 1970s.

Fears of an attack to probe our planet's ability to defend itself were running rampant at National Security and through the military chiefs of staff during the middle 1950s. After he retired from the army, even Gen. Douglas MacArthur got into the fray, urging the military to prepare itself for what he felt would be the next major war. He told the *New York Times* in 1955 that "The nations of the world will have to unite for the next war will be an interplanetary war. The nations of the Earth must someday make a common front against attack by people from other planets." The public took little notice of that comment, but it was, in fact, a disclosure of the strategic thinking of the military back in the 1950s and explains part of the paranoia the government was displaying about all information relating to the flying saucers and unidentified aircraft.

Part of the military response to what they perceived as threats from extraterrestrials was, first, to analyze the specific ways that alien spacecraft "passively" disrupt our defenses and worldwide communications through electrical and magnetic field interference and develop circuitry hardened against it. Second, General Trudeau and his counterparts in the other branches of the military at the Pentagon charged with strategic planning looked at the aggressive behaviors of the EBEs. They didn't just shadow or surveil our spacecraft in orbit; they buzzed us and tried to create such havoc with our communications systems that NASA more than once had to rethink astronaut safety in the Mercury and Gemini programs. Years later, there was even some speculation among Army Intelligence analysts who had been out of the NASA strategy loop that the Apollo moon-landing program was ultimately abandoned because there was no way to protect the astronauts from possible alien threats.

The alien spacecraft were also aggressively buzzing our frontline defenses in Eastern Europe, either looking for blind spots or weaknesses, or—which is what I believed because I was there and saw it with my own eyes—probing our radar to see how quickly we responded. We'd see blips shoot across our screens that we couldn't identify and suddenly they'd disappear. Then they'd reappear, only this time even closer to our airfields or missile launchers. Once we determined that we weren't being probed by Soviet or East German aircraft, we sometimes decided not to respond to the threats. Many times they'd just go away. But other times they would play cat and mouse, edging ever closer until we had to respond. That's what they were looking for, how quickly we could respond and pick them up on our targeting radars or catch up to them with our interceptors. Whenever we'd get just about there for an aerial sighting, they'd take off out of the atmosphere at speeds over 7,500 miles an hour. If we tried to follow, they'd play us along until our fliers had to return.

Our only successes in defending against them, back in the late 1950s and early 1960s, occurred when we were able to get a firm tracking radar lock. Then when we locked our targeting radars on, the signals that missiles were supposed to follow to the target, it somehow interfered with their navigational ability and the vehicle's flight became erratic. If we were especially fortunate and able to boost the signal before they broke away, we could actually bring them down. Sometimes we actually got lucky enough to score a hit with a missile before the UFO could take any evasive action, which an army air defense battalion did with an antiaircraft missile near Ramstein Air Force Base in Germany in May 1974. The spacecraft managed to crash-land in a valley. The craft was retrieved and flown back to Nellis Air Force Base in Nevada. The Roswell crash was different. There was much speculation that it was a combination of the desert lightning storm and our persistent tracking radars at Alamogordo and the 509th that helped bring down the alien vehicle over the New Mexico desert in 1947.

Then there were the suspected cattle mutilations and reported abductions, perhaps the most direct form of intervention in our culture short of a direct attack upon our installations. While debates broke out among the debunkers—who said these were a combination of hoaxes, attacks by everyday predators on cattle, psychological flashback memories of episodes of childhood abuse in the cases of reported abductees, and out-and-out fabrications of the media—field investigators found they could not explain away some of the cattle mutilations, especially where laser surgery seemed to be used, and psychologists found alarming similarities in the descriptions of abductees who had no knowledge of one another's stories. The military intelligence community regarded these stories of mutilations and abductions very seriously.

They worked up descriptions of at least three separate

scenarios in which (1) the EBEs were simply conducting scientific experiments on earthly life-forms and collecting whatever specimens they could without causing too much disruption and alerting us; (2) the EBEs were actively collecting specimens and conducting experiments so as to determine whether this was a hospitable environment for them to inhabit, and any disruption they caused was of no concern to them; and (3) all of the experimentation and specimen collection were the prelude to some kind of infiltration or invasion of our planet. We did not know their motives, but could only assume the worst and, therefore, needed to defend ourselves however we could.

While never disclosing it publicly, military intelligence analysts supported the view that Earth was already under some form of probing attack by one or more alien cultures who were testing both our ability and resolve to defend ourselves. Without ever directly addressing whether contacts between the aliens and Earth governments had already taken place—because the notes and minutes of the Hillenkoetter working group were never released to the Chiefs of Staff or to their intelligence officers—the heads of the armed services decided collectively that it was better to plan for war rather than be surprised.

At the same time, the civilian leaders of the nation's space program at NASA decided that military intelligence was overreacting to the shadowing and buzzing of our spacecraft. NASA, which had been holding as highly confidential any reports of extraterrestrial activity surrounding our space vehicles, nevertheless decided to adopt an internal official "wait and watch" attitude because they believed that it would have been impossible to launch an explicitly military defensive space program and still achieve the civilian scientific aims at the same time. So NASA agreed to go covert. As a cover, NASA, in 1961, agreed to cooperate with military planners to work a "second-tier" space program within and covered up by the civilian scientific missions. They agreed to open up a confidential "back-channel" communications link to military intelligence regarding any hostile activities conducted by the EBEs against our spacecraft even if these included only shadowing or surveillance. I was aware of this through my contacts in the military intelligence community.

What NASA didn't tell military intelligence, of course, was that they already had an even more classified back channel to the Hillenkoetter working group and were keeping them updated on every single alien spacecraft appearance the astronauts reported, especially during the early series of Apollo flights when the EBE craft began buzzing the lunar modules on successive missions after they thrusted out of earth orbit. Even though military intelligence was kept out of the operational loop between NASA and the working group, I and a few others still had contacts in the civilian intelligence community that kept us informed. And the army and air force managed to find at least 122 photos taken by astronauts on the moon that showed some evidence of an alien presence. It was a startling find and was one of many reasons that the Reagan administration pushed so hard for the Space Defense Initiative in 1981.

In 1960, upon the confidential approval of the working group and at the request of the National Security Agency, which was concerned about the vulnerability of its U2 flights, NASA agreed to allow some of its missions to become covers for military surveillance satellites. These satellites, although approved for surveillance of Soviet ICBM activity, were also supposed to spot alien activity in remote portions of the earth. Maybe, in the 1960s, we didn't have the technology we have now to intercept their ships, but by using new satellite surveillance techniques we believed we'd be able to pick up the signatures of an alien presence on the face of our planet. If we made it too difficult for them to set up shop with bases on Earth, military intelligence planners speculated, maybe they would simply go away. This was another example of how Cold War strategy was utilized for the dual purpose of trying to surveil extraterrestrial activity under the cover of surveilling Soviet activity.

However, throughout the 1960s, critical projects were started at the Foreign Technology desk to protect vital command-and-control systems, including the hardening of communications and defense computer circuitry by burying components sensitive to electromagnetic pulses, the same kind of energy generated after a nuclear explosion as well as by the EBE spacecraft. In fact, so important was our research into the effects of the electromagnetic pulse, or

EMP, that ever since the late 1950s the Department of Defense has been simulating EMP to determine how to protect the circuitry in its planes, tanks, missiles, and ships from being disabled by it. EMP generators were established at a number of facilities around the country, including the Harry Diamond Laboratories in Adelphia, Maryland, for the army and the EMP Empress I and II simulators for the navy in the middle of Chesapeake Bay and another one at China Lake in California. The air force set up EMP simulators at Kirkland Air Force Base in New Mexico and the army additional facilities at White Sands, New Mexico, and at the Redstone arsenal in Alabama.

We also initiated the crash development of night-vision equipment to enable our troops to see at night the same way the EBEs did, finally enabling us to get a footing, if not an equal footing, with the aliens so that we could force them to some kind of stalemate. It was only then that we began to realize what their intentions were and the startling secrets about their existence on this planet.

It was night vision that was on my mind that day as I was zipped through the sentry post at the main gate and very quickly buzzed into the development laboratories wing at Fort Belvoir by an army specialist 4 who seemed surprised that I wasn't in uniform.

"Colonel Corso," Dr. Paul Fredericks, technology-development consultant to the night-vision section at Fort Belvoir, said as he extended his hand and walked me over to what must have been his prized tobacco-colored leather chair. It was way oversized for his small office and was obviously his favorite seat. I was duly appreciative of the honor and courtesy he was according me. "General Trudeau told me you were bringing us some remarkable information about one of the projects we have in development here."

"I hope it's helpful to you, Dr. Fredericks," I began. "I'm not a physicist, but I think we have something that might speed up the research time line and show some new possibilities."

"Anything that could help, Colonel," he said as I opened up my briefcase and began to spread out what I had. "Anything at all."

CHAPTER 10

The U2 Program and Project Corona:

Spies in Space

"OF COURSE, GENERAL TRUDEAU HAS BEEN IN TOUCH WITH Don and the whole development team here," Dr. Fredericks continued as he watched me open the night-vision file that I'd taken out of my briefcase. "And I'm aware of the nature of the material you've got. It's not something we wanted to talk about over the phone."

"I appreciate your being discreet about this, Dr. Fredericks," I said. "If you think what I'm about to show you can help you in the development process, it's yours to use. But the arrangement will be that everything is originated here at Fort Belvoir. All R&D will do will be to provide the budget necessary to fund this development. You use your own sources to manufacture the product and take all the credit for the process."

"And this conversation?" Dr. Fredericks asked.

"Once you tell me you can use what I've brought and we get you the budget you require," I began, "this conversation never took place and you will take my name off your appointment schedule."

"Now you really *do* have my interest," he said with just the edge of a bemused sarcasm in his voice as if he'd been down this road many times before. "What did you bring in that briefcase that's so secret?"

And with that I held up the first of the army's 1947 sketches of the night viewer we pulled from the wreckage at Roswell. I handed it across to Dr. Fredericks, who looked at it and turned it around with his fingertips as if he were holding one of the Dead Sea Scrolls.

"You don't have to be so careful with it, Dr. Fredericks," I said. "I made a few thermal copies."

"Do you have the actual device?" he asked.

"Back at the Pentagon."

"Who was wearing this?" he continued.

"At the time, nobody," I told him. "According to the field report, they found this in the sand near one of the bodies."

"Bodies? At the Roswell crash?" Now he was completely incredulous. "General Trudeau didn't tell anyone about bodies."

"No, that's true," I said. "That's not information we give out. General Trudeau authorized me to answer any questions you have up to a certain level of security classification."

"We're not there yet," Dr. Fredericks asked and asserted at the same time.

"But we're close," I suggested. "I can talk about the device, talk about where it was found, but that's probably as far as I can go myself. If General Trudeau wants to give a background briefing and authorizes me to do so, then I can go deeper."

"Funny, but I always thought Roswell was a kind of legend. You know, they found something but maybe it was Russian," Dr. Fredericks said. Then he asked again if anyone at the Roswell retrieval had actually seen any of the creatures wearing the night-vision device in the sketches.

"No," I said. "There was a lot of debris that spilled out of the craft. The soldiers on the retrieval team looked through one of the seams that had been split open running along the craft's lengthwise axis and they saw view ports built into the hull. Well, what astonished them was that when they looked through the view ports, they could see daylight, or a greenish, hazy kind of diffused light that looked like dusk, but outside it was completely dark."

Paul Fredericks was on the edge of his seat now.

"No one at the crash site knew anything about the night viewers the Germans were developing during the war," I explained. "So even the officers on the retrieval team were amazed at what they were seeing. When they autopsied the alien at the 509th and pulled off these 'eyepieces,' is the only word I can use for them, they realized that they were a complicated set of reflectors that gathered all the available light and turned them into nighttime image intensifiers." I continued, pointing to the sketch in Paul Fredericks's hands. "Some medical officer tried to look through it down a darkened hall and it made the images stand out, but nothing was ever done with it and they packed it away with the rest of the alien."

"Did they perform any analysis on this when they brought it back?" Fredericks asked.

"Some," I told him. "But they had no facilities at the 509th and had to wait until they brought it back to Wright. It wasn't until the intelligence boys at the Air Materiel Command got hold of it that they realized that this was something the Germans were trying to deploy."

"But this is far more sophisticated," Dr. Fredericks said. "The Germans weren't even close to something like this."

"Yes, sir," I said. "Not even close. And that's what got the intelligence people at Wright so concerned. Just how close were the Germans about to get when the war ended? What else had they gotten their hands on? Did they have help?"

"Or," Dr. Fredericks said very slowly, "did they find a crash just like we found?"

"That's exactly the point, Dr. Fredericks," I said. "What did they find?"

"And if the Germans could get their hands on this material, what about the Soviets?" he asked. But he was talking to himself now, talking in a way that made him sound as if he were really thinking out loud. "Why not the Chinese or any of our European allies? Just how much of this stuff is out there?" he finally asked me.

"We don't have any of those answers," I told him. "At least not those of us in the army. And for obvious reasons nobody's walking around sharing this information back and forth among the services or with any other agencies. We have what we have, and that's as far as we're willing to go."

"And you don't want me talking about this or trying to sniff around for any information," he said.

"If we thought you were going to do that I wouldn't even be here," I said. "I have these reports here and descriptions of the device. I'll leave them with you. If you think you can work these into your development program, I'll have the material itself sent over and then it's out of our hands completely. Farm it out to wherever you want it developed. Offer your defense contractor the right to patent it. Never tell them where you got it or what its origin might be. As far as we're concerned whoever comes up with the night viewers you ultimately contract with to build can own the whole product and slap their name on it. All we want to do is get this thing developed. That's it."

"May I?" Dr. Fredericks asked, reaching for the reports I'd spread out on the arm of the leather chair.

I handed them across in a bundle, and he flipped through them as if he were my old college professor looking at a term paper, humphing, grunting, and nodding at every page.

"That's more about how they handled the alien at Wright Field than about the eyepieces themselves," I said. "Because in reality, they didn't know what made the thing tick and they didn't really want to tear it apart."

"So they just threw it in a package?" he asked.

"Basically, that's exactly what happened," I said. "At first they didn't know how it was supposed to work. Or maybe they thought it would turn human beings blind or something. They were that afraid. After a while, they just let it stay in dead storage and hoped someone else would take it off their hands."

"And that'd be you," Dr. Fredericks said.

"Actually," I told him, "that'd be you, if you want it."

"I need to read this material more thoroughly and see where we can slip your night vision into the project without causing a ripple on the surface," Dr. Fredericks explained.

"How easy will that be?" I asked.

"At Fort Belvoir," he answered, "teams here are taught to keep their own thoughts to themselves. If you tell them this is a piece of foreign technology our intelligence boys got from some other country and we're supposed to make it disappear into what we're doing, that's the story."

"Nobody asks any questions?" I pushed.

"Nobody asks questions under any circumstances," he said. "It would move along faster and create its own little development bureaucracy if we had the budget to turn it into a crash development project with a real development phase deadline."

"Then what happens?" I asked.

"It's just like Santa's workshop on the first day of winter. None of the elves looks up from his workbench until it's done. Then the next project comes along and everybody forgets. By the time the troops are wearing these things in the field and they're handing out the gold watches over a prime rib at the Potomac Inn, night vision is just one big happy memory with the details rewritten to fit the view of history that serves the moment. No one will ever even guess, Colonel Corso," he said. "From the moment your boys hand the material over, it goes into the developmental soup at Fort Belvoir and comes out the other end as a weapon in the field."

I stood up and closed my briefcase while he walked around his desk. "So what are you going to recommend to General Trudeau?" he asked.

"I'd like to suggest we send the device over, you come up with the budget you need, and General Trudeau finds the allocation," I said.

"And you?" he said.

"It was a pleasure not meeting you, Dr. Fredericks," I told him. "Of course, there will be a liaison over in Army R&D who will officially be placed in charge of night-vision development. He will report to General Trudeau and anything I need to know I'll find out from the general. I look forward to seeing the development reports as they come out. Congratulations on your new piece of technology. And congratulations to the company who winds up with this defense contract."

"Congratulations, indeed," Dr. Fredericks said.

We shook hands and he walked me out of his office into the corridor. For a moment, it was like stepping out of the surreal into the real. We'd just stitched our own piece of fabric over reality, created a piece of history. The technology boys in research and development at Fort Belvoir would receive a device from one of their consultants who would whisper to them that this was liberated from one of our enemies. Don't ask any questions. But it was just the thing that the lab people at Fort Belvoir were looking for to show them how a finished device might look. Can they come up with a reverse-engineering plan? Is there a company they're already working with on night vision? And within a few months, some company, whoever it might be, would wind up with a plan in place, a development budget, and a new identity for the strange-looking eyepieces that turned up in my Roswell files. It might take five or so years, but when it came rolling off the assembly line somewhere in Pennsylvania, Maryland, Ohio, or wherever, it would be "Made in the USA" and I'd read about it in the papers or see it on television.

Night vision was the first project we actually seeded during the first year of my tenure at Foreign Technology. It would turn out to be easier than most because of the history of German development during the war and the research already done through the 1950s. By the time I brought the Roswell night viewer to Fort Belvoir, it fit right in through the scam of an existing development program and no one was the wiser. The actual weapons-development program at Fort Belvoir served as the cover for the dissemination of Roswell technology so perfectly that the only distortion anyone could find as he went back through the history is what might seem like a sudden acceleration in the development program itself shortly after 1961. Night vision got a boost in funding, a new officer was assigned to the project by General Trudeau, and General Trudeau's name starts turning up on a regular basis as one of the apparent benefactors of the program. By 1963, when he and I were gone from the Pentagon, the project was at Martin Marietta Electronics—now part of Lockheed Martin—and already on its way through the initial deployment that would take place in Europe and Vietnam.

But I didn't know that as I drove through the Fort Belvoir gate and headed back to my Pentagon office. I only felt satisfied that it looked like we had successfully inserted one of our own Foreign Technology projects into an ongoing development stream already under way and had camouflaged our appropriation of a piece of alien technology. At this point, I believed, we'd kept it out of the hands of the Soviets for the time being, and the aliens, if they were monitoring what we were doing, maybe didn't know what we were doing with it either. It would give us time.

I headed north along the Potomac and through the green woods of Fairfax County, Virginia, back to a desk that was quickly piling up with other projects that needed disposition. One of them, which was running parallel with the night vision I'd just handed off, was the embryonic "Project Corona," an idea whose time was suddenly thrust upon us by the shooting down of a U2 surveillance plane and the capture of its pilot, Francis Gary Powers.

The air force and the CIA had been running the U2 program for a while during the Eisenhower administration, and the reports and photos routinely crossed my desk at the National Security Council. Like so many other events during the Cold War, the U2 didn't have just a single purpose, the surveillance of the Soviet Union to monitor their guided-missile development program. It had a triple intent. Of course, we wanted to know exactly what the Soviets were up to, but we also wanted to test their air defense capability. We wanted to know how accurately their radars could track the U2 and whether any of their missiles could bring it down. So we deliberately provoked them by making our presence known when we wanted them to fire at us. Could they shoot us down? Cameras on the U2 picked up the launch of enemy surface-to-air missiles as the pilot flew over sensitive installations where the Soviets had to challenge us or cede to us the control of top classified zones in their airspace.

So we played gamesmanship with them, probing their defenses, deliberately sacrificing pilots who we believed died when their planes were shot down, and always denying what we were doing even as Khrushchev screamed at Eisenhower that the U2 program was putting Khrushchev himself at risk inside the Kremlin. "We can deal with each other," the Communist Party chairman told Ike. "But not if you force me out of office." But as much as Eisenhower hated the U2 program and the jeopardy into which it placed our pilots, the President had to accommodate himself to one of the other agendas of the surveillance: the ongoing search for any evidence of extraterrestrial spacecraft landings or crashes within the vastness of the Soviet Union. We also wanted to see whether the Soviets were harvesting any of the alien aircraft technology for themselves. That's what made the U2 program too valuable to give up until we had an alternative. And the alternative, although it was an air force and not an army program, was part of a shared R&D between our intelligence services and the National Security Council/CIA apparatus. And it was already in development within Lockheed in a division they called "skunk works."

Because we had set up our U2 flights to provoke the Soviets and because we knew that ultimately we would start to lose pilots and planes, the National Security staff began looking aggressively for a more secure surveillance program as early as 1957, my last year at the White House. Intelligence decided to take orbital satellite photos of Soviet installations, but only if they could get a bird up there that would be reliable. Also, we didn't want to let the Soviets know we were turning earth orbit into a surveillance facility because we didn't want to encourage them to go after our satellites. So the trick was to get a satellite up there in complete secrecy. But how could you do that with the whole world watching?

The army and air force had an idea. Lockheed had already shown that it could develop a surveillance plane, the U2 and eventually the SR71, out of the public view and run those flights without too much interference from Senate watchdog committees and out of the presence of any newspaper reporters. Could they do the same thing with a satellite? And if they could, would the satellite recon photos be as reliable as the photos we were getting from the U2s?

Normally, I would have said that if the army were putting up a satellite, it could do anything it wanted because everything we did under our intelligence blanket remained relatively secure. However, both the army and the air force were effectively put out of the satellite-launching business toward the end of the Eisenhower administration by the civilian National Aeronautics and Space Agency under a pooled resources crash program to get satellites up into space to show the world the flag. The Soviets had beaten us in the race initially with Sputnik, and the failed army and navy attempts to launch satellites only made us look worse. After the navy's first attempt to launch a satellite, I learned for a fact that when the *New York Daily News* ran the full-page headline, "Oh Dear," after the satellite rose a few inches, fell back onto the launchpad, and blew up into smithereens, no one was laughing harder than Nikita Khrushchev.

After a few of these attempts, the National Security Council advised President Eisenhower to throw in the towel, pool all the national scientific resources he could, and turn the U.S. entry into the space race over to a civilian agency. The military services had learned their lesson about competing over the same technology the hard way and had to stand back and watch NASA take over.

NASA had some immediate successes, and before the end of the Eisenhower administration in 1960, they had managed to put satellites in orbit and experiment with the effects of orbital flight on animals in far more sophisticated ways than the army's V2 experiments with small primates at Alamogordo in the late 1940s and early 1950s. As the army and air force intelligence offices looked at the successes of these NASA satellites and at the increasing vulnerabilities of the U2 flights, they saw the possible answer to their need for a fail-safe surveillance program. When NASA began its Discoverer orbiter program, launching a payload into low orbit and returning it, the military services thought they saw a solution. If they could somehow manage to build a workable photo-recon satellite small enough to fit into the very limited space inside the Discoverer payload capsule, recover the surveillance device when the orbiter returned to Earth, and install the entire military-spying program within a civilian scientific exploration program that was getting a lot of attention from the newspapers without alerting the public to the military's secret agenda, they would have their covert surveillance.

We knew that the Soviets would very quickly find out about the program, but that wasn't such a bad thing. We reasoned that there was no way, given the CIA's penetration by the KGB, to keep the program completely covert, but if the Soviets knew we were able to watch them it might keep them honest. And Khrushchev wouldn't have to worry about our deliberately violating his airspace, so he was off the hook at the Kremlin and thankful for it. All we had to do was keep it out of the public arena and we'd be home free. The whole program rested on our being able to slip what we now called "Corona" into the existing Discoverer program without a whisper in the air, the Soviets would go along without a protest, and we would get our surveillance photos.

We added an additional incentive for the Soviets to discourage them from getting their friends in the CIA to leak the story to friendly journalists and blowing the cover on the whole operation. We encouraged them to participate with us in the hidden agenda of Corona: surveillance of potential alien crash landings. Army Intelligence, upon Eisenhower's and the NSC's express approval, let it be known to their counterparts in the Soviet military that any aerial intelligence we developed as a result of Corona that revealed the presence of aliens on Soviet territory would be shared with the military. What they did with the information, we said, we really didn't care. But the military was more than grateful. The professional military didn't trust the commissars in the Communist Party any more than we did and hated being under their collective thumb. Thus, in a perverse way, although we were tipping off the Russian military about alien activity in their territory, we really weren't sharing information with the Communists because of the deep division within the Soviet government between the Communist Party and the military.

Our incentive worked and the KGB encouraged the CIA—even I was surprised at how effectively they worked together—not to leak the story. Now it was up to the air force and the skunk-works division at Lockheed to build the Corona surveillance satellite out of the public arena and load the vehicle into the Discoverer rocket right under the noses of the American press. It was one of the trickiest operations of the Cold War because the Russians knew what we were doing, NASA was making the entire project happen, but the American press, hungry for even the smallest tidbit of spaceflight information, had to be kept completely in the dark. If necessary, we had to lie to them, provide them with cover stories, completely trick them into thinking that all the American people had to think about was the little chimp that was blasted into orbit wearing his custom-sized space helmet. And we didn't have much time to do it because we knew the Soviets were trying to embarrass Ike at the end of his term by bringing down one of our U2 planes with a live pilot inside. We were now in a race against the Soviets to replace the U2 with the Corona, even though the Soviets understood and accepted what we were doing every step of the way. It was one of the ironies of the Cold War.

The engineers at Lockheed designed the satellite camera package to fit neatly into the payload cone of the Discoverer capsule. They worked under brutal time constraints because President Eisenhower was putting pressure on the National Security Council to cut off the U2 overflights completely. The old general knew it was just a matter of time before the Soviets would capture a living American pilot, extract his confession, and march him in front of the television cameras to the humiliation of the United States. Eisenhower was a man of his word who disliked politicians because they always sought the expedient solution, not the most honorable one. Eisenhower disliked expedience for expediency's sake and always preferred to take the most directly honest path whenever he could. But, as Khrushchev complained about the U2 flights, Ike always denied we were sending them. It was such an obvious lie that Khrushchev kept goading Eisenhower about exposing himself that way. "We will shoot one of them down, you'll see," he kept telling Eisenhower whenever he complained. "Then what will you say?"

But President Eisenhower denied the existence of the U2, put down the telephone, and turned on his own staff, furious that they had put him into such an untenable situation. "Stop the flights," he ordered. But the CIA kept pushing for one more flight. It was serving a purpose, they argued. They were learning about the Russian air defense system at the same time they were surveilling possible areas of alien spacecraft activity. With or without the Russians' knowledge, the U2s denied the extraterrestrials a complete camouflage because of our high-resolution aerial surveillance. I don't know whether we actually found any evidence of an alien landing on Russian territory from our U2 surveillance, but the extraterrestrials certainly could see that we were able to surveil the Soviet Union, and their knowledge of our capability served as a deterrent to roaming the vast areas of the Soviet Union with impunity.

The CIA claimed the U2s were so important to our national security that they were even ready to sacrifice one of their own pilots. However, I also believe that the KGB moles who had penetrated them wanted Eisenhower to be embarrassed before the entire world. And when Francis Gary Powers took off in May 1960, they had their chance.

There is still a great deal of doubt about the shootdown of Powers's U2. His mission was to fly over the most sensitive Soviet missile installations and make himself a target. We believed the Russian SAMs couldn't reach his altitude. But, whether Powers fell asleep at the stick because of oxygen deprivation or whether his CIA controllers forced him to a lower altitude to get better photos or even to make himself a more provocative target, we'll never know. I believe that Powers was probably startled out of a low-oxygen lethargy by the explosion of a SAM close enough to force him to lose control. His plane was not hit by the missile. The U2 was the type of aircraft that was very difficult to fly. Powers probably pulled into a stall and was unable to bring it back. As his plane spun toward the ground and Powers became too disoriented to regain control, he pulled on the lever next to his seat, blew the canopy off, and ejected.

Powers was captured alive, paraded before cameras, and forced to confess that he was spying on the Soviet Union. Khrushchev had his excuse to cancel a summit meeting with Eisenhower and put on one of the great performances of his career in front of the Supreme Soviet. Eisenhower, as he had most feared, was publicly humiliated and forced to admit to Khrushchev that he had sent the U2s over the Soviet Union. He promised Khrushchev that the U2 flights would end, eliminating a valuable surveillance tool and potentially blinding us not only to what the Soviet Union was doing but potentially to what the extraterrestrials were doing in Asia as well. It was a terrible experience for the old man, who believed he had been compromised by his own administration.

All the while during the final months of preparations before Gary Powers's U2 flight, NASA was completing the engineering details to insert the Corona payload into the Discoverer payload. If all went well, the first launch of Corona would give the National Security Council the results they wanted and the U2 program would come to an end because it had been made obsolete by Corona. Then Gary Powers was shot down and the U2 program came to an end because Eisenhower terminated it. We were blind. Then Discoverer was launched, and those of us in the army and air force missile programs who were aware of Corona and what was at stake in the mission held our collective breaths. If it worked, we had eyes. If it failed, our best surveillance opportunity would have failed.

You can imagine the jubilation at the Pentagon when the Corona payload was recovered and we developed the first photos. They were better than what we had gotten from the U2, and the Corona was completely invisible to the Soviets. Khrushchev hid the information from his own Supreme Soviet, and Eisenhower certainly didn't make a public statement to the American people. We were back in the photo-intelligence business, and in addition to keeping tabs on Soviet missile developments, we had a way to track any possible EBE attempt to set up a base in the remotest parts of Asia, Africa, or South America. We were gaining parity with the EBEs, a small victory, but a victory nevertheless.

What satisfied me the most about Project Corona, I thought as I reached the outskirts of Washington on my way back from Fort Belvoir, was that it was elegant as well as successful. Just like the ease with which we had slipped the Roswell night visor into the development and engineering stream at Fort Belvoir, so had we slipped the Corona photo-surveillance payload directly into the ongoing Discoverer program, reverse-engineering Discoverer to make the payload fit. No one realized what we had accomplished or how effectively the military utilized traditional programs as a cover for their own secret weapons-development systems.

At the same time, we knew we were gaining on the aliens. With each successful start of a new project, some based on the Roswell technology, others initiated specifically to counter the alien capabilities we had discovered at Roswell, we believed we were advancing our game piece to the next square. We believed that no matter how hostile the aliens' intentions were, they didn't have the raw power to launch a global war against us. They would study us, infiltrate us, wear us down until we might not be able to resist them, but they had neither the intention nor the capability, we believed, of destroying the planet so as to take it for themselves. In that, we held the upper hand.

But what we needed was a real outpost in a location that would enable us to establish a strategic advantage, a base to strike at them far enough away so that we wouldn't create a panic on Earth. We needed a base on the moon. It was something the army had dreamed about from the very first months after our encounters with the aliens outside of Roswell and something we had tried to fund without the public's knowledge. It was an ambitious project that had bounced around from skeptic to skeptic inside the military for over a year before it landed in front of me. And when I took over the Foreign Technology desk, it was a project we almost had.

CHAPTER 11

Project Moon Base

"I ENVISION EXPEDITIOUS DEVELOPMENT OF THE PROPOSAL TO establish a lunar outpost to be of critical importance to the U.S. Army of the future. This evaluation is apparently shared by the Chief of Staff in view of his expeditious approval and enthusiastic endorsement of initiation of the study," General Trudeau wrote to the chief of ordnance in March 1959, in support of the army's "Project HORIZON," a strategic plan for deploying a military outpost on the surface of the moon. It was the army's most ambitious response to the threat from extraterrestrials and, by the time I arrived at the Pentagon, it was one of the projects that General Trudeau had handed off to me to get moving.

"The boys at NASA are taking over the whole rocket-launching business, Phil," he said. "And the army's not even getting the scraps left on the table."

I had just left the White House when the National Aeronautics and Space Act was passed in 1958, and I knew what that had portended. It transferred the responsibility of space from the military services to a civilian-run agency that was supposed to fulfill the U.S. promises to other countries for the demilitarization of space. It was a laudable goal, anyone would argue: demilitarize space so that countries could explore and experiment without the risk of losing their space vehicles or satellites to hostile activities. For the United States and the Russians the agreement meant that our respective astronauts and cosmonauts wouldn't make war on each other. Good idea. But someone forgot to tell it to the extraterrestrials, who had been systematically violating our planet's airspace for decades, if not centuries, and had already set up a base of operations on the moon.

For General Trudeau and much of the U.S. military command, the Soviets' ability to put high-payload vehicles and cosmonauts into orbit with relative ease was a frightening prospect. Unless the United States challenged Soviet technology with our own ongoing launch program and expanded our satellite surveillance, the army believed it would cede an all-important strategic advantage to the Soviet Union. By 1960, we were reaching a critical juncture. Because of the development window and the time it took to get projects through development, programs started too late in the 1960s would be hopelessly obsolete by 1970, when the Soviets were expected to have established a presence in space.

As in the U2 program, we had another agenda that concerned us more than just the Soviets' ability to threaten us with a nuclear-missile capability from space. We were also very much aware of the ability of a dominant military power on Earth to establish its own version of a treaty with extraterrestrials. We had already seen how Stalin negotiated a separate nonaggression pact with Hitler, allowing the Germans to stabilize its Eastern front and invade Western Europe. We didn't want to see Khrushchev gain so much unchallenged power in space that the extraterrestrials would readily agree to some kind of accommodation with him guaranteeing both of them a degree of freedom to dominate the political affairs of our planet. This may seem paranoid now, in the 1990s, but in the late 1950s this was exactly the thinking of the military intelligence community.

General Trudeau's concerns were the concerns of anybody who knew the truth about an alien presence around our planet and their abilities to drop on top of us from out of nowhere just like they had done in Roswell, in Washington, D.C., in 1952, and in countless other places around the world. And we didn't know if any one of these sightings could turn into a full-fledged landing in force or if an invasion hadn't already begun. If they could turn the Soviet government into a client state with a proxy army, there might be no checking their ability to exercise their will to colonize our planet, appropriate our natural resources, or, if the cattle mutilations and stories of abductions were true, conduct with complete impunity an organized experimentation or testing program on the life-forms of this planet. In the absence of any information to disprove our fears, it was the military's obligation to project the worst possible scenario. That's why the army pushed for Project HORIZON. We had to have a plan.

The Horizon documents were straightforward in expressing their concerns: We needed to put a fully armed military outpost on the moon first because if the Soviets achieved this objective before we did, we would be in the position of having to storm a hill or secure a military position. We would rather be the defenders of a strongly fortified enclave than the attackers. Our outpost had to be strong enough to withstand an assault and have enough personnel to conduct scientific experiments and continual surveillance of the earth and its airspace.

Initially, General Trudeau argued, the outpost must be of sufficient size and contain sufficient equipment to permit the survival and moderate constructive activity of from ten to twenty personnel at a minimum. It must allow for expansion of the permanent facilities, resupply, and rotation of personnel to guarantee the maximum amount of time for a sustained occupancy. The general not only wanted the outpost to establish a beachhead on the moon, he wanted it to be permanent and able to sustain itself for long periods without support from the earth. Therefore, location and design were critical and required, in the army's view, a triangulation station of moon-to-Earth baseline space surveillance system that facilitated: (1) communication with and optimum observation of the earth, (2) routine travel between the moon and the earth, (3) the best possible exploration capability not only of the immediate area of the lunar surface but long-range exploration expeditions and, most importantly from the army's perspective, (4) the military defense of the moon base. The army's primary objective was to establish the first *permanent* manned installation on the moon and nothing less. The military potential of the moon was paramount, but the mission allowed for an ongoing investigation of the commercial and scientific potentials of the outpost as well.

The army wanted to make Horizon conform to existing national policy on space exploration, even insofar as the demilitarization of space was concerned. But it was tough because all of us in the military services who had come in contact with the Roswell file believed that we were already under some form of attack. Demilitarizing space only meant playing into the hands of a culture that had displayed a hostile intent toward us. But we also realized that overtly establishing a military presence in space would encourage the Soviets to match us step for step and result in an arms race in outer space that would exacerbate Cold War tensions. Armaments in space might be more difficult to control, and the chance of an accidental military exchange could have easily precipitated a crisis on Earth. Thus, the whole problem of what to do about establishing a military presence in space was a conundrum. Horizon was the army's attempt to accomplish its military objectives within the context of the government's demilitarization policy.

The army faced another obstacle in its plans from the members of the Roswell working group who were still establishing and enforcing policy at levels above top secret. The working group correctly saw that any independent military expedition into space, especially for the purpose of establishing an outpost on the moon, had a high probability of encountering extraterrestrials. In this encounter, there was no guarantee that a military exchange would not ensue or, at the very least, a military report would be filed. Even if these reports were kept top secret, given the military bureaucracy and the presence of legislative oversight it was highly unlikely that the press would not learn about military encounters with aliens. Thus, the basic premise of the working group and its entire mission, the camouflage of our discovery of alien life-forms visiting and probably threatening Earth, would be undermined and years of successful operations might easily be brought to an unsatisfactory end. No, the working group would rather have the exploration of space in the hands of a civilian agency whose bureaucracy could be more easily controlled and whose personnel would be handpicked, at least at the outset, by the members of the working group.

Thus, the stage was set for a byzantine bureaucratic struggle among members of the same organizations but with different levels of security clearance, policy objectives, and even knowledge of what had taken place in years gone by. And underlying it all was the basic assumption that the world's civilian population was not ready to learn the real truth about the existence of extraterrestrial cultures and the likely threat these cultures posed to life on Earth. General Trudeau was as undaunted as I had ever seen him. In Korea, he charged back up Pork Chop Hill into the face of an enemy attack so fierce that the soldiers who had volunteered to go up with him believed they were going to breathe their last. But they couldn't let him go up there alone, which is exactly what he was set to do when he threw away his helmet and clasped one on from a wounded sergeant. He chambered the first round into his automatic and said, "I'm going. Who's with me?" I imagined he had the same look on his face now, as he handed me the report for Project Horizon, as he did then. "We're going, Phil," he said, and that was all I needed to hear.

When the civilian space agency supporters told the army that all of the issues the military raised about the need to establish a presence first would be accomplished with civilian missions, General Trudeau argued that the civilian plans did not explicitly call for a base on the moon, only for the possibility of an outpost in earth orbit that may or may not be capable of serving as a way station for flights to the moon or to other planets. And the time frame for the construction of an orbiting space station made it seem obsolete even before it reached the drawing boards. Besides, General Trudeau told the scientists on Eisenhower's aeronautics and space advisory committee toward the end of the President's administration, you can't trust a civilian-run agency to complete a military mission. It hadn't happened in the past and it wouldn't happen in the future. If you wanted a military operation completed, only the military could do it. President Eisenhower understood that kind of logic.

In the late 1950s, the White House had forwarded queries to General Trudeau about the army's research and development policy regarding Project Horizon and why, specifically, the military needed to be on the moon and why a civilian mission couldn't accomplish most of the scientific objectives. This was at the time when the White House was supporting the National Aeronautics and Space Act and was supporting the creation of the civilian National Aeronautics and Space Administration.

General Trudeau responded that he couldn't immediately lay out the full extent of the military potential. "But," he wrote in the report, "it is probable that observation of the Earth and space vehicles from the moon will prove to be highly advantageous."

Later he wrote that by using a moon-to-Earth baseline, space surveillance by triangulation—in other words, using a point of reference on Earth and a point of reference on the moon to pinpoint the positions of enemy missiles, satellites, or spacecraft—promised greater range and accuracy of observation. Instead of having only one point of observation, we would have an additional angle because we would have a base on the moon as another point of observation. This was especially the case for the types of lunar and Mars missions NASA was planning as early as 1960. He said that the types of earth-based tracking and control networks currently in the planning stages were already inadequate for the deep space operations that were also in the planning stages in the civilian agencies. So, it made no sense to spend money developing communications and control networks that would be obsolete for the very purposes for which they were being designed. Military communications would be improved immeasurably by the use of a moon-based relay station that would cover a broader range and probably be more resistant to attack during a conventional or nuclear war that took place on Earth. But General Trudeau had the real bombshell waiting to be dropped.

"The employment of moon-based weapons systems

against Earth or *space targets* may prove to be feasible and desirable," he wrote the army chief of ordnance, revealing for the first time that he believed, along with Douglas MacArthur, that the army might be called upon to fight a war in space as well as on Earth. General Trudeau foresaw the possibility that a moon-based communications network would have an advantage in tracking guided missiles launched from Earth, but he also realized that weapons could be fired from space, and not just by Earth governments but by extraterrestrial craft. It was the moon-base project, he believed, that would be able to protect civilian populations and military forces on Earth from attacks launched either from earth orbit or from space. But a moon-based defense initiative had an added feature.

"Moon-based military power will be a strong deterrent to war because of the extreme difficulty, from the enemy point of view, of eliminating our ability to retaliate," he hypothesized. "Any military operations on the moon will be difficult to counter by the enemy because of the difficulty of his reaching the moon, if our forces are already present and have means of countering a landing or of neutralizing any hostile forces that have landed." And, the general told me, this would apply whether those hostile forces were the Soviets, the Chinese, or the EBEs. The situation would be reversed, however, "if hostile forces are permitted to arrive first. They can militarily counter our landings and attempt to deny us politically the use of their property."

The army conceived of the development of a moon base as an endeavor similar to the building of the atomic bomb: a vast amount of resources applied to one particular mission, complete secrecy about the nature of the mission, and a crash program to complete the mission before the end of the next decade. He said that the establishment of the outpost should be a special project having authority and priority similar to the Manhattan Project in World War II. Once established, the lunar base would be operated under the control of a unified space command, which was an extension of current military command-and-control policy, and still is. Space, specifically an imaginary sphere of space encompassing the earth and the moon, would be considered a military theater governed by whatever military rules were in force at that time. The control of all U.S. military forces by a unified command had already been in effect by the late 1950s, so General Trudeau's plan for a unified military space command was no exception to an ongoing practice. The only difference was that the general didn't want the unified command to exercise authority solely over the moon base itself; he wanted it extended to control and utilize exclusively military satellites, military space vehicles, space surveillance systems, and the entire logistical network installed to support these military assets.

To the general, being second to the Soviet Union in deploying and supporting a permanent lunar outpost would have been "disastrous" not only to our national prestige but to our very democratic system itself. In Arthur Trudeau's estimation, the Soviet Union was currently planning to fortify a lunar base by the middle 1960s and declare it Soviet territory. He believed that if the United States tried to land on the moon, especially if we tried to establish a base of operations there, the Soviets would have propagandized the event as an act of war, an invasion of its territory, and would have tried to characterize the United States as the aggressor and our presence as a hostile act. If they defended the moon as one of their colonies, or if they were the proxy force on behalf of the extraterrestrials with whom they had forged a military treaty, the United States would be in a weakened position. Thus, General Trudeau concluded and so advised his chief of the Ordnance Missile Command, it was of the utmost urgency that the U.S. Army devise a feasible plan to have a manned landing on the lunar surface by spring 1965, with a fully operational lunar outpost deployed on the moon by late 1966 at a cost over an eight-and-a-half-year period of $6 billion.

The first two astronauts, the spearhead of the scouting crew, were scheduled to touch down on the lunar surface in April 1965, in an area near the lunar equator where, according to the surveys, the army believed the terrain would support multiple landing and liftoff facilities and the construction of a cylindrical, ranch-house type of structure with tubular walls built beneath the surface into a crevice that would house an initial twelve personnel. The bulk of the construction materials for the lunar outpost, about

300,000 pounds, would already be on the site, having been transported there over the previous three months. According to the army plan, an additional 190,000 pounds of cargo would be sent to the moon from April 1965 through November 1966. And from December 1966 through December 1967, another 266,000 pounds of cargo and supplies would be scheduled to arrive at the now operational moon base.

It is April 1965, and a lunar vehicle with a crew of two astronauts has just touched down on the moon's surface. Although the vehicle has an immediate liftoff capability to return the astronauts to Earth, their scouting from orbit has determined that the area is safe and that there are no threats from either the Soviets or any extraterrestrials. The radio crackles with the team's first instructions.

"This is Horizon control, Moonbase. You are go for the first twenty-four hours," Horizon control at the Cocoa Beach, Florida, Cape Canaveral Space Command Center advises the astronauts. They secure their lander, which, if they receive the go to stay for additional periods, will ultimately become their cabin for the next two months as the construction crews arrive from Earth to begin the assembly of the lunar outpost.

However, even before the first manned cargo ships arrive, the advance crew of two astronauts will confirm the condition of the cargo that has already been delivered to the site, refine the environmental studies that have been conducted by the unmanned surveillance probes, and verify that the initial measurements and assumptions for the site of the moon base are correct.

By July 1965, the first crew of nine men arrive to begin laying the cylindrical tubes in the crevice beneath the surface and install the two portable atomic reactors that will power the entire outpost. A number of factors influenced the army's decision to sink the main structures beneath the lunar surface. The most important of these were the uniform temperatures, the insulation of the lunar surface material itself, protection from a potentially hazardous shower of small meteors and meteorites, camouflage and security, and protection from the kinds of radiation particles that are normally prevented from reaching Earth by our atmosphere.

Army engineers designed the cylindrical housing units to look and act like vacuum tank thermos bottles with a double wall with a special insulation between. The thermos design would prevent heat loss and so insulate the housing unit so that just the heat radiated by the internal artificial lighting system would be more than adequate to maintain a comfortable temperature inside. The crew's atmosphere was to be maintained by insulated tanks containing liquid oxygen and nitrogen with the waste moisture and carbon dioxide absorbed by solid chemicals and recycled through a dehumidifier. Eventually, as the base became more permanent and new crews were rotated in and out, a more efficient recycling system was to be installed.

The initial construction crew was assigned to live in a temporary configuration of cylindrical quarters as their numbers were increased by an additional six men and more supplies. Like the permanent facility, the temporary construction cabin would be buried in a crevice beneath the lunar surface, but it would be smaller than the permanent cabin and have none of the laboratory facilities that were to be built in the permanent structure. From the component parts already shipped to the landing site, the construction crew was to assemble a lunar surface rover, a digging and trenching vehicle—similar to a backhoe—and a forklift type of vehicle that would also serve as a type of crane. With just these three devices, the army believed, a crew of fifteen workers could assemble a permanent outpost out of prefabricated components. The Horizon plan for construction of facilities in a weightless, airless environment ultimately became the model for the construction of both the Russian *Mir* and American *Freedom* space stations.

While the construction of the permanent subsurface structure was under way, other members of the crew would lay out the multiantenna communications system that would rely on geosynchronous Earth satellites to relay transmissions back and forth from Earth ground stations. Lunar-based tracking and surveillance radar equipment would also maintain a constant vigilance of the earth and be able to track any orbital vehicles from the earth's surface as well as space vehicles entering the planet's atmosphere from outer space. Members of the crew would communicate with each other and with the outpost itself by radios mounted in the helmets of their space suits.

By the time the army was proposing Project Horizon, army engineers had already selected a number of launch sites. Instead of Cape Canaveral, the army chose an equatorial location because the earth spins fastest at the equator and this would provide added thrust to any rocket with an especially heavy payload. The army chose a secret location in Brazil where it wanted to start construction on an eight-launchpad facility that would house the entire project. The spacecraft would be monitored and controlled from the facilities at Cocoa Beach, where the army and navy were already launching their satellites.

We broke the program into six separate phases beginning with the June 1959 initial feasibility, which was written in response to General Trudeau's first proposal and became Phase I of the entire plan. Phase II, scheduled to be completed in early 1960, when I was to take over the project, called for a detailed development and funding plan in conjunction with preliminary experimentation on some of the essential components. During this phase, I had planned to use our regular Army R&D procedures to manage and review the testing and make sure that we could do what we said we could do under the initial feasibility study.

In Phase III, we scheduled the complete development of the hardware and the system integration for the entire project. This included the rockets, the space capsules, all of the lunar transportation and construction vehicles, the launch facilities at the proposed site in Brazil, and the lunar outpost components for both the temporary and the permanent bases. Also included in this phase was the development of all of the communications systems, including relay stations, surveillance systems, and the personal protective and communications gear that the astronauts would use. And finally, Phase III called for the engineering of all the actual procedures needed for Horizon to be successful such as the orbital rendezvous, orbital fueling of lunar transportation vehicles, transfer of cargo in orbit, and launching and testing of cargo rockets.

Under Phase IV, scheduled for 1965, the first lunar landing was to take place. The establishment of the first two-man lunar observation outpost and the construction of the preliminary living and working quarters for the first detachment of the crew were all slated for completion. The plans stated that by the end of this phase, "a manned lunar outpost will have been established."

Phases V and VI were the operational phases of the project and were scheduled to be completed over a two-year period beginning in December 1966 and winding up in January 1968. Under these phases, the lunar outpost would progress from the preliminary construction phases to the construction of the permanent facilities. These facilities begin the surveillance of Earth, establish our military presence by the emplacement of fortified positions on the moon, and begin the first scientific experiments and exploration. In Phase VI, based upon the success of the permanent outpost and the exploration of the lunar terrain, the army planned to expand the outpost with more landings and additional facilities and report on the results of biological and chemical testing and the first attempts to exploit the moon as a commercial entity. The army also believed, because that was the way we in R&D believed we could pay back the enormous development overhead we incurred, that by commercially exploiting the moon, perhaps through the same kind of federal land-leasing deals the Department of the Interior currently grants for oil and mineral exploration, we could put the billions of dollars spent back into the federal coffers.

Project Horizon also outlined the development of an Earth-orbiting station as an ancillary project to support the lunar landing missions. Under the "Orbital Station" specifications, the Army Ordnance project developers suggested the launching and assembly of an "austere, basic" orbital platform that would provide astronaut crews on their way to the moon with a rendezvous point for exchanging and increasing their payloads, refueling, and relaunching their spacecraft. The orbiting station would also be important in the early cargo shipment stages of Project Horizon where army crews could handle the cargo loading in the weight-lessness of space faster and easier than they could on Earth. Cargo could be shipped up separately, travel in earth orbit with the station, and then be reassembled by crews who would live in their own spaceship cabins instead of in the space station and then return to Earth when the refueling and reassembly of payloads was complete.

If the preliminary basic space station were successful, the army envisioned a more elaborate, sophisticated facility that would have its own scientific and military mission and serve as a relay station for crews on their way to or from the lunar outpost. This station would have an enhanced military capability and enable the United States to dominate the airspace over its enemies, blind its enemies' satellites, and shoot down its missiles. The army also saw the enhanced orbiting space station as another component in an elaborate defense against extraterrestrials, especially if the military were able to develop high-energy lasers and the particle-beam weapon we had seen aboard the Roswell spacecraft. The space station would, according to the army plan, effectively provide the platform for testing Earth-to-space weapons, and these, General Trudeau and I agreed, would be primarily directed against the hostile extraterrestrials who were the real threat to our planet.

In its plan for a separate administration and management structure within the structure of the army, Project Horizon was designed to be the largest research, development, and deployment operation in the army's history. Larger than the Manhattan Project, Horizon could easily have become a completely separate unit within the army itself. As such, Horizon was perceived as an immediate threat to the other branches of the military as well as to the civilian space agencies. The navy had its own pet plan for establishing undersea bases that would harvest the commercial and scientific opportunities at the bottom of the oceans while at the same time, and more importantly, establishing an antisubmarine defense that would counter the threat from Soviet nuclear submarines. We suspected that the navy plans, like our own plans for a moon base, also gave the navy the capability of carrying out surveillance tracking of unidentified undersea objects if, in fact, that's what the EBEs were sending to Earth.

Despite the civilian opposition to the army's plan, General Trudeau wrote that the army had no choice but to advocate its plans for a moon base. "The United States intelligence community agrees that the Soviet Union may accomplish a manned lunar landing at any time after 1965." This, he said, would establish a Soviet precedent for claiming the lunar surface as Soviet territory which, even in and of itself, could precipitate the next war if the United States also tried to establish a presence there. Being second was no option. "As the Congress has noted," General Trudeau continued, "we are caught in a stream in which we have no choice but to proceed."

However, as hard as we tried to get Project Horizon into full funding and development, we were stopped. The nation's space program had become the property of the civilian space agency, and NASA had its own agenda and its own schedule for space exploration. We were successful in discrete projects like Corona, but it would not relinquish to the army the control necessary to establish a moon base under the terms of a Project Horizon.

I became General Trudeau's point man for the project in Washington. I was able to lobby for it, and Horizon also became an effective cover for all of the technological development I was overseeing out of the Roswell file. No one knew just how much of the Roswell technology would wind up getting into development because of the military issues Horizon implicitly proposed about the presence of extraterrestrials and their hostile intentions. After his first full year in office, President Kennedy also saw the value in Project Horizon even though he was in no position to dismantle NASA or order NASA to cede control to the army for the development of a base on the moon.

But I think we eventually made our point to the President because he ultimately saw the value in a moon base. Shortly after I testified before the Senate in a closed, top-secret session about how the KGB had penetrated the CIA and was actually dictating some of our intelligence estimates since before the Korean War, Attorney General Robert

Kennedy, who read that secret testimony, asked me to come over to the Justice Department for a visit.

We came to a meeting of the minds that day. I know that I convinced him that the official intelligence the President was receiving through his agencies was not only faulty, it was deliberately flawed. Robert Kennedy began to see that those of us over at the Pentagon were not just a bunch of old soldiers looking for a war. He saw that we really did see a threat and that the United States was truly compromised by Soviet penetration of our most secret agencies. We didn't talk about Roswell or any aliens. I never told him about extraterrestrials, but I was able to convince him that if the Soviets got to the moon before we did, victory in the Cold War might just belong to them by the end of this decade. Bobby Kennedy suspected that there was another agenda to the army's desire to deploy a lunar outpost for military as well as for scientific and commercial purposes and, without ever acknowledging that agenda, promised that he would talk about it with the President.

I can only tell you that it was a mark of achievement for me personally when President John Kennedy announced to the nation shortly after my meeting with Bobby at the Justice Department that it was one of his goals that the United States put a manned expedition on the moon before the end of the 1960s. He got it! Maybe he couldn't let the army have another Manhattan Project. That was another era and another war. But Jack Kennedy did understand, I believe, the real consequences of the Cold War and what might have happened if the Russians had put a manned lander on the moon before we did.

The way history turned out, it was our lunar expeditions, one after the other throughout the 1960s, that not only caught the world's attention but showed all our enemies that the United States was determined to stake out its territory and defend the moon. Nobody was looking for an out-and-out war, especially the EBEs who tried to scare us away from the moon and their own base there more times than even I know. They buzzed our ships, interfered with our communications, and sought to threaten us by their physical presence. But we continued and persevered. Ultimately, we reached the moon and sent enough manned expeditions to explore the lunar surface that they effectively challenged the EBEs for control over our own skies and sphere of space, the very sphere General Trudeau was talking about in the Project Horizon memoranda ten years earlier. And although the Horizon proposal projected a lunar landing by 1967, it presupposed that the army would begin creating the bureaucracy to manage the effort and build the hardware as early as 1959. Because of NASA and civilian management of space exploration, the United States took longer to reach the moon than we had originally assumed and, of course, never did build the permanent base we had planned for in the original Horizon proposal.

I knew, even though I was no longer in the army in 1969, that our success at lunar exploration had demonstrated that we were exercising control and that the EBEs would not have free rein over our skies. It also demonstrated that if there were any deals to be made, any proxy relationships to establish, the Soviets were not the ones to deal with. By the beginning of the 1970s, as the Apollo lunar landings continued, it was clear that the tide had turned and we had gained some of the advantage in dealing with the EBEs that we were seeking way back in the 1950s.

But for me, back in 1961, staring at the mammoth Project Horizon report on my desk and realizing that the entire civilian science establishment was mobilizing against this endeavor, I knew that small victories would have to suffice until the big ones could be won. And I took out the printed silicon wafers we'd pulled from the Roswell spacecraft wreckage and told myself that these would comprise the next project I would get into development. I barely knew what they were, but, if the scientists at White Sands Proving Grounds were right about what they portended, this was a victory we would relish long after the political battles over Project Horizon were over.

CHAPTER 12

The Integrated Circuit Chip:

From the Roswell Crash Site to Silicon Valley

WITH THE NIGHT-VISION IMAGE INTENSIFIER PROJECT UNDER way at Fort Belvoir and the Project Horizon team trying to swim upstream against the tide of civilian management of the U.S. space program, I turned my attention to the next of the Roswell crash fragments that looked especially intriguing: the charred semiconductor wafers that had broken off some larger device. I hadn't made these my priorities at first, not knowing what they really were, until General Trudeau asked me to take a closer look.

"Talk to some of the rocket scientists down at Alamogordo about these things, Phil," he said. "I think they'll know what we should do with them."

I knew that in the days immediately following the crash, General Twining had met with the Alamogordo group of the Air Materiel Command and had described some of the debris to them. But I didn't know how detailed his descriptions were or whether they even knew about the wafers we had in our file.

"I want to talk to some of the scientists up here, too," I said. "Especially, I want to see some of the engineers from the defense contractors. Maybe they can figure out what the engineering process is for these things."

"Go over to Bell Labs, Phil," General Trudeau also suggested. "The transistor came out of their shop and these things look a lot like transistorized circuits."

I'd heard that General Twining had worked very closely with both Bell Labs and Motorola on communications research during the war, afterwards at the Alamogordo test site for V2 missile launches, and after the Roswell crash. Whether he had brought them any material from the crash or showed them the tiny silicon chips was a matter of pure speculation. I only know that the entire field of circuit miniaturization took a giant leap in 1947 with the invention of the transistor and the first solid-state components. By the late 1950s, transistors had replaced the vacuum tube in radios and had turned the wall-sized wooden box of the 1940s into the portable plastic radio you could hear blaring away at the shore on a hot July Sunday. The electronics industry had taken a major technological jump in less than ten years, and I had to wonder privately whether any Roswell material had gotten out that I didn't know about prior to my taking over Foreign Technology in 1961.

I didn't realize it at first when I showed those silicon wafers to General Trudeau, but I was to become very quickly and intimately involved with the burgeoning computer industry and a very small, completely invisible, cog in an assembly-line process that fifteen years later would result in the first microcomputer systems and the personal computer revolution.

Over the course of the years since I joined the army in 1942, my career took me through the stages of vacuum-tube-based devices, like our radios and radars in World War II, to component chassis. These were large circuitry units that, if they went down, could be changed in sections, smaller sections, and finally to tiny transistors and transistorized electronic components. The first army computers I saw were room-sized, clanking vacuum-tube monsters that were always breaking down and, by today's standards, took an eternity to calculate even the simplest of answers. They were simply oil-filled data pots. But they amazed those of us who had never seen computers work before.

At Red Canyon and in Germany, the tracking and targeting radars we used were controlled by new transistorized chassis computers that were compact enough to fit onto a truck and travel with the battalion. So when I opened up my nut file and saw the charred matte gray quarter-sized, cracker-shaped silicon wafers with the gridlines etched onto them like tiny printed lines on the cover of a matchbook, I could make an educated guess about their function even though I'd never seen anything of the like before. I knew, however, that our rocket scientists and the university researchers who worked with the development laboratories at Bell, Motorola, and IBM would more than understand the primary function of these chips and figure out what we needed to do to make some of our own.

But first I called Professor Hermann Oberth for basic background on what, if any, development might have taken place after the Roswell crash. Dr. Oberth knew the Alamogordo scientists and probably received secondhand the substance of the conversations General Twining had with his Alamogordo group in the hours after the retrieval of the vehicle. And if General Twining described some of the debris, did he describe these little silicon chips? And if he did, in those months when the ENIAC—the first working computer—was just cranking up at the Aberdeen Ordnance Testing Grounds in Maryland, what did the scientists make of those chips?

"They saw these at the Walker Field hangar," Dr. Oberth told me. "All of them at Alamogordo flew over to Roswell with General Twining to oversee the shipment to Wright Field."

Oberth described what happened that day after the crash when a team of AMC rocket scientists pored over the bits and pieces of debris from the site. Some of the debris was packed for flight on B29s. Other material, especially the crates that wound up at Fort Riley, were loaded onto deuce-and-a-halfs for the drive. Dr. Oberth said that years later, von Braun had told him how those scientists who literally had to stand in line to have their equations processed by the experimental computer in Aberdeen Maryland were in awe of the microscopic circuitry etched into the charred wafer chips that had spilled out of the craft.

Von Braun had asked General Twining whether anyone at Bell Labs was going to be contacted about this find. Twining seemed surprised at first, but when von Braun told him about the experiments on solid-state components— material whose electrons don't need to be excited by heat in order to conduct current—Twining became intrigued. What if these chips were components of a very advanced solid-state circuitry? von Braun asked him. What if one of the reasons the army could find no electronic wiring on the craft were the layers of these wafers that ran throughout the ship? These circuit chips could be the nervous system of the craft, carrying signals and transmitting commands just like the nervous system in a human body.

General Twining's only experience had been with the heavily insulated vacuum-tube devices from World War II, where the multistrand wires were covered with cloth. He'd never seen metallic printed chips like these before. How did they work? he'd asked von Braun.

The German scientist wasn't sure, although he guessed they worked on the same principle as the transistors that laboratories were trying to develop to the point where they could be manufactured commercially. It would completely transform the electronics industry, von Braun explained to General Twining, nothing short of a revolution. The Germans had been desperately trying to develop circuitry of this sort during the war, but Hitler, convinced the war would be over by 1941, told the German computer researchers that the *Wehrmacht* had no need for computers that had a development timetable greater than one year. They'd all be celebrating victory in Berlin before the end of the year.

But the research into solid-state components that the Germans had been doing and the early work at Bell Labs was nothing compared to the marvel that Twining had shown von Braun and the other rocket scientists in New Mexico. Under the magnifying glass, the group thought they saw not just a single solid-state switch but a whole system of switches integrated into each other and comprising what looked like an entire circuit or system of circuits. They couldn't be sure because no one had ever seen anything even remotely like this before. But it showed them an image of what the future of electronics could be if a way could be found to manufacture this kind of circuit on Earth. Suddenly, the huge guidance-control systems necessary to control the flight of a rocket, which, in 1947, were too big to be squeezed into the fuselage of the rocket, could be miniaturized so that the rocket could have its own automatic guidance system. If we could duplicate what the EBEs had, we, too, would have the ability to explore space. In effect, the reverse-engineering of solid-state integrated circuitry began in the weeks and months after the crash even though William Shockley at Bell Labs was already working on a version of his transistor as early as 1946.

In the summer of 1947, the scientists at Alamogordo were only aware of the solid-state circuit research under way at Bell Labs and Motorola. So they pointed Nathan Twining to research scientists at both companies and agreed to help him conduct the very early briefings into the nature of the Roswell find. The army, very covertly, turned some of the components over to research engineers for an inspection, and by the early 1950s the transistor had been invented and transistorized circuits were now turning up in consumer products as well as in military electronics systems. The era of the vacuum tube, the single piece of eighty-year-old technology upon which an entire generation of communications devices including television and digital computers was built, was now coming to a close with the discovery in the desert of an entirely new technology.

The radio vacuum tube was a legacy of nineteenth-century experimentation with electric current. Like many historic scientific discoveries, the theory behind the vacuum tube was uncovered almost by chance, and nobody really knew what it was or cared much about it until years later. The radio vacuum tube probably reached its greatest utility from the 1930s through the 1950s, until the technology we discovered at Roswell made it all but obsolete. The principle behind the radio vacuum tube, first discovered by Thomas Edison in the 1880s while he was experimenting with different components for his incandescent lightbulb, was that current, which typically flowed in either direction across a conductive material such as a wire, could be made to flow in only one direction when passed through a vacuum. This directed flow of current, called the "Edison effect," is the scientific principle behind the illumination of the filament material inside the vacuum of the incandescent lightbulb, a technology that has remained remarkably the same for over a hundred years.

But the lightbulb technology that Edison discovered back in the 1880s, then put aside only to experiment with it again in the early twentieth century, also had another equally important function. Because the flow of electrons across the single filament wire went in only one direction, the vacuum tube was also a type of automatic switch. Excite the flow of electrons across the wire and the current flowed only in the direction you wanted it to. You didn't need to throw a switch to turn on a circuit manually because the vacuum tube could do that for you. Edison had actually discovered the first automatic switching device, which could be applied to hundreds of electronic products from the radio sets that I grew up with in the 1920s to the communications networks and radar banks of World War II and to the television sets of the 1950s. In fact, the radio tube was the single component that enabled us to begin the worldwide communications network that was already in place by the early twentieth century.

Radio vacuum tubes also had another important application that wasn't discovered until experimenters in the infant science of computers first recognized the need for them in the 1930s and then again in the 1940s. Because they were switches, opening and closing circuits, they could be programmed to reconfigure a computer to accomplish different tasks. The computer itself had, in principle, remained essentially the same type of calculating device that Charles Babbage first invented in the 1830s. It was a set of internal gears or wheels that acted as counters and a section of "memory" that stored numbers until it was their turn to be processed. Babbage's computer was operated manually by a technician who threw mechanical switches in order to input raw numbers and execute the program that processed the numbers.

The simple principle behind the first computer, called by its inventor the "Analytical Engine," was that the same machine could process an infinite variety and types of calculations by reconfiguring its parts through a switching mechanism. The machine had a component for inputting numbers or instructions to the processor; the processor itself, which completed the calculations; a central control unit, or CPU, that organized and sequenced the tasks to make sure the machine was doing the right job at the right time; a memory area for storing numbers; and finally a component that output the results of the calculations to a type of printer: the same basic components you find in all computers even today.

The same machine could add, subtract, multiply, or divide and even store numbers from one arithmetical process to the next. It could even store the arithmetical computation instructions themselves from job to job. And Babbage borrowed a punch-card process invented by Joseph Jacquard for programming weaving looms. Babbage's programs could be stored on series of punch cards and fed into the computer to control the sequence of processing numbers. Though this may sound like a startling invention, it was Industrial Revolution technology that began in the late eighteenth century for the purely utilitarian challenge of processing large numbers for the British military. Yet, in concept, it was an entirely new principle in machine design that very quietly started the digital revolution.

Because Babbage's machine was hand powered and cumbersome, little was done with it through the nineteenth century, and by the 1880s, Babbage himself would be forgotten. However, the practical application of electricity to mechanical appliances and the delivery of electrical power along supply grids, invented by Thomas Edison and refined by Nikola Tesla, gave new life to the calculation machine. The concept of an automatic calculation machine would inspire American inventors to devise their own electrically powered calculators to process large numbers in a competition to calculate the 1890 U.S. Census. The winner of the competition was Herman Hollerith, whose electrically powered calculator was a monster device that not only processed numbers but displayed the progress of the process on large clocks for all to see. He was so successful that the large railroad companies hired him to process their numbers. By the turn of the century his company, the Computing Tabulating and Recording Company, had become the single largest developer of automatic calculating machines. By 1929, when Hollerith died, his company had become the automation conglomerate, IBM.

Right about the time of Hollerith's death, a German engineer named Konrad Zuse approached some of the same challenges that had confronted Charles Babbage a hundred years earlier: how to build his own version of a universal computing machine that could reconfigure itself depending upon the type of calculation the operator wanted to perform. Zuse decided that instead of working with a machine that operated on the decimal system, which limited the types of arithmetic calculations it could perform, his machine would use only two numbers, 0 and 1, the binary system. This meant that he could process any type of mathematical equation through the opening or closing of a series of electromagnetic relays, switches that would act as valves or gates either letting current through or shutting it off. These relays were the same types of devices that the large telephone companies, like the Bell system in the United States, were using as the basis of their networks. By marrying an electrical power supply and electric switches to the architecture of Babbage's Analytical Engine and basing his computations in a binary instead of a decimal system, Zuse had come up with the European version of the first electrical digital computer, an entirely new device. It was just three years before the German invasion of Poland and the outbreak of World War II.

In the United States at about the same time as Zuse was assembling his first computer in his parents' living room, Harvard mathematics professor Howard Aiken was trying to reconstruct a theoretical version of Babbage's computer, also using electromagnetic relays as switching devices and relying on a binary number system. The difference between Aiken and Zuse was that Aiken had academic credentials and his background as an innovative mathematician got him into the office of Thomas Watson, president of IBM, to whom he presented his proposal for the first American digital computer. Watson was impressed, authorized a budget for $1 million, and, right before the attack on Pearl Harbor, the project design was started up at Cambridge,

Massachusetts. It was then moved to IBM headquarters in New York during the war.

Because of their theoretical ability to calculate large sets of numbers in a relatively short period of time, digital computers were drafted into the war effort in the United Kingdom as a code-breaking device. By 1943, at the same time that IBM's first shiny stainless-steel version of Aiken's computer was up and running in Endicott, New York, the British were using their dedicated cryptoanalytical Colossus computer to break the German codes and decipher the code-creating ability of the German Enigma—the code machine that the Nazis believed made their transmissions indecipherable to the Allies. Unlike the IBM-Aiken computer at Harvard and Konrad Zuse's experimental computer in Berlin, the Colossus used radio vacuum tubes as relay switches and was, therefore, hundreds of times faster than any experimental computer using electromagnetic relays. The Colossus, therefore, was a true breakthrough because it married the speed of vacuum-tube technology with the component design of the Analytical Engine to create the first modern-era digital computer.

The British used the Colossus so effectively that they quickly felt the need to build more of them to process the increasingly large volume of encrypted transmissions the Germans were sending, ignorant of the fact that the Allies were decoding every word and outsmarting them at every turn. I would argue even to this day that the technological advantage the Allies enjoyed in intelligence-gathering apparatus, specifically code-breaking computers and radar, enabled us to win the war despite Hitler's initial successes and his early weapon advantages. The Allies' use of the digital computer in World War II was an example of how a superior technological advantage can make the difference between victory and defeat no matter what kinds of weapons or numbers of troops the enemy is able to deploy.

The American and British experience with computers during the war and our government's commitment to developing a viable digital computer led to the creation, in the years immediately following the war, of a computer called the Electronic Numerical Integrator and Calculator, or ENIAC. ENIAC was the brainchild of Howard Aiken and

Rome, 1945. Capt. Philip Corso receives his bronze star from Brig. Gen. Brown.

Tokyo, 1953. From left, 1st Lt. Howard Steele Jr., Maj. Corso, Col. Kalle Rasmussen, Lt. Col. John Thames, and 1st Lt. Lee Sherman after a military awards ceremony.

Germany, 1958. Thirteen-year-old Philip Corso Jr. shows off his science project: a homemade walking, talking, radio-controlled robot. Phil Jr.'s ability to work with electrical motors continues to this day.

Germany, 1960. Lt. Col. Corso, right, Inspector General of the 7th Army, visits an army helicopter base.

Lt. Col. Corso exchanges formalities with base officers.

From left, Edward O'Connor, Lt. Col. Corso, Lt. Gen. Arthur
Trudeau, and Victor Fediay at the general's new offices in
Pittsburgh, where he was president of Gulf Oil Research.
Corso gave Fediay, an advisor to the staff of the Senate
Foreign Relations Committee, a list of questions about UFOs
to ask the Soviets in Moscow. On his return from Russia,
Fediay said that the KGB general he spoke to saw the list and
asked him, "Are you trying to get me killed?"

Reconnaissance photos of the moon that were taken as part of the Project HORIZON proposal for establishing a permanent military base on the lunar surface.

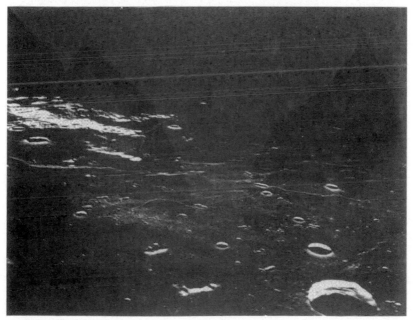

Lt. Col. Corso was never able to confirm the veracity of the following purported UFO surveillance photos, which were in Army Intelligence files as support material for the R&D project to harvest the Roswell alien technology for military purposes.

NATIONAL ARCHIVES

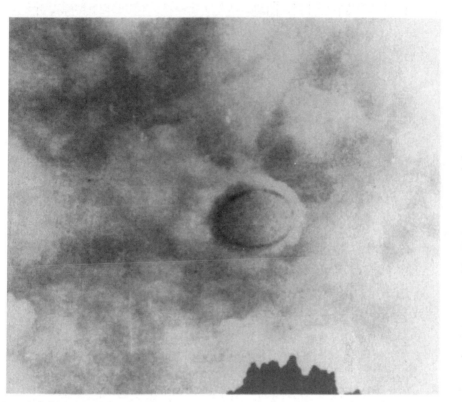

NATIONAL ARCHIVES

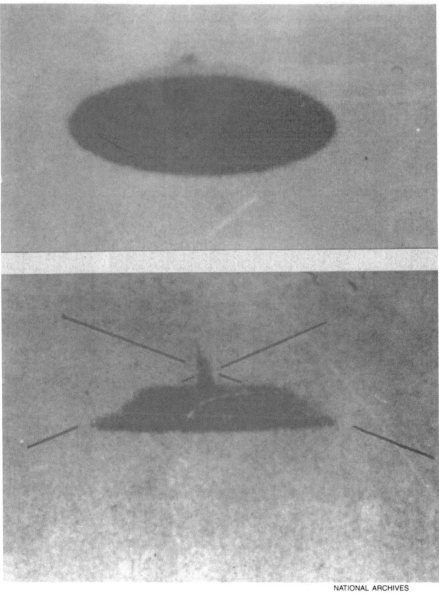

one of the army's early R&D brain-trust advisers, the late mathematician John von Neumann. Although it operated on a decimal instead of a binary system and had a very small memory, it relied on radio vacuum-tube switching technology. For its time it was the first of what today are called "number crunchers."

When measured against the way computers developed over the years since its first installation, especially the personal computers of today, ENIAC was something of a real dinosaur. It was loud, hot, cumbersome, fitful, and required the power supply of an entire town to keep it going. It couldn't stay up for very long because the radio tubes, always unreliable even under the best working conditions, would blow out after only a few hours' work and had to be replaced. But the machine worked, it crunched the numbers it was fed, and it showed the way for the next model, which reflected the sophisticated symbolic architectural design of John von Neumann.

Von Neumann had suggested that instead of feeding the computer the programs you wanted it to run every time you turned it on, the programs themselves could be stored in the computer permanently. By treating the programs themselves as components of the machine, stored right in the hardware, the computer could change between programs, or the routines of subprograms, as necessary in order to solve problems. This meant that larger routines could be processed into subroutines, which themselves could be organized into templates to solve similar problems. In complex applications, programs could call up other programs again and again without the need of human intervention and could even change the subprograms to fit the application. Von Neumann had invented block programming, the basis for the sophisticated engineering and business programming of the late 1950s and 1960s and the great, great grandmother of today's object-oriented programming.

By 1947, it had all come together: the design of the machine, the electrical power supply, the radio vacuum-tube technology, the logic of machine processing, von Neumann's mathematical architecture, and practical applications for the computer's use. But just a few years shy of the midpoint of the century, the computer itself was the product of eighteenth- and nineteenth-century thinking and technology. In fact, given the shortcomings of the radio tube and the enormous power demands and cooling requirements to keep the computer working, the development of the computer seemed to have come to a dead end. Although IBM and Bell Labs were investing huge sums of development money into designing a computer that had a lower operational and maintenance overhead, it seemed, given the technology of the digital computer circa 1947, that there was no place it could go. It was simply an expensive-to-build, expensive-to-run, lumbering elephant at the end of the line. And then an alien spacecraft fell out of the skies over Roswell, scattered across the desert floor, and in one evening everything changed.

In 1948 the first junction transistor—a microscopically thin silicon sandwich of n-type silicon, in which some of the atoms have an extra electron, and p-type silicon, in which some of the atoms have one less electron—was devised by physicist William Shockley. The invention was credited to Bell Telephone Laboratories, and, as if by magic, the dead end that had stopped the development of the dinosaur-like ENIAC generation of computers melted away and an entirely new generation of miniaturized circuitry began. Where the radio-tube circuit required an enormous power supply to heat it up because heat generated the electricity, the transistor required very low levels of powers and no heating-up time because the transistor amplified the stream of electrons that flowed into its base. Because it required only a low level of current, it could be powered by batteries. Because it didn't rely on a heat source to generate current and it was so small, many transistors could be packed into a very small space, allowing for the miniaturization of circuitry components. Finally, because it didn't burn out like the radio tube, it was much more reliable. Thus, within months after the Roswell crash and the first exposure of the silicon-wafer technology to companies already involved in the research and development of computers, the limitations on the size and power of the computer suddenly dropped like the removal of a roadblock on a highway and the next generation of computers went into development. This set up for Army R&D, especially during the years I was there, the opportunity for us to encourage that development with defense contracts calling for the implementation of integrated-circuit devices into subsequent generations of weapons systems.

More than one historian of the microcomputer age has written that no one before 1947 foresaw the invention of the transistor or had even dreamed about an entirely new technology that relied upon semiconductors, which were silicon based and not carbon based like the Edison incandescent tube. Bigger than the idea of a calculating machine or an Analytical Engine or any combination of the components that made up the first computers of the 1930s and 1940s, the invention of the transistor and its natural evolution to the silicon chip of integrated circuitry was beyond what anyone could call a quantum leap of technology. The entire development arc of the radio tube, from Edison's first experiments with filament for his incandescent lightbulb to the vacuum tubes that formed the switching mechanisms of ENIAC, lasted about fifty years. The development of the silicon transistor seemed to come upon us in a matter of months. And, had I not seen the silicon wafers from the Roswell crash with my own eyes, held them in my own hands, talked about them with Hermann Oberth, Wernher von Braun, or Hans Kohler, and heard the reports from these now dead scientists of the meetings between Nathan Twining, Vannevar Bush, and researchers at Bell Labs, I would have thought the invention of the transistor was a miracle. I know now how it came about.

As history revealed, the invention of the transistor was only the beginning of an integrated-circuit technology that developed through the 1950s and continues right through to the present. By the time I became personally involved in 1961, the American marketplace had already witnessed the retooling of Japan and Germany in the 1950s and Korea and Taiwan in the late 1950s through the early 1960s. General Trudeau was concerned about this, not because he considered these countries our economic enemies but because he believed that American industry would suffer as a result of its complacency about basic research and development. He expressed this to me on many occasions during our meetings, and history has proved him to be correct.

General Trudeau believed that the American industrial economy enjoyed a harvest of technology in the years immediately following World War II, the effects of which were still under way in the 1960s, but that it would soon slow down because R&D was an inherently costly undertaking that didn't immediately contribute to a company's bottom line. And you had to have a good bottom line, General Trudeau always said, to keep your stockholders happy or else they would revolt and throw the existing management team right out of the company. By throwing their efforts into the bottom line, Trudeau said, the big American industries were actually destroying themselves just like a family that spends all its savings.

"You have to keep on investing in yourself, Phil," the general would like to say when he'd look up from his *Wall Street Journal* before our morning meetings and remark about how stock analysts always liked to place their value on the wrong thing. "Sure, these companies have to make a profit, but you look at the Japanese and the Germans and they know the value of basic research," he once said to me. "American companies expect the government to pay for all their research, and that's what you and I have to do if we want to keep them working. But there's going to come a time when we can't afford to pay for it any longer. Then who's going to foot the bill?"

General Trudeau was worrying about how the drive for new electronics products based upon miniaturized circuitry was creating entirely new markets that were shutting out American companies. He said that it was becoming cheaper for American companies to have their products manufactured for them in Asia, where companies had already retooled after the war to produce transistorized components, than for American companies, which had heavily invested in the manufacturing technology of the nineteenth century, to do it themselves. He knew that the requirement for space exploration, for challenging the hostile EBEs in their own territory, relied on the development of an integrated-circuit technology so that the electronic components of spacecraft could be miniaturized to fit the size requirements of rocket-propelled vehicles. The race to develop more intelligent missiles and ordnance also required the development of new types of circuitry that could be packed into smaller and smaller spaces. But retooled Japanese and German industries were the only ones able to take immediate advantage of what General Trudeau called the "new electronics."

For American industry to get onto the playing field the basic research would have to be paid for by the military. It was something General Trudeau was willing to fight for at the Pentagon because he knew that was the only way we could get the weapons only a handful of us knew we needed to fight a skirmish war against aliens only a handful of us knew we were fighting. Arthur Trudeau was a battlefield general engaged in a lonely military campaign that national policy and secrecy laws forbade him even to talk about. And as the gulf of time widened between the Roswell crash and the concerns over postwar economic expansion, even the people who were fighting the war alongside General Trudeau were, one by one, beginning to die away. Industry could fight the war for us, General Trudeau believed, if it was properly seeded with ideas and the money to develop them. By 1961, we had turned our attention to the integrated circuit.

Government military weapons spending and the requirements of space exploration had already heavily funded the transistorized component circuit. The radars and missiles I was commanding at Red Canyon, New Mexico, in 1958 relied on miniaturized components for their reliability and portability. New generations of tracking radars on the drawing boards in 1960 were even more sophisticated and electronically intelligent than the weapons I was aiming at Soviet targets in Germany. In the United States, Japanese and Taiwanese radios that fit into the palm of your hand were on the market. Computers like ENIAC, once the size of a small warehouse, now occupied rooms no larger than closets and, while still generating heat, no longer blew out because of overheated radio vacuum tubes. Minicomputers, helped by government R&D funding, were still a few years away from market, but were already in a design phase. Television sets and stereophonic phonographs that offered solid-state electronics were coming on the market, and companies like IBM, Sperry-Rand, and NCR were beginning to bring electronic office machines onto the market. It was the beginning of a new age of electronics, helped, in part, by government funding of basic research into the development and manufacture of integrated-circuit products. But the real prize, the development of what actually had been recovered at Roswell, was still a few years away. When it arrived, again spurred by the requirements of military weapons development and space travel, it caused another revolution.

The history of the printed circuit and the microprocessor is also the history of a technology that allowed engineers to squeeze more and more circuitry into a smaller and smaller space. It's the history of the integrated circuit, which developed throughout the 1960s, evolved into large-scale integration by the early 1970s, very large-scale integration by the middle 1970s, just before the emergence of the first real personal computers, and ultra large-scale integration by the early 1980s. Today's 200-plus-megahertz, multigigabyte hard-drive desktop computers are the results of the integrated-circuit technology that began in the 1960s and has continued to the present. The jump from the basic transistorized integrated printed circuit of the 1960s to large-scale integration was made possible by the development of the microprocessor in 1972.

Once the development process of engineering a more tightly compacted circuit had been inspired by the invention of the transistor in 1948, and fueled by the need to develop better, faster, and smaller computers, it continued on a natural progression until the engineers at Intel developed the first microprocessor, a four-bit central processing unit called the 4004, in 1972. This year marked the beginning of the microcomputer industry, although the first personal microcomputers didn't appear on the market until the development of Intel's 8080A. That computer chip was the heart of the Altair computer, the first product to package a version of a high-level programming language called BASIC, which allowed nonengineering types to program the machine and create applications for it. Soon companies like Motorola and Zilog had their own microprocessors on the market, and by 1977 the Motorola 6502-powered Apple II was on the market, joined by the 8080A

Radio Shack, the Commodore PET, the Atari, and the Heathkit. Operationally, at its very heart, the microprocessor shares the same binary-processing functions and large arrays of digital switches as its ancestors, the big mainframes of the 1950s and 1960s and the transistorized minis of the late 1960s and early 1970s. Functionally, the microprocessor also shares the same kinds of tasks as Charles Babbage's Analytical Engine of the 1830s: reading numbers, storing numbers, logically processing numbers, and outputting the results. The microprocessor just puts everything into a much smaller space and moves it along at a much faster speed.

In 1979, Apple Computer had begun selling the first home computer floppy-disk operating system for data and program storage that kicked the microcomputer revolution into a higher gear. Not only could users input data via a keyboard or tape cassette player, they could store relatively large amounts of data, such as documents or mathematical projections, on transportable, erasable, and interchangeable Mylar disks that the computer was able to read. Now the computer reached beyond the electronics hobbyist into the workplace. By the end of the year, MicroPro's introduction of the first fully functional word processor called WordStar, and Personal Software's release of the very first electronic spreadsheet called VisiCalc, so transformed the workplace that the desktop computer became a necessity for any young executive on his or her way up the corporate ladder. And by the early 1980s, with the introduction of the Apple Macintosh and the object-oriented computer environment, not only the workplace but the whole world looked like a very different place than it did in the early 1960s. Even Dr. Vannevar Bush's concept of a type of research query language based not on a linear outline but on an intellectual relationship to something embedded in a body of text became a reality with the release of a computer program by Apple called HyperCard.

It was as if from the year 1947 to 1980 a fundamental paradigm shift in the ability of humankind to process information took place. Computers themselves almost became something like a silicon-based life-form, inspiring the carbon-based life-forms on planet Earth to develop them, grow them, and even help them reproduce. With computer-directed process-control programs now in place in virtually all major industries, software that writes software, neural-network-based expert systems that learn from their own experience in the real world, and current experiments under way to grow almost microscopically thin silicon-based chips in the weightless environment of earth orbit may be the forerunner of a time when automated orbital factories routinely grow and harvest new silicon material for micro-processors more sophisticated than we can even imagine at the present. Were all of this to be true, could it not be argued that the silicon wafers we recovered from Roswell were the real masters and space travelers and the EBE creatures their hosts or servants? Once implanted successfully on Earth, our culture having reached a point of readiness through its development of the first digital computers, would not the natural development stream, starting from the invention of the transistor, have carried us to the point where we achieve a symbiotic relationship with the silicon material that carries our data and enables us to become more creative and successful?

Maybe the Roswell crash, which helped us develop the technological basis for the weapons systems to protect our planet from the EBEs, was also the mechanism for success-fully implanting a completely alien nonhumanoid life-form that survives from host to host like a virus, a digital Ebola that we humans will carry to another planet someday. Or what if an enemy wanted to implant the perfect spying or sabotage mechanism into a culture? Then the implantation of the microchip-based circuit into our technology by the EBEs would be the perfect method. Was it implanted as sabotage or as something akin to the gift of fire? Maybe the Roswell crash in 1947 was an event waiting to happen, like poisoned fruit dropping from the tree into a playground. Once bitten, the poison takes effect.

"Hold your horses, Phil," General Trudeau would say when I would speculate too much. "Remember, you've got a bunch of scientists you need to talk to and the people at Bell Labs are waiting to see your report when you've finished talking to the Alamogordo group."

It was 1961 and the miniaturization of computer and electronic circuitry had already begun, but my report to the general and appointments he was arranging for me at Sperry-Rand, Hughes, and Bell Labs were for meetings with scientists to determine how their respective companies were proceeding with applying miniaturized circuitry into designs for weapons systems. The inspiration for microcircuitry had fallen out of the sky at Roswell and set the development of digital computers off in an entirely new direction. It was my job now to use the process of weapons development, especially the development of guidance systems for ballistic missiles, to implement the application of microcircuitry systems to these new generations of weapons. General Trudeau and I were among the first scouts in what would be the electronic battlefield of the 1980s.

"Don't worry, General, I've got my appointments all set up," I told him. I knew how carried away I could get, but I was an intelligence officer first, and that meant you start with a blank page and fill it in. "But I think the people at Bell Labs have already seen these things before." And they actually did—in 1947.

CHAPTER 13

The Laser

As I worked my way through the list of items in my nut file, writing advisory reports and recommendations to General Trudeau about the potential of each item, I lost all concept of time. I could see, as I drove up and down the Potomac shore to Fort Belvoir to check on the progress of night vision at Martin Marietta, that the summer was coming to an end and the leaves had started to change color. I could also see that now it was already dark when I left the Pentagon. And it was dark now when I set out for the Pentagon every morning. I'd gotten into the habit of taking different routes to work just to make sure that if the CIA had put a tail on me, I'd make him work harder to stay up with me.

General Trudeau and I had settled down into a long daily routine ourselves at R&D. We had our early-morning meetings about the Roswell file—he also called it the "junk pile" because it was filled with so much debris and pieces of items that had broken away from larger components—but we had buried the Roswell material development projects themselves so deep inside the regular functions of the R&D division that not even the other officers who worked with us every day knew what was going on. We'd categorized the work we did so carefully that when it came time to discuss anything about Roswell, even if it had a bearing on some other item we were working on at the time, we made sure that either no one was at the office, or we were at a place where we wouldn't have to stop talking just because someone came into the room.

My responsibility at Foreign Technology was to feed R&D's ongoing project development with information and intelligence from sources outside the regular army channels. These ran in interconnected rings through the Pentagon to defense industry contractors to testing operations at army bases and to researchers at universities or independent laboratories who were under contract with us. If we were developing methods of preserving food, always trying to come up with a better way to prepare field rations, and the Italians and Germans had a process that seemed to work, it was my job to learn about it and slip the information into the development process. Even when there was no official development process under way for a specific item, if something I learned was appropriate to any one of the army's major commands, whether it was the Medical Corps, the Signal Corps, the motor pool, ordnance, or even the Quartermaster Corps, it was also my job to find a way to make that information appropriate and drop it in without so much as a splash. This made the perfect cover for what I was doing with the Roswell file as long as I could find ways to slip the Roswell technology into the development process so invisibly no one would ever able to find the Roswell on-ramp to the information highway.

For all the world to see, General Trudeau and I regularly met to review the ongoing projects in Army R&D, those we had inherited from the previous command and those we wanted to initiate on our watch. Officers who'd been assigned to R&D before we arrived had their own projects already in development, too, and the general had assigned me the task of feeding those projects with information and intelligence, no matter where it came from, without disturbing either what the officers were doing or interfering with their staffs. It was tricky because I had to work in the dark, undercover even from my own colleagues whose reputations would have been destroyed if word leaked out that they were dealing in "flying saucer stuff." Yet at the same time, most high-ranking officers at the Pentagon and key members of their staffs knew that Roswell technology was floating through most of the new projects under development. They were also vaguely, if not specifically, aware of what had happened at Roswell itself and of the current version of the Hillenkoetter/Bush/Twining working group, which had personnel stationed at the Pentagon to keep tabs on what the military was doing.

Uniting what I called my official "day job" at R&D on regular projects and my undercover job in the Roswell file was my official, but many times informal, role as General Trudeau's deputy at the division. In that job, I would carry out the general's orders as they related to the division and not specifically to any one project or another. If General Trudeau needed information to help him redefine his budgetary priorities or assemble information to help compile supplementary development budgets, he'd often ask me to help or at least give him advice. And I functioned as the general's intelligence officer as well, supporting him at meetings with information, helping him present position papers, assisting him whenever he had to hold briefings or meet with congressional committees, and defending him and the division against the almost weekly attacks on our turf from officers in the other military branches or from the civilian development and intelligence agencies. Everybody wanted to know what we knew, what we were spending, and what we were spending it on. And we had no quarrel with telling anybody who wanted to know exactly what kinds of goods the American people were getting for their money except when it came to one category—Roswell. That's when the mantle of darkness would fall and our memories about where certain things came from became very dim, as it did with the dramatic improvement in night-vision technology shortly after the summer of 1961. Even our own people became very frustrated with us when General Trudeau would turn to me at a meeting and say, "You know that night-vision information you sent over to Fort Belvoir a while back? Where did you find that file, Phil?" And if I couldn't play dumb and say, "I don't think I ever came across this before, must be someone else in charge," then I'd simply shrug and say, "I don't know, General, must have been in the files somewhere. I'll have to go back and look."

It was an act, and many of the officers who suspected we had a stash of information somewhere knew we were covering up something. But if they were career, they also knew how to play the Pentagon version of steal the bacon. We had it and we were hiding it. No one would find out anything unless we let them. So the general would typically hand off anything having to do with military intelligence information to me and I would usually find a way not only to lose the answer but to lose the question as well. We became so practiced at this that entirely new inventions could find their way into development at many different places at the same time without anyone's ever becoming aware of the source of the technology, especially the officer who was assigned the task of project manager within our very own division.

The CIA got so frustrated at not getting any information out of us that they began keeping closer tabs on the Russian attachés floating around Washington and working under their KGB controllers at the embassies and consulates. Because the CIA knew how thoroughly our universities had been penetrated they figured they'd get information on the rebound by photographing what was inside the photocopiers at the Russian embassy in Washington. And sure enough, from the rumor mill circulating around the exchange of scientists between industry and academia, the CIA knew that we were onto something at Army R&D and kept the circle as tight around us as they possibly could. So I had to keep close tabs on the general, not letting him go into meetings, any meetings, unprotected and always making sure that the CIA knew that they would have to climb over me to get to General Trudeau and anything he knew. And the CIA knew that I knew what they were doing and where their loyalties lay and also knew that it would have to come to a showdown someday.

General Trudeau and I had quickly established our routine in early 1961, and our categorization of how we did our jobs seemed to be working. Night vision was under development at Fort Belvoir, and researchers who worked with us had made sure that the silicon wafer chips had gotten to their colleagues at Bell Labs and assured us that a new generation of transistorized circuitry was already finding its way into development. The silicon chips were a covert reintroduction to the people at Bell Labs because the initial introduction of the integrated-circuit chips from the Roswell crash had reached defense contractors as early as 1947 in the weeks after the material reached Wright Field.

A similar history of introduction and reintroduction had occurred with stimulated-energy radiation, a weapon the early analysts believed they were looking at in the wreckage of the Roswell craft. Since directed-energy radiation was a technology we'd already deployed in World War II, seeing what they thought was a superadvanced version of that technology, so advanced as to be in a completely different realm, so excited the analysts at Wright Field that they wanted to get it out to research scientists as quickly as possible, which they did. And by the early 1950s, a version of stimulated-energy radiation had found its way into the scientific community, which was developing new products around the process of microwave generation.

Most Americans who were alive in the 1950s remember the introduction of the microwave oven that helped us "live better electrically" in our new modern kitchens. One of the miracle appliances that burst onto the scene in the 1950s promised to cook food in less than half the time of conventional ovens, even when the food had been completely frozen. Marketed under a variety of brand names including the now-historic "Radar Range," the microwave oven cooked whatever was inside not by the application of pure heat, the way conventional ovens did, but by bombarding the food with showers of tiny waves of electromagnetic radiation, usually only a centimeter or so long. The waves would pass through the food, exciting the water molecules deep inside and causing them to align and realign, back and forth, with greater velocity. The molecular activity generated heat from within and the food cooked from the inside out. Once you enclosed it in the right kind of container to keep all the moisture from evaporating, you had a quick-cooked meal.

The theory behind the microwave oven that started us down the long and profitable path of stimulated-energy research was formulated in 1945 with the first commercial microwave ovens rolling off the line at Raytheon in Massachusetts in 1947 before any dissemination of either intelligence or material from the crash of the Roswell spacecraft. But in the wreckage of that craft, the scientists from the test-firing range at Alamogordo reported that the inhabitants of the craft seemed to use very advanced wave stimulation instrumentation that, according to their analysis, bore a relationship to the physics of a basic microwave generator. The retrieval team that pulled the wreckage out of the desert also found a short, stubby, internally powered flashlight device that threw a pencil-thin, intense beam of light for a short distance that could actually cut through metal. This, the engineers at Wright Field believed, was also based on wave stimulation. The questions then were, how did the EBEs use wave stimulation and how could we adapt it to military uses or slip it into the product development already under way?

By 1954, when I was at the White House, the National Security Council was already receiving reports of a theory, developed by Charles H. Townes, that described how the atoms of a gas could be excited to extraordinarily high energy levels by the application of bursts of energy. The gas would release its excess energy as microwaves of a very precise frequency that could be controlled. In theory, we thought, the energy beam could be a signal to carry communications or an amplifier for the signal. When the first maser was assembled at Bell Laboratories in 1956, it was used as a timer because of the very exact calibration of the wave frequency.

The maser, however, was only a forerunner of the product that was to come, the laser, which would revolutionize every aspect of technology it touched. It would also prove to be a weapon that would help us deploy a realistic threat to the EBEs who seemed poised to trigger a nuclear war between the superpowers. Where the maser was an amplification of generated microwaves, the laser was an amplification of light, and theories about how this might be accomplished were circulating widely throughout the weapons-development community even before Bell Labs produced the first maser.

I had seen the descriptions of the EBE laser in reports about the Roswell crash, a beam of light so thin that you couldn't even see it until it landed on a target. What was the purpose of this light generator? the Alamogordo group had asked. It looked like a targeting or communications device, seemed to have an almost limitless range, and, if the right power source could be found to amplify the light beam to where it could penetrate metal, the device could be used as a drill, a welder, or even a devastating weapon.

Even while I was at the White House, all three branches of the military were working with researchers in university laboratories to develop a working laser. In theory, exciting the atoms of an element to produce light energy in the same way that atoms of a gas were excited to produce microwaves, lasers offered the tantalizing promise of a directed-energy beam that had such a wide variety of applications it could become an almost universal utility for all divisions of the military, even controlling warehouse inventory for the Quartermaster Corps. Finally, in 1958, the year after I left the White House, there was a surge in research activity, especially at Columbia University where, two years later, physicist Theodore Maiman constructed the first working laser.

The first practical demonstration of the laser took place in 1960, and by the time I got to the Pentagon, General Trudeau had put it on our list of priorities to develop for military purposes. Also, because stimulated-energy radiation devices were among the cache of technological debris we recovered from Roswell, the U.S. development of the laser encompassed the special urgent requirements of my Roswell mission. I had to write a report to General Trudeau suggesting ways the EBEs might have used laser technology in their missions on this planet and how we could develop similar uses for it under the guise of a conventional development program. In other words, once we guessed how the aliens were using it, it was to become our developmental model for similar applications.

We believed that the EBEs used lasers for navigation, by

bouncing beams off distant objects in space and homing in on them to triangulate a course; for communication, by using the laser beam as a carrier signal or as a signal in and of itself; for surveillance, by painting potential targets with a beam; and for power transmission, illumination, and even data storage. The strength and integrity of the laser beam should have served as the EBEs' primary method of communication over vast distances or even as a way of storing communications in packages for later delivery. However, it was the EBEs' use of directed energy as a medical tool and ultimately as a potential weapon that sent shivers up and down our spines because to our minds it was evidence of the aliens' hostile intentions. Whether they saw us as true enemies to be destroyed or regarded all life on our planet as laboratory specimens to be experimented with, the results from the animal carcasses picked up in the field by our military nuclear, biological, and chemical recovery teams and the civilian intelligence investigators could have been very much the same.

In the Pentagon from 1961 to 1963, I reviewed field reports from local and state police agencies about the discoveries of dead cattle whose carcasses looked as though they had been systematically mutilated and reports from people who claimed to have been abducted by aliens and experimented on. One of the common threads in these stories were reports by the self-described abductees of being subjected to some sort of probing or even a form of surgery with controlled, intense, pencil-thin beams of light. Local police reported that when veterinarians were called to the scene to examine the dead cattle left in fields, they often found evidence not just that the animal's blood had been drained but that entire organs were removed with such surgical skill that it couldn't have been the work of predators or vandals removing the organs for some depraved ritual. Where there was evidence of crime of someone staging a bizarre hoax, it was usually obvious from the clumsiness of the attempt and the deliberate staging of the carcass. And in the overwhelming majority of instances where the animal was killed by a predator who consumed its blood and carried away internal organs, the evidence of teeth marks or of a brief life-and-death struggle was also a clear indicator of what had happened. But in those cases where investigators claimed to have been baffled by what they found, the removal of the organs and the draining of the animal's blood—where blood had been completely drained—were so sophisticated that there was almost no peripheral damage to the surrounding tissue. There was even some speculation, in the early 1960s, that whatever device the EBEs had employed, it didn't even cut through the surrounding tissue. We had no medical instruments that even remotely approached what the aliens could do. It was as though some device had simply excised the organs with techniques that even went beyond our own surgical precision.

While I was on the White House National Security staff and later when I was at the Pentagon, I was intrigued by these reports. I also remember that both civilian and military intelligence personnel attached to the staffs of individuals who worked for the Hillenkoetter and Twining working group on UFOs in the 1950s were actively engaging in research into the kinds of surgical methods that would produce "crime scene evidence" like this. Could have been the Russians, they thought at first. Given the tense climate of the Cold War, a fear that the Soviets were experimenting with American livestock to develop some form of toxin or biological weapon that would devastate our cattle population was not unduly paranoid. It's sufficient to say, without going into any detail, that we were thinking about the same kinds of weapons, so it was not far-fetched to say that we were projecting our own doomsday strategies onto what the Russians might have done.

But it wasn't the Soviets who were going after our cattle. In fact the Soviet strategy for destabilizing the United States was so sophisticated that it was only a strategy of playing nuclear chicken with the Soviets that forced them to back down in the end. It was the EBEs who were experimenting with organ harvesting, possibly for transplant into other species or for processing into some sort of nutrient package or even to create some sort of hybrid biological entity. This is what people attached to the working group thought in the 1950s and 1960s, and even though we had no solid intelligence at the time that we were right, we operated on the assumption that no one takes an organ just for the sheer pleasure of removing it. Although the first public reports of cattle mutilations surfaced around 1967 in Colorado, at the White House we were reading about the mutilation stories that had been kept out of press as far back as the middle 1950s, especially in the area around Colorado. There was speculation, also, that maybe pharmaceutical companies were responsible because they could utilize the organs and soft tissues in biological experimentation, but we dismissed that because the companies had their own farms and could grow anything they wanted. Our intelligence organizations and especially the working group believed that the cattle mutilations that could not be obviously explained away as pranks, predators, or ritual slaughter were the results of interventions by extraterrestrials who were harvesting specific organs or for experimentation. So if our cattle were important enough to the EBEs to get them to expose what they were doing, it was an important thing for us to understand why. The EBEs were nothing if not coldly and clinically efficient—their methodology reminded us of the Nazis—and they didn't waste time sitting around on the ground where they were most vulnerable to attack or capture unless they had a darn good reason for doing so.

We didn't know their reasons back in the 1950s and 1960s and can only make educated guesses about them now, but back then we were driven by a terror that unless we found ways to defend ourselves against the EBEs we would be corralled by them and used for replacement tissue or as a source of nutrition. In 1997 this may sound like a nightmare out of a flying saucer horror movie, but in 1957 this was our thinking both in the White House and in the military. We didn't know, but we had irrefutable evidence that EBEs were landing on farms, harvesting vital organs from livestock, and then just leaving the carcasses on the ground because they knew we couldn't do anything about it.

The mutilations that interested the National Security personnel seemed to have the same kind of modus operandi. Whoever went after the animals seemed most interested in the mammary, digestive, and reproductive organs, especially the uteruses from cows. In many cases the eyes or throats were removed in a type of surgery in which the demarcation line was almost microscopically thin and the surrounding tissue showed that the incision had super-heated and then blackened as it cooled. But the crime scene and forensic specialists noted that in any type of cut by a predatory animal or a human—even a skilled surgeon—one would find evidence of some trauma in the surrounding tissue such as swelling, contusions, or other forms of abrasion. In these reports of mutilations, forensic examination showed no evidence of collateral trauma or even inflammation. Therefore, they believed, the cuts to extract the tissue were made so quickly and wounds were sealed so fast that the surrounding tissue never was destroyed. This meant that whoever was operating on these animals did so in a matter of minutes. It was rare, therefore, that police would ever catch them in the act. So if we couldn't protect our livestock or react intelligently to the stories of human abductions, except to debunk them and make the abductees themselves think they were delusional, we had to find weapons that would put us on a more equal footing with the EBEs. One of those weapons, which had a wide application potential, was the laser—light amplification through stimulated energy radiation—the device the army found in the Roswell spacecraft and would later develop as a weapon in cooperation with Hughes Aircraft.

Shortly after the first successful demonstration of a ruby red laser at Columbia University, the three military branches realized they had a winner. The following year, the results of the tests at Columbia, the industry interest in developing laser-based products, and the Roswell report on stimulated energy all merged on my desk. Now it was my turn to get involved and assemble the information to support laser product development with military funds before the whole operation was turned over to one of the R&D specialists who would take the product through its next stages. That was the way our backfield worked: I fed the play, made sure the snap got off, and then faded in behind the blockers. By the time the ball carrier had made his way into the secondary, I was already off the field. I never got the Heisman Trophy, but I sure as hell moved the ball.

I began by listing the needs of the army for what the laser might be able to accomplish. Based on what the army analysts reported they saw in the Roswell ship, it seemed to me obvious that if the Roswell laser was a cutting or surgical tool, the beam could also be utilized as an advanced rapid-firing weapon. With a beam so precise and directed, the laser would also make an excellent range finder and target manager for artillery. If the beam was capable of instantaneous readjustment and fed into a computer, it would also be the perfect targeting system for a tank, especially a tank on the move. Typically, a tank must stop before it can fire because the gunner needs to have a fixed firing platform from which he calculates range, direction, and other compensating factors. The laser can do all that while the vehicle is moving and should therefore enable a tank to stay on the move while firing. And if a laser can paint a target from a tank and find the range, I speculated, it can do the same for a helicopter from air to air and air to ground.

I suggested to General Trudeau that all the research we were conducting into helicopter tactics, especially into the role of helicopters as infantry support gun and rocket platforms, dovetailed perfectly with the possibilities of the laser as a range-finding mechanism. We could paint friendly troops to locate them, identify our foes, and illuminate potential targets with light invisible to all but our own gunners. At the same time, our own bombs or missiles can home in on the laser image we project onto a target, like a heat-seeking missile. Once painted, the target could evade the laser-guided rocket or shell only with great difficulty. For a stationary target such as a fortification or artillery redoubt, a laser-guided shell would be particularly devastating because we could take it out with one or two rounds instead of having to go back again and again to make sure we'd found the target.

As a signal, a laser is so intense, refined, and perfectly stable that it is almost impervious to any kind of disturbance. For this reason, I wrote General Trudeau, the EBEs must have used an advanced form of a laser for their communication, and we can, too. The intensity of the beam and its highly refined focus mean that it can be aimed with minute precision. Amplifying the power to boost the signal should not distort the beam's aim, which makes it perfect for straight-line long-distance communication.

Lasers also have high capacities for carrying multiple signals. Therefore, I wrote the general, we can pack a greater number of transmission bands into a laser signal than we can with our conventional signal carriers. This meant that we could literally flood a battlefield with different kinds of communication channels, each carrying different kinds of communication, some not even invented yet, and have them securely carried by laser signals. For command and control on the increasingly sophisticated electronic battlefield the army was predicting for the 1970s, lasers would become the Signal Corps workhorses.

General Trudeau said that he was also interested in an item from one of the specification reports that other military observers wrote that said that lasers could also serve as projection devices for large-screen displays. Lasers were so bright that displays could be shown in rooms that didn't have to be darkened. The general saw the possibility of fully lit situation rooms with large-screen displays from satellite radar transmissions. The room would allow computer operators to see what they were doing at their keyboards while seeing the displays and listening to the briefing.

I suggested that the army cartography division would be particularly interested in the accuracy of the laser-derived measurements for maps. That same measurement ability would also be able to generate digital data for ground-hugging infantry support helicopters or low-flying planes. Aircraft that could stay close to the ground could avoid enemy radar and stay concealed until the last minute. But unless there was a method for accurately charting the topography, aircraft could find themselves scraping treetops or crashing into the side of a hill. If a laser could accurately transmit topographic features to altitude control and navigational computers on board attack aircraft, it would keep the aircraft safely above any ground obstacles but close enough to the ground to remain concealed. This ground-hugging capability that I suggested to General Trudeau had been suggested to me from the analysis reports of UFOs that also had this capability. It was what enabled them to hover close to the ground and to move rapidly at speeds over a thousand miles an hour at treetop level without hitting anything. The laser-type devices aboard the UFO instantly fed the craft with the topographic features of the landscape and the craft automatically adjusted to the terrain.

In late 1961, General Trudeau asked me to visit Fort Belvoir again, this time to meet a Dr. Mark Johnston, one of aeronautical research scientists from Hughes Aircraft. Fort Belvoir was one of the safe houses for the Office of R&D to conduct meetings in because it was a secure military facility. My comings and goings there on Army R&D business were completely routine, even to the CIA surveillance teams that would occasionally pick up my car coming out of the Pentagon, and could be covered in our daily logs with references to the ongoing projects that served as covers. My meeting with Johnston, for example, was to talk about the Hughes helicopter-development program, not to give him my reports on the laser measuring devices we believed were in the Roswell spacecraft. I briefed Johnston on what the scientific team from Alamogordo believed was on the spacecraft, asked him not to talk about it, and suggested that the Hughes team developing the navigational radars for the helicopter project consider using the newly developed lasers as terrain measuring apparatus and for target acquisition.

"Yes, of course," I assured him. "The Office of R&D would have a development budget for the laser project if the R&D team at Hughes thought our idea was feasible and they could develop it."

And that's exactly what happened. Using the positive results from the Columbia University test and the army weapons specifications we drew up in R&D for the requirements of a range-finder, targeting, and tracking weapon, and with research grants from the Pentagon, Hughes signed on as one of the contractors for the military laser. Today, the laser has become the HEL, or High Energy Laser, deployed by the army's Space Defense Command as, among other things, an antisatellite/antiwarhead weapon.

My meeting at Hughes was quick and direct. Like so many of the research scientists I met with from Hughes, Dow, IBM, and Bell, Johnston disappeared behind the workbenches, computer screens, or test tubes of the company's back room and out of my sight forever. When General Trudeau would ask me to follow up on the project months later, a different company representative would meet with me and the project would look just like any other Army R&D–initiated research contract. Any traces of Roswell or the nut file would be gone, and the project would have been slipped into the normal R&D functioning. Of course this device didn't come out of the Roswell incident. The incident was only a myth; it never took place. This came out of the Foreign Technology desk, something the Italians or French were working on and we picked up through intelligence sources.

Our work with laser products was becoming so successful by the end of 1961 that General Trudeau was urging me to spread the wealth around as many army bases as I could. I spoke to weapons experts at Fort Riley, Kansas, for example, about the use of lasers by troops in the field. Maybe as range finders, we suggested, or even as ways to lock onto a target the way the air force was experimenting with something they were calling "smart bombs." By 1964, after seeing the research into the feasibility of lasers that we had commissioned, handheld range finders were being tested at army bases around the country, and today, police forces use laser sights on their weapons. Lasers became one of the army's great successes.

In one of our final pushes for the development of laser-based weapons systems, we argued successfully for a budget to develop laser tracking systems for incoming missiles. This was a project we fought hard for, over political opposition as well as opposition from the other military branches, which were looking at our proposal as a conventional method of tracking missiles. The laser was too new, they argued. Atmospheric interference or heavy clouds would distort the laser over long distances, they said. Or, they said, it would simply take too much power and would have no portability. General Trudeau and I had another agenda for this project that we couldn't readily share with anybody. We believed that lasers could be used not just to track incoming missiles—that was obvious. We saw the lasers too as our best weapon for not only tracking UFOs from the ground, from aircraft, or from satellites but, if we could boost the power to the necessary levels, for shooting them down. Shoot down a few of them, we speculated, and they wouldn't violate our airspaces with such impunity. Equip our fighter planes or interceptors with laser-firing mechanisms and we could pose a credible threat to them. Equip our satellites with laser firing mechanisms and we could triangulate a firing pattern on the UFOs that might even keep them away from our orbiting spacecraft. But all of this was speculation in late 1961.

Only a very few people in the other branches of R&D even had a hint about what we were proposing. The National Aeronautics and Space Administration had its own plans for developing laser tracking systems and didn't want to share any development budget with the military, so there was very little help forthcoming from NASA. The air force and navy were guarding their own development budgets for laser weapons, and we couldn't trust the civilian intelligence agencies at all. So General Trudeau and I began advocating a plan as a cover to develop laser tracking and other sophisticated types of surveillance projects. It was outrageous on the surface, but it quickly found its adherents, and its real agenda could be completely masked. We could never call it an anti-UFO device so we named it the antimissile missile. It was one of the most successful projects ever to come out of Army R&D. It owed most of its theory to our discovery of the laser in the Roswell wreckage.

CHAPTER 14

The Antimissile Missile Project

THERE WERE TIMES DURING MY TENURE AT THE PENTAGON when something in the Roswell file had such resonance in my life that it made me question whether there was some larger plan for my work. I've read about the concept of synchronicity or confluence in the years since I retired from the military and how things or events tend to cluster around a common thread. Such a common thread was the development of the antimissile missile that encompassed my work in R&D at the Pentagon, my brief stint as a staff adviser to Senator Strom Thurmond, and my years in Rome during the war and occupation as the assistant chief of staff, Intelligence (G-2), Rome Area Allied Command.

In early 1963, just after I left the Pentagon, Senator Strom Thurmond asked me to join his staff as a consultant and adviser on military and national security issues. Congress had just appropriated $300 million to turn a fledgling plan to investigate the feasibility of an antimissile missile program into a full development project. But it ran right into a concrete barrier just as soon as it left the Senate. Secretary of Defense Robert McNamara flatly refused to spend the money because, he said, not only would it intensify the

U.S.-Soviet arms race, it would actually offend the Kremlin because it would put them on notice that we were trying to deploy a first-strike capability while neutralizing their ICBMs. Worse, he said to the Congress, the United States military simply didn't need the weapon in the first place.

Senator Thurmond was incensed and I was deeply worried. McNamara just didn't get it. He was completely misinformed about how the Soviets reacted to any weapons deployment on our part. They didn't negotiate with us out of a sense of cooperation, only a sense of necessity that it was in their best interests to do so. If they thought we could knock out their ICBMs, that, more than anything, would keep them honest. Hadn't they backed down over Cuba because they saw that Kennedy actually meant business when he screwed up his resolve to order the navy to enforce the blockade? But the CIA had McNamara's ear and was giving him exactly the information the disinformation specialists in the Kremlin wanted him to have: don't develop the antimissile missile.

General Trudeau and I had a secret agenda we had worked up the previous year at the Pentagon. The antimissile missile, utilizing laser targeting and tracking, was supposed to be the perfect mechanism for getting the funds to develop a laser-beam weapon we could ultimately use to fire on UFOs. At least that was the way we'd planned it. The general had gotten it through the Pentagon bureaucracy while I covered his flank on the legislative side, testifying before the Armed Services Committee on the efficacy of a weapon that was capable of protecting American strategic forces with an umbrella. If any country were foolish enough to attack the United States, the antimissile missile would blunt their offensive and enable us not only to devastate their military forces but hold their population centers hostage as well.

Not so, said the Defense Department. The deployment of an antimissile missile would encourage our enemies to attack our cities first and devastate our civilian population. What did it matter if we had the ability to strike back when the damage to us had already been done? The only thing that was keeping our civilian population centers safe was each side's ability to hold the other's nuclear forces hostage.

If both sides devastated one another's nuclear forces, it would give each side time to stop before a mutual destruction of the civilian populations.

But the secretary of defense didn't understand war. He especially hadn't seen what lessons the Soviets learned during World War II when their population centers had been devastated and people were reduced to the point of starvation and cannibalized one another for food. That kind of experience doesn't toughen you against the ravages of war, it educates you. The Soviets' only hope for a victory in the Cold War was in our putting down our guard and capitulating to them. By refusing to go forward with the antimissile missile, the secretary of defense was listening to arguments that were spoon-fed to him, certainly without his knowledge, by people in the civilian intelligence community who were being manipulated by the KGB.

Senator Thurmond's reaction to Bob McNamara's refusal to spend the antimissile missile appropriation was to hold subcommittee hearings on this issue to find out why. The Defense Department didn't want to disclose classified information about the capabilities of a proposed weapon and our defense policy before a public session of Congress. So Fred Buzhardt, who years later became President Nixon's counsel, suggested that Senator Thurmond invoke a senatorial privilege to close a session of the Senate so that the issue of the antimissile missile could be discussed in private before the full Senate. But first, we had to request specific information from the Department of Defense, and that task, because I was the Senator's adviser for military affairs, fell to me. No one knew that I was actually the officer who had initially prepared the information for the antimissile missile program to begin with and probably knew more about the documents than anyone because less than a year earlier I had prepared them myself.

The first meeting with the Defense Department was held in my new office in the basement of the Capitol Building. Secretary McNamara sent his own scientific adviser, Harold Brown, who would later become the secretary of defense himself, along with an army colonel who had become the project officer for the antimissile missile development program. Brown didn't know who I was, but his assistant from the army certainly did.

"Colonel," the army project officer began as soon as I asked him a question about the request we'd sent for information, and Harold Brown sat up straight in his chair. Gradually, like chipping away parts of a granite block, I asked the project officer about the specific details of the antimissile missile program, how much of the budget allocation from previous Pentagon funding they'd already spent, and what their development timetable would be if the current appropriation were spent for the current phase of the project. Then I asked more technical questions about the research into ground-based radars, satellite-based radars, speculation into Soviet counter-antimissile missile strategies, and Soviet development of even bigger and more mobile ICBMs that would present more imperative targets for any antimissile missile system because we couldn't take them out in a first strike. Mounted on railway cars or trucks, mobile Soviet missiles would be almost impossible to track even though they would have to remain stationary for the liquid fueling process to be completed.

"I see that my assistant keeps on calling you colonel, Mr. Corso," Harold Brown said. "And you certainly seem to know a lot of details on this subject."

"Yes, sir," I said. "I only retired from the army a couple of months ago but while I was at the Pentagon, I was the acting projects officer for the antimissile missile program."

"Then there's no use in holding back," Harold Brown said and finally smiled for the first time in our meeting. He reached into his pocket and pulled out a folded envelope. "Here are your copies of the complete details of the project about which we briefed President Kennedy. It's all here. And I presume this is what you are looking for, officially," he said with a special emphasis on "officially." He knew that I knew what was in that envelope but couldn't disclose it before the Senate because it contained classified information and I would be breaching the National Security Act. However, by his giving me the material, much of it based on information that I had developed myself and had privately briefed Attorney General Robert Kennedy on in 1962,

Brown was giving me the full authorization to disclose. He probably realized that in private sessions, I had talked generally about what was in the army file on the antimissile missile—that was a form of senatorial privilege as long as it wasn't abused—but that I couldn't go formal with it. Now I could, and I appreciated Harold Brown's candor.

The battle over the appropriation was about to be joined, but I couldn't look over the contents of the envelope, some of which were my own notes, without thinking back to the sequence of events that led to this meeting and to the project that ultimately was developed as a result of it. It began earlier in 1962 as I was working down the list of the priorities I had set for myself in the nut file. In it was a medical report about the creatures that I was trying to save until I had gotten all of the tangible items from Roswell into the development process.

It was a report on the possible function and apparent structure of the alien brain, a report that marveled at the similarities between the EBE brain and the human brain. However, one item in the report threw me for a complete loop. The medical examiner wrote that measurements of brain activity taken from the EBE who was still barely alive at Roswell showed that its electronic signature, at least what they were able to measure with equipment in 1947, displayed a signal similar to what we would call long, low-frequency waves. And the examiner referred to a description by one of the Roswell Army Air Field doctors that the creature's brain lobes seem to have been not just physiologically and neurologically integrated but integrated by an electromagnetic current as well.

I would have loved to dismiss this as the speculation of a doctor who had no experience with this type of analysis and certainly no experience with alien beings. Therefore, whatever he wrote was nonsense and not worth the time it took to respond to it. File it back in the cabinet and get on to other issues that could be turned into viable projects. But the medical examiner's report was more disturbing than I was ready to admit because it took me back to a time when I was the assistant chief of staff in Rome and made friends with some of the members of the graduate faculty at the University of Rome.

I was a twenty-five-year-old captain at the time, a former engineering undergraduate, way in over my head and learning my job responsibilities each day, keeping one step ahead of my boss so he wouldn't find out that I didn't really know anything. In one of my visits to the university I met Dr. Gislero Flesch, a professor of criminology and anthropology who lectured me on what he called his theory and experiments on "the basis of life." It was a wild and, I thought, supernatural theory on what he called the filament within each cell. The filament was activated by some cosmic action or form of electromagnetic radiation that bombarded the earth continuously from outer space and resonated against a constant refresh of electrical activity from the brain.

"Capitaine," he would say whenever he began some formal explanation. I also thought that he was always surprised that someone so young could actually be dispatched from the New World to administer law and justice in Rome, the capital of the ancient world. The old professor also was scrupulous about showing everyone, including his dimmest of students, extraordinary respect. "The electromagnetic forces in the body are the least understood," he continued. "Yet they account for more activity than anyone realizes."

As an engineering student whose whole experience with energy had to do with verifiable experiments, I was more than skeptical at first. How can you measure an electrical activity in the brain that you cannot see? How can invisible waves of energy that you can't feel or see excite certain areas of the human cell, and what was their purpose?

Professor Flesch introduced me to Professor Casmiro Franck, one of the first scientists to ever photograph brain waves. Professor Franck became a friend because during my days in Rome, fighting off Gestapo agents, Communist partisans, and the local crime families and crime chieftains, I was always engaged in some type of warfare. But when I had time off, I wanted to meet people, to stretch my experience, to fall in love with the city of my own ancestors I had been assigned to protect. So I sought out a network of friends to whom I could relate and from whom I could learn. Professor Franck was just such a man.

In Franck's first experiments he had used a rabbit brain as a test subject. He measured what he said were the long, low-frequency waves animal brains generate and described how he was able to trace the paths these waves took when they were transmitted from the brain to the animal's voluntary muscles. Certain muscles, Professor Franck said, were attuned to respond to certain brain wavelengths, waves of a specific frequency. In cases of muscle paralysis, it's not the muscle that's necessarily damaged, it's the muscle's tuning mechanism that becomes disabled so that it no longer picks up the right frequency. It's like a radio, he said. If the radio can't pick up a signal, the radio isn't necessarily broken; its antenna or the crystal may need to be adjusted to the correct frequency. I was a guest at his laboratory more than a few times and watched him carry out his experiments with live rabbits, interfering with their brains' electromagnetic wave propagation by implanting electrodes and seeing which muscles became cataleptic and which responded. He said it was the frequency that was being altered because once the animal was removed from the experimental table, it could walk and hop as if nothing had ever happened.

Then Professor Franck introduced me to another one of his colleagues, the celebrated research biologist and physician Doctor Castellani, who had many years earlier isolated and identified the disease called "sleeping sickness" and perfected what during the 1930s and 1940s became known as "Castellani Ointments" as treatments for a variety of skin diseases. Where other doctors, he said, had focused on treating only the symptoms they could see on the skin, Doctor Castellani said that the problems of many skin rashes, psoriasis, or inflammations that looked like bacterial infections were, in fact, correctable by changing the skin's electromagnetic resonance. The ointments, he said, didn't attack the infection with drugs; they were chemical reactants that changed the electrostatic condition of the skin, allowing the long, low-frequency waves from the brain to do the healing.

All three men were using these electromagnetic waves to promote healing in ways I considered astounding. They made claims about the ability of electromagnetic treatments to affect the speed at which cells divide and tumors grow. They claimed that through directed electromagnetic wave propagation they could cure heart disease, arthritis, all types of bacteriological infections that interfered with cell function, and even certain forms of cancer.

If this sounds like something supernatural in 1997, imagine how it must have sounded to the ears of a young and inexperienced intelligence officer in 1944 who was so far out of his element that the older, seasoned British intelligence laughed at his age. They laughed until they saw what happened to the Gestapo agents who were trying to reinfiltrate Rome behind the Allied front lines and met up with my men on the back streets and alleys. That's when the laughing stopped.

I spent many hours with Professors Flesch, Franck, and Castellani in Rome and watched them experiment with all kinds of small animals. They didn't have the research funds nor the endorsments of the medical societies to allow them to expand their work or to treat patients with their unconventional methods. Thus, much of their work found its way into research monographs, articles in academic journals, or university lectures at symposiums. And I left Rome in the spring of 1947, said my good-byes to the friends I had made at the University of Rome, and put their work—relegated once again to the supernatural—out of my mind as I concentrated on my new jobs at Fort Riley, the White House, Red Canyon, Germany, and the Pentagon. Then on the day that I came across the speculative report on the structure of the alien brain from Roswell, everything Professors Flesch, Franck, and Castellani said came back to me like a clap of thunder. Here I was again, staring at a piece of loose-leaf paper that was staring right back at me and forcing me to consider ideas and notions from over ten years ago that challenged everything science back then was telling us about the way the brain worked.

While I reviewed the reports about the autopsied alien brain and what the medical examiner thought the low-frequency waves meant when he applied current to the tissue, I also saw reports from an army military liaison attached to the Stalingrad consulate office that described

Soviet experiments with psychics who were attempting to exercise some form of kinetic mind control over objects traveling through the air, directing them from one spot to another. These reports, written in the late 1950s, gave General Trudeau a lot of concern because they showed the Soviets were onto something.

"These fellas don't waste their time, Phil," the general told me at one of our morning briefings after I had dropped off the reports the day before so he could look them over. "If they're looking into this stuff, then they know there's something there."

"You don't think this report is just a lot of speculation?" I asked. I knew from the expression on his face that it was a question I shouldn't have asked.

"If you thought this was just speculation, Colonel," he said very abruptly, "then you wouldn't be passing the buck up to me to tell you that." General Trudeau had a way of bringing you up short when he thought you said something stupid. And what I had said was very stupid for an officer with my training and experience. He also knew I was worried or else I wouldn't have tried to back off so quickly. "You're right to be worried about this," he said, his tone softening when he saw how I was looking at him. "You'd be right if you sat in your office and sweated bullets over what this means. And you know exactly what worries the both of us. Do I have to say it?"

No, he didn't. It was obvious. If the Soviets had gotten their hands on some of the apparatus from any one of the alien spacecraft that had gone down since 1947—and I didn't know how many there were—they'd have figured out by now that the aliens had used some form of brain-wave control for navigation. How they directed their thoughts or translated them into an electronic circuit, we didn't know. But we knew that there were no steering wheels or conventional methods of control on the spacecraft, and the headbands we found with the electronic sensors on them were designed to pick up some form of signal from the brain. The analysts at Wright Field believed that the sensors on the headbands corresponded with points on the multilobed alien brain that generated low-frequency waves, so the headbands formed an integral part of the circuit. If we were able to figure that out, the Soviets were certainly capable of figuring that out as well. Besides, the general didn't have to say it because I thought it: What if the Soviets, all alone in space the way they were in the early 1960s, had some communication with the aliens that we didn't have? Who said the EBEs had to be anti-Communist anyway?

General Trudeau also shared with me some intelligence reports that described antimissile missile tests the Soviets had conducted with very powerful tracking radar. We'd known about their radars because I'd seen them work during exercises in Germany when each side would test the other's responses over the East German border. Their radars and their ability to lock onto aircraft was just as good as ours. But what the general showed me were reports that described the Soviets firing intercept missiles at incoming ICBM vehicles and exploding the intercept warheads so as to knock out the navigational systems on the aggressor missiles. One of those test intercepts had been conducted successfully right through an atomic cloud on one of the Soviet missile test ranges in Asia. This was especially disturbing because anyone who knows anything about the nature of an atomic cloud knows that the electromagnetic pulse immediately knocks out any form of electronics. That's also how we knew what the signatures were of the alien UFOs that buzzed our ships and bases. So much of our nonhardened power was knocked out by the pulse that we knew an electromagnetic wave had hit us. So if the Soviets could harden their antimissile missile guidance system to home in on a target through an electromagnetically charged atomic cloud, they were using a technology significantly more advanced than ours, and it spelled trouble.

"When you were in Germany commanding the Nike battalion," the general asked me, still holding the reports in his hand, "you experimented with tight evasive maneuvers in drone target practice, didn't you?"

The general's memory served him correctly. Our antiaircraft battalion deployed the Nike, one of the most advanced guided antiaircraft missiles of its time. The Nike was a radar-guided missile. And the Hawk was a heat-seeking missile that could be locked onto its target by tracking radar and then, when launched, would home in on the target's heat exhaust. So, even if a pilot tried to evade the missiles, the fast-moving Hawk warheads would catch up to him and blow off his engine. If it were a tail-engine fighter, it would effectively end his mission and he'd probably have to eject. If it were a wing-engined bomber, then, with one of his wing-mounted engines shot off, the pilot would probably have to turn for home because he wouldn't have the power to carry the payload of bombs to the target.

"When we were shooting at drones in simulated bombing formation, we scored a perfect shootdown again and again, but when pilots used extremely fast evasive maneuvers against our missiles, we couldn't hit them," I said.

"Explain how that worked," he asked.

"Nike antiaircraft missiles move like boats on water," I explained. "They cut wide arcs and get an angle to home in on their targets. Any early evasive maneuvers the fighter pilot makes, the missile compensates for and stays on course toward his heat source. But if the pilot is able to evade at the very last minute of the Nike's trajectory, the missile will fly right by and can't recover. Bomber pilots have to stay in formation and keep on course if they're going to hit their target and have enough fuel to get home, so their evasive patterns are strictly limited. For fighter pilots, it's much easier so any MiG, just like any of our Phantoms, can outmaneuver a Nike any day."

"So if the Soviets have something that can take out missile warheads through an atomic cloud and are using devices that may have come from an alien technology, we have something to worry about," the general said.

"We'd have a lot to worry about," I agreed. "We have nothing even remotely like this, except for the laser tracking system, but that's years away from any sort of deployment even assuming we can get the President to ask Congress to give us the money to develop it."

General Trudeau slammed his palm on the desk with enough force to shake the entire office. I'm sure his clerk sitting just outside thought I was getting bawled out for something, but that was the general's way of reinforcing a decision he was making. "Phil, you are the antimissile

missile projects officer for the time being. I don't care whatever the hell else you have to do, you write me up a report on what we discussed here and then put together a proposal I can use to get us some money to develop this thing," he said. "I know we're on the right track, even if we're in a strange arena. Thought control," he said, speculating about how the power of the human brain could be harnessed to the navigation of a guided missile. "Well, if the Russians are looking at it seriously, then we'd better do the same thing before they blindside us like the did with Sputnik."

"Why me?" I said to myself as I walked down the stairs to my office. This was like an assignment to write a term paper when there wasn't even any research you could use and still be called sane. I had to write about the hardware and systems applications of navigational control, not medical or biological functions per se, but that made it all the more difficult. I remembered my son telling me that he was able to fix gasoline engines that had broken down and electrical motors that were no longer putting out power because he believed the moving parts spoke to him. As way out as I thought that sounded at the time, walking back to my office now and thinking about what the Soviets were playing with, maybe my kid didn't sound so crazy after all. It was something I'd have to research.

If the information that Professors Flesch, Franck, and Castellani conveyed to me back in Rome fifteen years ago had any validity, then the vague references in the Roswell report that I'd read probably had validity as well. So I began.

"The references to EBE brain function in the medical examiner's reports from Roswell," I wrote in my opening memo to General Trudeau,

suggest new avenues of research to us in the guidance and navigational control of machines. The electromagnetic integration of the alien brain lobes and the possible integration with other brain functions including kinesthetic capability—the ability to move objects—over long distance is startling and sounds more like science fiction than fact. But if we can establish a correlation with long, low-frequency waves and this electromagnetic integration, it will be a way to identify a measurable phenomenon with a process we do not understand. Initially, I recommend we study the phenomenon in an effort to apply our findings to gathering and utilizing any data we can develop concerning long, low-frequency waves and electromagnetic integration so as to marry it to our existing guidance and control hardware systems and create a new state of the art in missile tracking.

A caveat: The Central Intelligence Agency has begun a program in which they work with "seers," as they call them, parapsychologists who they expect will give them the same capability as the KGB's "Psychotronic Technology" training. Both intelligence agencies are skirting the edges of our military's approach and we must be careful not to let our research fall into their cauldron. We would be discredited and possibly stopped from proceeding both from efforts from our own side and from protests by the Soviets should they find out. Therefore I recommend that the background of our experimentation with long low-frequency brain waves and any source material be completely expunged along with any historical data relevant to this analysis.

My basis for our proposed antimissile missile was the Soviets' own success with controlling the trajectory of an ICBM warhead in flight and the success they had in targeting incoming warheads with their own antimissile missile in development.

"In recent months," I wrote,

it has come to our attention that the Soviets can change the trajectory of an ICBM after launch once it is on its way to a target. In addition, the Soviets have twice tested an antimissile missile fired through an atomic cloud at an approaching ICBM. Therefore, a technical proposal must be drawn up as soon as possible for:

1. An antimissile missile that will be able to lock onto an incoming ICBM and stay locked on through all evasive maneuvers and destroy it before it reaches its target, and

2. All circuitry must be hardened to withstand radiation, blast, heat, and electromagnetic pulse from an atomic detonation up to and including the intensity of the Russian bomb explosion of 60 megatons.

Premise:

Our present antiaircraft missiles centered around the Nike-Ajax, Nike-Hercules, and the Hawk are not adequate against ICBMs thus rendering us virtually defenseless against such an attack. Present systems cannot remain locked onto an incoming ICBM or find the target to destroy if it changes trajectory, which capability the latest Soviet test models indicate the enemy may be able to deploy within the decade. Our spy satellites will be able to locate the Soviet warheads once they are launched, but the Soviets are also developing the capability to disable our surveillance satellites either with orbiting nuclear weapons to destroy them or send them out of orbit. At the very least, Soviet capability to generate an electromagnetic pulse through a nuclear detonation in space will render our satellites electronically blind. Secret intelligence reports confirm that the Soviets have already disabled two of our satellites and one launched by the British. We, therefore, have a two-fold problem, not only must the antimissile missile circuitry be hardened but the spy satellite circuitry must also be hardened from radiation, ion emissions, and ELM pulses. But because of the nuclear test ban treaty, the United States will not have the opportunity to run actual tests so we will have to scale our data up from our existing test results to arrive at figures we can only assume are accurate.

When General Trudeau read my full report, he asked me to speak to the scientists who consulted with us as part of a brain trust and develop a technical discussion, as speculative as we needed it to be with no restrictions whatsoever, in which we integrated what we had in our Roswell files with what intelligence we had on the types of testing the Soviets were conducting.

"Don't worry about how it's going to be circulated, Phil," General Trudeau assured me. "I want to show it to only a few members of the House and Senate Defense appropriations committees and they've promised to keep it confidential."

"I know you want this right away, General," I said. "Can I have the rest of the day to work on it?"

"You can have until tomorrow morning," he said. "Because after lunch tomorrow you and I are meeting with the Senate subcommittee and I want to read them this report."

I told my wife that I'd be home late in the morning for a change of uniform and then I was going over to Capitol Hill for a meeting. Then I ordered up a couple of sandwiches, put a new pot of coffee on, and settled in at the office for a long night.

"The present design and configuration of our ICBMs is adequate," I wrote onto my legal pad, crossed out the sentence, and then wrote it again. "However internal changes are necessary, especially within the warhead capsule."

What I would recommend would be nothing less than radical. We needed an entirely new navigational computer system that would take advantage of the transistorized circuitry now coming into development and projected for the marketplace by the late 1960s.

I suggested we model the missile's onboard computer on the design of an actual dual-hemisphere brain with one hemisphere or lobe receiving global positioning data from orbiting satellites. The other hemisphere will control the missile functions such as thrusters, positioning changes, and booster stage separation. It will receive data through a low-frequency transmission from the other lobe. The control lobe will also transmit missile flight telemetry to the positioning lobe so that the two computers will function together in tandem. This, I reasoned, would make the system more difficult to jam. If our global positioning satellite detected a threat from an incoming antimissile missile, it would relay that information to the warhead, whose control computer would direct the thrusters to fire so as to take evasive action before the final target approach.

Inasmuch as I believed it was through the application and amplification of low-frequency brain waves that the EBEs navigated the craft that we found at Roswell, our implementation of this technology might enable us also to use our brains to control the flight of objects. We could use some form of a brain-wave system to navigate our ICBM warhead final-stage vehicles if their onboard radar detected a threat from an antiballistic missile. We could also use this system to home in on incoming enemy warhead launchers even if they were capable of taking some evasive action.

If we designed the missile the way I suggested, by the time it had been locked into its final trajectory, its detonation would be set so that even if it were knocked off course it would still explode and cause enough collateral damage that it would count as a hit. Enough of our ICBMs could get through, we reasoned, so as to overwhelm not only the Soviet guided-missile forces but pose a realistic threat to their population centers. Meanwhile, the technology we developed for changing the flights of our incoming ICBMs could be applied as a template to our own antimissile missiles so as to neutralize any Soviet missile threat.

My conclusion: "An appropriation of $300 million must be requested for the coming FY 1963 as a urgent crash development appropriation."

I read my own notes from the envelope handed over by Harold Brown and looked back at him.

"Colonel," Brown's assistant said. "We understand the urgency of your request last year and we appreciate your reasons for fighting for it now."

"But the Defense Department is simply not going to allow the army to go forward with an antimissile missile at this time. Not in 1963," Mr. Brown said.

"When?" I asked.

"At a time," the army colonel said, "when the impact of

our deploying this system will be greater than it is now. The Russians know we have a bead on the type of satellites they're putting up and we can take them out in a heartbeat, much faster than they can take out ours."

I began to answer, but Harold Brown got up to leave. We shook hands and he walked toward the door. The army colonel remained in front of my desk. "Maybe just you and I can have a word, Colonel Corso," he said. My own associate on Senator Thurmond's committee left the office also.

"In the Pentagon, we understand that your early research into the technology of the antiballistic missile is the real reason for your support, Colonel Corso," the project manager said. "It's in good hands."

But I can tell you he didn't know the real reason, the EBEs. Only General Trudeau understood the secret agenda that lay beneath the research into the project.

"But when do you think development will start?" I asked.

"In just a couple of years we'll have lunar spacecraft orbiting the moon," he said. "We'll have orbiting satellites mapping every inch of the Soviet Union. We'll see what they can throw against us. Then we'll have exactly the kind of antimissile missile you proposed because then even the Congress will see the reason for it."

"But until then . . ." I began.

"Until then," the colonel said, "all we can do is wait."

It would take another twenty years for the beginnings of an antimissile to be deployed. And it would also take a president who was willing to recognize the threat from the extraterrestrials to force an antimissile weapon through a hostile Congress.

CHAPTER 15

My Last Year in R&D:

The Hoover Files, Fiber Optics, Supertenacity, and Other Artifacts

I BARELY PICKED MY HEAD UP FROM THE PILES OF TECHNICAL proposals on my desk during the winter months of 1961. The work didn't even stop for the Christmas holiday, when most of Washington likes to take a break and head for the West Virginia mountains or the Maryland countryside. I was traveling a lot during the final months of 1961, seeing weapons undergo testing at proving grounds around the country, meeting with university researchers on such diverse items as the preservation of food or the conversion of spent atomic-pile material into weapons, and developing intelligence reports for General Trudeau on the kinds of technologies that might shape weapons development into the next decade.

With my other eye, I was keeping a lookout for any reports going to the Air Intelligence Command about UFO sightings that I thought Army Intelligence should be thinking about. The AIC was the next step in classification from the Project Blue Book people. Its job, besides the obvious task of moving any urgent UFO reports up the ladder of secrecy to the next levels where they would disappear behind the veil of camouflage, was to classify the type of event or incident the sighting seemed to indicate. Usually that meant separating real aircraft sightings that needed to be investigated for pure military intelligence purposes from either true UFO sightings that needed to be processed by whatever elements of the original working group were on watch or false sightings that needed to be sent back down to Blue Book to be debunked. The AIC loved it when it had actual false sightings it could send back: an obvious meteorite that they could confirm, some visual anomaly having to do with an alignment of planets, or, best of all, a couple of clowns somewhere that decided to pull a Halloween prank and scare the locals. There were guys running around wheatfields with snowshoes or submitting photos of flying frozen pie tins to the local papers. Then the folks at Blue Book could release the story to the press, and everybody patted themselves on the back for the job they were all doing. Life could be fun in the early 1960s, especially if you didn't know the truth.

Moving into 1962, Army Intelligence was lit up with rumors about potential threats coming in from all over the place. The anti-Castro Cubans were mad about the President's refusal to support the Bay of Pigs invasion and were looking for revenge; Castro was mad about the Bay of Pigs invasion and was looking to get back at us; Khrushchev was still furious about the U2 and the Bay of Pigs and thinking Kennedy was a pushover, would soon jump on an opportunity to force us into some humiliating compromise. The Russians were on the verge of sending manned spacecraft into extended orbital flights and robot probes out to explore Venus. We were way behind in the space race and none of the services had the budget or the ability to get us back into the fight. NASA was telling the President they would have to dig in, develop the technology base, and, by the middle of the decade, put on a show for the whole world. But now, as the year turned, it was all silent running until we could put something up we could brag about.

The army was making ominous noises about events in Southeast Asia. The more the army pushed to get troops on the ground, the more the Kennedy administration refused to get involved. The army was telling the President we would eventually be sucked into a war we could not win and the events would control us instead of our controlling them. Later that same year, I would be offered the job of director of intelligence for the Army Special Forces units already operating in the Southeast Asian theater. At about the same time the army said it was going to name Gen. Arthur Trudeau as the commander of all U.S. forces in South Vietnam. As our names were being circulated, General Trudeau confided to me that he doubted we would get the jobs. And if we did, he said, it would be a toss-up as to who would be the most unhappy, the Vietcong or the U.S. Army.

"If they send us over there, Phil," he said after one of our morning briefings, "one of two things will happen. Either we'll both get court-martialed or we'll win the damn war. Either way the army's not going to like the way we do business."

As usual, General Trudeau was right. Before the end of 1962 and right about the time the old man was making up his mind whether to retire or not, his name was vetoed as the commander of all U.S. forces in Vietnam and I was told to stay at my desk. The handwriting was on the wall: Vietnam was going to be a political war run by the disinformation specialists at the CIA and fought under a cloud of unknowing. Unfortunately, history proved us to be correct. By the time Richard Nixon surrendered to the Chinese and we crawled out of Southeast Asia a few years later, we would learn, I hope for the last time, what it was like to be humiliated on the battlefield and then eviscerated at the negotiating table.

The new year brought J. Edgar Hoover over to the Pentagon. The FBI director was growing increasingly anxious at all the Roswell stories circulating like ice-cold currents deep under the ocean throughout NASA and the civilian intelligence agencies. Somebody was conspiring about something, and that meant the FBI should get involved, especially if the CIA was messing around in domestic issues. Hoover didn't like the CIA and he especially didn't like the cozy relationship he thought President Kennedy had with the CIA because he believed his boss, the President's brother, was keeping him on a short leash when it came to taking on the agency about territorial issues. Hoover knew, but didn't believe, that after the Bay of Pigs,

Kennedy had become very suspicious of the intelligence information he was getting from the CIA. By the end of 1962, the President would learn from his own brother, who would learn from me, just how deliberately flawed the information coming out of the CIA was. And I would also learn, when I worked for Senator Russell on the Warren Commission in 1964, how that had sealed his fate.

But in 1962, still near the height of his power, J. Edgar Hoover was as territorial as any lifetime bureaucrat in Washington could be. And when somebody stepped on his toes, or when he thought someone had stepped on his toes, he kept kicking them until the guy was dead. Even his own agents knew what it was like to get on his bad side. I was as territorial in my own way as the FBI director was in his, and during my years at the White House under President Eisenhower, we had established a professional relationship. If he needed to know something that bore on some KGB agent nosing around the government, I helped him out. If I needed to find something out on the q.t. about somebody I needed to take out of the bureaucratic loop, he would tell me what he knew. We never established any formal relationships in the 1950s, but we let each know who we thought the bad guys were.

In the 1950s, Hoover got interested in the rumors about Roswell because anything the CIA got their teeth into made him nervous. If it were only the military running a cover-up, he could live with that, although he thought the military never should have run the OSS during World War II. But once he suspected the CIA was part of the Roswell story, he wanted in. But in my years on the White House staff, there wasn't much I could tell him. It wouldn't be until 1961 that I got my hands on what really happened at Roswell, and then I didn't have to contact him. He called me.

We found we could help each other. Besides being territorial, J. Edgar Hoover was an information fanatic. If there was a bit of information floating around, whether it was rumor or truth, Hoover was obsessive about putting it into his files. Information was such a valuable commodity to him, he was willing to trade for it with anybody in government he trusted. I wanted information, too. I was going out to meetings with scientists and university researchers whose loyalties I couldn't verify. I had to be very circumspect about the technological information I was delivering, and many times I needed to know whether a particular chemist or physicist had ever been suspected of dealing with the Communists or, worse, was on the payroll of the CIA.

In retrospect I can see how all this smacks of the thinking of Senator Joe McCarthy, but I was at the White House during the army McCarthy hearings and I can tell you straight out that Joe McCarthy—unwittingly—was the best friend the Communists ever had in government. Single-handedly, Senator McCarthy helped give respectability to a bunch of people who would never have had it otherwise. He turned behaving in contempt of Congress into a heroic act by his very tactics, and the Communists in government were laughing at the free rein he gave them. All they had to do was provide him with a human sacrifice every now and then, someone completely unimportant or actually inno-cent of any wrongdoing, and McCarthy pilloried them on television. But when he turned against the U.S. Army, he crossed into my territory and we had to shut him down.

The Communists used McCarthy to give them good press and open up an area where they could work while the anti-Communists were made to look like fools. I told this to Robert Kennedy, who as a young lawyer had been a member of Roy Cohn's investigative staff working for the McCarthy subcommittee and who had learned firsthand what it was like to be completely misled into self-destructive behavior. It was a mistake, he confided to me, that he would never make again. Unfortunately, his brother's enemies were his own, and he was misled into thinking that being president would allow him to settle the score.

But in January of 1962 all that was on my mind was reestablishing a relationship with J. Edgar Hoover so that I could pursue my agenda while keeping a lookout for who might be dangerous out there in the academic community. Now I had something to bargain with for the information I wanted. Not only did I have the bits and pieces of the Roswell story that I knew Hoover wanted, I also had information about the domestic activities of the CIA. Hoover was more than interested in sharing information, and we continued to talk right through 1962 until I left the army and went over to Senator Thurmond's staff. Our relationship continued right through 1963. And in 1964, when I was an investigator for Senator Russell on the Warren Commission and Hoover was pursuing his own independent investigation into the President's assassination, he and I could only stare at one another again on either side of the abyss of that crime. Stacked up against the enormity of what had happened, Hoover and I both understood that there are some battles you cannot win. So you leave them alone so you can fight another day.

I'm not sure whether J. Edgar Hoover ever really believed that the Roswell story was true, an absolute conspiracy to cover up something else, or just a delusion that became mass hysteria out there in the desert. There were so many details buried in army memos and maintained under layers of cover stories fabricated by military intelligence experts that he couldn't possibly know the truth. But like the good cop that he was, he took information wherever he could find it and kept on searching for something that made sense. If the army saw a threat to our society, then Hoover thought there was a threat. And whenever he could follow up a report of a sighting with a very discreet appearance by a pair of FBI agents to interview the witnesses and get away with it, he did. He was more than willing to share that information with me, and that was how I found out about some of the unpublicized cattle mutilation stories in the early 1960s.

My J. Edgar Hoover connection was important to me as I began my work in the early weeks of 1962 because the level of research into the types of projects we were developing became very intense. The rumors of General Trudeau's appointment to the Southeast Asia command and my selection as intelligence director for the Green Berets in Southeast Asia, as vague and unconfirmed as they were, set a deadline for the general and me to push our projects forward because we knew we had only a year or so left on our tenure at R&D. So when the FBI director and I would talk, I had questions ready to ask. No information we ever shared was in writing, and any notes that I took from the conversations we had I later destroyed after committing them to memory or taking action on the things he said. Even to this day, although FBI agents have contacted me about records supposedly still left in the old files, I don't know what notes the FBI director took about our conversations and what specific actions he ever took. Because we trusted each other and remained in contact once every six months or so even after I left government service, I never followed up on anything I said and never asked for any verification of information in the files. I think Hoover appreciated that.

By February of 1962 I had lined my nut file projects up for an end run that would take me to the end of the year and either South Vietnam or retirement. The first folder on the desktop was the "glass filaments."

Fiber Optics

Members of the retrieval team who foraged around inside the spacecraft on the morning of the discovery told Colonel Blanchard back at the 509th that they were amazed they couldn't find any conventional wiring. Where were the electrical connections? they asked, because obviously the vehicle had electronics. They didn't understand the function of the printed circuit wafers they found, but, even more important, they were completely mystified by the single glass filaments that ran through the panels of the ship. At first, some of the scientists thought that they comprised the missing wiring that also had the engineers so confused as they packed the craft for shipping. Maybe they were part of the wiring harness that was broken in the crash. But these filaments had a strange property to them.

The wire harness seemed to have broken loose from a control panel and was separated into twelve frayed filaments that looked something like quartz. When, back at the 509th's hangar, officers from the retrieval team applied light to one end of the filament, the other end emitted a specific color. Different filaments emitted different colors. The fibers—in reality glass crystal tubes—led to a type of junction box where the fibers separated and went to different parts of the control panel that seemed to acknowledge electrically the different color pulsing through the tube.

Since the engineers evaluating the material at Roswell knew that each color of light had its own specific wavelength, they guessed that the frequency of the light wave activated a specific component of the spacecraft's control panel. But beyond that, the engineers and scientists were baffled. They couldn't even determine the spacecraft's power source, let alone what generated the power for the light tubes. And, the most amazing thing of all was that the filaments not only were flexible but still emitted light even when they were bent back and forth like a paper clip. How could light be made to bend? the engineers wondered. This was one of the physical mysteries of the Roswell craft that stayed hidden through the 1950s until one of the Signal Corps liaisons, who routinely briefed General Trudeau on the kinds of developments the Signal Corps was looking for, told us about experiments in optical fibers going on at Bell Labs.

The technology was still very new, Hans Kohler told me during a private briefing in early 1962, but the promise of using light as a carrier of all kinds of signals through single-filament glass strands was holding great promise. He explained that the premise of optical fibers was to have a filament of glass so fine and free of any impurities that nothing would impede the light beam moving along the center of the shaft. You also had to have a powerful light source at one end, he explained, to generate the signal, and I thought of the successful ruby laser that had been tested at Columbia University. I knew the EBEs had integrated the two technologies for their glass-cable transmission inside the spacecraft.

"But what makes the light bend?" I asked Professor Kohler, still incredulous that the aliens seem to have been able to defy one of our own laws of physics. "Is it some kind of an illusion?"

"It's not a trick at all," the scientist explained. "It only looks like an illusion because the fibers are so fine, you can't see the different layers without a microscope."

He showed me, when I gave him the broken pieces of filament that I still had in my nut file, that each strand, which looked like one solid piece of material enclosing the circumference of a tiny tube, was actually double layered.

When you looked down the center of the shaft you could see that around the outside of the filament was another layer of glass. Dr. Kohler explained that the individual light rays are reflected back toward the center by the layer of glass around the outside of the fiber so that the light can't escape. By running the glass fibers around corners and, in the case of the Roswell spacecraft, through the interior walls of the ship, the aliens were able to bend light and focus it just like you can direct the flow of water through a supply pipe. I'd never seen anything like that before in my life.

Kohler explained that, just like lasers, the light can be made to carry any sort of signal: light, sound, and even digital information.

"There's no resistance to the signal," he explained. "And you can fit more information on to the light beam."

I asked him how the EBEs might have used this type of technology. He suggested that all ship's communication, visual images, telemetry, and any amplified signals that the vehicles sent or received from other craft or from bases on the moon or on earth would use these glass fiber cables.

"They seem to have an enormous capacity for carrying any kind of load," he suggested. "And if a laser can amplify the signal, in their most refined form, these cables can carry a multiplicity of signals at the same time."

I was more than impressed. Even before asking him about the specific types of applications these might have for the army, I could see how they could make battlefield communications more secure because the signals would be stronger and less vulnerable to interference. Then Professor Kohler began suggesting the uses of these fibers to carry visual images photographed in tiny cameras from the weapons themselves to controlling devices at the launcher.

"Imagine," he said, "being able to fire a missile and actually see through the missile's eye where it's going. Imagine being able to lock onto a target visually and even as it tries to evade the missile, you can see it and make final adjustments." And Kohler went on to describe the potential of how fiber-optics-based sensors could someday keep track of enemy movements on the ground, carry data-heavy visual signals from surveillance satellites, and pack very complicated multichannel communications systems into small spaces. "The whole space program is dependent upon carrying data, voice, and image," he said. "But now, it takes too much space to store all the relays and switches and there's too much impedance to the signal. It limits what we can do on a mission. But imagine if we could adapt this technology to our own uses."

Then he looked me very squarely in the eye and said the very thing that I was thinking. "You know this is *their* technology. It's part of what enables them to have exploration missions. If it became *our* technology, too, we'd be able to, maybe we could keep up with them a little better."

Then he asked me for the army's commitment. He explained that some of our research laboratories were already looking into the properties of glass as a signal conductor and this would not have to be research that was started from complete scratch. Those kinds of start-ups gave us concern at R&D because unless we covered them up completely, it would look like there was a complete break in a technological path. How do you explain that? But if there's research already going on, no matter how basic, then just showing someone at the company one of these pieces of technology could give them all they need to reverse-engineer it so that it became our technology. But we'd have to support it as part of an arms-development research contract if the company didn't already have a budget. This is what I wanted to do with this glass-filament technology.

"Where is the best research on optical fibers being done?" I asked him.

"Bell Labs," he answered. "It'll take another thirty years to develop it, but one day most of the telephone traffic will be carried on fiber-optic cable."

Army R&D had contacts at Bell just like other contractors we worked with, so I wrote a short memo and proposal to General Trudeau on the potential of optical fibers for a range of products that Professor Kohler and I discussed. I described the properties of what had been previously called a wiring harness, explained how it carried laser signals, and, most importantly, how these fibers actually bent a stream of light around a corner and conducted it the same way a wire conducts an electrical current. Imagine conducting a beam of high-intensity single-frequency light the same way you'd run a water line to a new bathroom, I wrote. Imagine the power and flexibility it provided the EBEs, especially when they used the light signal as a carrier for other coded information.

This would enable the military to re-create its entire communications infrastructure and allow our new surveillance satellites to feed *and store* potential targeting information right into frontline command-and-control installations. The navy would be able to see the deployment of an entire enemy fleet, the air force could look down on approaching enemy squadrons and target them from above even if our planes were still on the ground, and for the army it would give us an undreamed-of strategic advantage. We could survey an entire battlefield, track the movements of troops from small patrols to entire divisions, and plot the deployments of tanks, artillery, and helicopters at the same time. The value of fiber-optic communication to the military would be immeasurable. And, I added, I was almost certain that a development push from the army to facilitate research on the complete reengineering of our country's already antiquated telephone system would not be seen by any company as an unwarranted intrusion. I didn't have to wait long for the general's response.

"Do it," he ordered. "And get this under way fast. I'll get you all the development allocation you need. Tell them that." And before the end of that week, I had an appointment with a systems researcher at the Western Electric research facility outside of Princeton, New Jersey, right down the road from the Institute for Advanced Study. I told him it came out of foreign technology, something that the intelligence people picked up from new weapons the East Germans were developing but thought we could use.

"If what you think you have," he said over the phone, "is that interesting and shows us where our research is going, we'd be silly not to lend you an ear for an afternoon."

"I'll need less than an afternoon to show you what I got," I said. Then I packed my Roswell field reports into my briefcase, got myself an airline ticket for a flight to Newark Airport, and I was on my way.

Supertenacity Fibers

Even before the 1960s, when I was still on the National Security staff, the army had begun to look for fibers for flak jackets, shrapnel-proof body armor, even parachutes, and a protective skin for other military items. Silk had always been the material of choice for parachutes because it was light, yet had an incredible tensile strength that allowed it to stretch, keep shape, and yet withstand tremendous forces. Whether the army's search for what they called a "tenacity fiber" was prompted purely by its need to find better protection for its troops or because of what the retrieval team found at Roswell, I do not know. I suspect, however, that it was the discovery at the crash site that began the army's search.

Among the items in my Roswell file that we retained from the retrieval were strands of a fiber that even razors couldn't cut through. When I looked at it under a magnifying glass, its dull grayness and almost matte finish belied the almost supernatural properties of this fiber. You could stretch it, twist it around objects, and subject it to a level of torque that would rend any other fiber, but this held up. Then, when you released the tension, it snapped back to its original length without any loss of tension in its original form. It reminded me of the filaments in a spiderweb. We became very interested in this material and began to study a variety of technologies, including spider silks because they, alone in nature, exhibit natural supertenacity properties.

The spider's spinning of its silk begins in its abdominal glands as a protein that the spider extrudes through a narrow tube that forces all the molecules to align in the same direction, turning the protein into a rodlike, very long, single thread with a structure not unlike a crystal. The extrusion process not only aligns the protein molecules, the molecules are very compressed, occupying much less space than conventionally sized molecules. This combination of lengthwise aligned and supercompressed molecules gives this thread an incredible tenacity and the ability to stretch under enormous pressure while retaining its tensile strength and integrity. A single strand of this spider's silk thread would have to be stretched nearly fifty miles before breaking and if stretched around the entire globe, it would weigh only fifteen ounces.

Clearly, when the scientists at Roswell saw how this fiber—not cloth, not silk, but something like a ceramic—had encased the ship and formed the outer skin layer of the EBEs, they realized it was a very promising avenue for research. When I examined the material and recognized its similarity to spider thread, I realized that a key to producing this commercially would be to synthesize the protein and find a way to simulate the extrusion process. General Trudeau encouraged me to start contacting plastics and ceramics manufacturers, especially Monsanto and Dow, to find out who was doing research on supertenacity materials, especially at university laboratories. My quick poll paid off.

I not only discovered that Monsanto was looking for a way to develop a mass-production process for a simulated spider silk, I also learned that they were already working with the army. Army researchers from the Medical Corps were trying to replicate the chemistry of the spider gene to produce the silk-manufacturing protein. Years later, after I'd left the army, researchers at the University of Wyoming and Dow Corning also began experiments on cloning the silk-manufacturing gene and developing a process to extrude the silk fibers into a usable substance that could be fabricated into a cloth.

Our research and development liaison in the Medical Corps told me that the replication of a supertenacity fiber was still years away back in 1962, but that any help from Foreign Technology that we could give the Medical Corps would find its way to the companies they were working with and probably wouldn't require a separate R&D budget. The development funding through U.S. government medical and biological research grants was more than adequate, the Medical Corps officer told me, to finance the research unless we needed to develop an emergency crash program. But I still remained fascinated by the prospect that something similar to a web spinner had spun the strands of supertenacity fabric around the spaceship. I knew that whatever that secret was, amalgamating a skin out of some sort of fabric or ceramic around our aircraft would give them the protection that the Roswell craft had and still be relatively lightweight.

Again, I didn't find out about it until much later, but research into that very type of fabrication was already under way by a scientist who would, years later, win a Nobel Prize. At a meeting of the American Physical Society three years before, Dr. Richard Feynman gave a theoretical speculative assessment of the possibilities of creating substances whose molecular structure was so condensed that the resulting material might have radically different properties from the noncompressed version of the same material. For example, Feynman suggested, if scientists could create material in which the molecular structures were not only compressed but arranged differently from conventional molecular structures, the scientists might be able to alter the physical properties of the substance to suit specific applications.

This seemed like brand-new stuff to the American Physical Society. In reality, though, compressed molecular structures were one of the discoveries that had been made by some of the original scientific analytical groups both at Alamogordo right after the Roswell crash and at the Air Materiel Command at Wright Field, which took delivery of the material. As a young atomic physicist, Richard Feynman was a colleague of many of the postwar atomic specialists who were in the army's and then the air force's guided-missile program as well as the nuclear weapons program in the 1950s. Although I never saw any memos to this effect, Feynman was reported to have been in contact with members of the Alamogordo group of the Air Materiel Command and knew about some of the finds at the Roswell crash site. Whether these discoveries suggested theories to him about the potential properties of compressed molecular structures or whether his ideas were also extensions of his theories about the quantum mechanics behavior of electrons, for which he won the Nobel Prize, I don't know. But Dr. Feynman's theories about compressed molecular structures dovetailed with the army efforts to replicate the supertenacity fiber composition and extrusion processes.

By the middle of the 1960s work was under way not only at large industrial ceramics and chemical companies in the United States but in university research laboratories here, and in Europe, Asia, and India.

With my questions about who was conducting research into supertenacity fibers answered and learning where that research was taking place, I could turn my attention to other applications of the technology to see whether the army could help move the development along faster or whether any collateral development was possible to create products in advance of the supertenacity fibers. Our scientists told us that one way to simulate the effect of supertenacity was in the cross-alignment of composite layers of fabric. This idea was the premise for the army's search for a type of body armor that would protect against the skin-piercing injuries of explosive shrapnel and rounds fired from guns.

"Now this won't protect you against contusions," General Trudeau told me after a meeting with Army Medical Corps researchers at Walter Reed. "And the concussive shock from an impact will still be strong enough to kill anybody, but at least it's supposed to keep the round from tearing through your body."

I thought about the many blunt-trauma wounds you see in a battle and could imagine the impact a large round would leave even if it couldn't penetrate the skin. But through the general's impetus and the contacts he set up for me at Du Pont and Monsanto, we aggressively pursued the research into the development of a cross-aligned material for bulletproof vests. I hand-carried the field descriptions of the fabric found at Roswell to my meetings at these companies and showed the actual fabric to scientists who visited us in Washington. This was not an item we wanted to risk carrying around the country. By 1965, Du Pont had announced the creation of the Kevlar fabric that, by 1973, was brought to market as the Kevlar bulletproof vest that's in common use today in the armed services and law-enforcement agencies. I don't know how many thousands of lives have been saved, but every time I hear of a police officer whose Kevlar vest protected him from a fatal chest or back wound, I think back to those days when we were just beginning to consider the value of cross-aligned layers of supertenacity material and am thankful that our office played a part in the product's development.

Our search for supertenacity materials also resulted in the development of composite plastics and ceramics that withstood heat and the pressures of high-speed air maneuvers and were also invisible to radar. The cross-stitched supertenacity fibers on the skin of the Roswell vehicle, which I believe had been spun on, also became an impetus for an entirely new generation of attack and strategic aircraft as well as composite materials for future designs of attack helicopters.

One of the great rumors that floated around for years after the Roswell story became public with the testimony of retired Army Air Force major Jesse Marcel before he died was that Stealth technology aircraft were the result of what we learned at Roswell. That is true, but it was not a direct transfer of technology. Army Intelligence knew that under certain conditions the EBE spacecraft had the ability to hide their radar signature, but we didn't know how they did it. We also had pieces of the Roswell spacecraft's skin, which was a composite of supertenacity molecular-aligned fibers. As far as I know, we've still not managed to re-create the exact process to manufacture this composite, just like we've not been able to duplicate the electromagnetic drive and navigation system that enabled the Roswell vehicle to fly even though we have that vehicle and others at either Norton, Edwards, and Nellis Air Force bases. But through the study of how this material worked and what its properties are, we've replicated composites and rolled an entirely new generation of aircraft off the assembly line.

Although the American public first heard about the existence of a Stealth technology in President Jimmy Carter's campaign against President Ford in 1976, we didn't see the Stealth in action until the air attacks on Iraq during the Persian Gulf War. There, the Stealth fighter, completely invisible to Iraqi radar, launched the first high-risk assaults on the Iraqi air force air-defense system and operated with almost complete impunity. Invisible to radar, invisible to heat-seeking missiles, striking out of the night sky like demons, the Stealth fighters, with their flying-wing almost crescent shaped, look uncannily like the space vehicle that crashed into the arroyo outside of Roswell. But appearances aside, the composite skin of the Stealth that helps make it invisible to almost all forms of detection was inspired by the Army R&D research into the skin of the Roswell aircraft that we sectioned apart for distribution to laboratories around the country.

Depleted-Uranium Invisible Artillery Shells

For the air force, Stealth technology meant that aircraft could approach a target invisible to radar and maintain that advantage throughout the mission. For the army, Stealth technology for its helicopters provides an incredible advantage in mounting search-and-destroy, Special Forces recon, or counterinsurgency missions deep into enemy territory. But the possibility of a Stealth artillery shell, which we conceived of at R&D in 1962, would have allowed us something armies have sought ever since the first deployment of artillery by a Western European army at Henry V's victory at Agincourt in the early fifteenth century. Certainly Napoleon would have wanted this ability when he deployed his artillery against the British line at Waterloo. So would the Germans in World War I when their artillery pounded the Allied forces hunkered down in their trenches and again at the Battle of the Bulge in 1944 when those of us stationed in Rome could only pray that our boys could hang on until the clouds broke and our bombers could hit the German emplacements.

In all artillery battles, once a shell is fired, it can be tracked by an observer back to its source and then return fire can be directed against whoever is firing. But as the range of artillery increased and we found ways to camouflage guns, we became proficient in hiding artillery until the advent of battlefield radar, which allows the trajectory of shells to be tracked back to their source. But imagine if the shell were composed of a material that rendered it invisible to radar? That was the possibility we proposed to General Trudeau: an invisible artillery shell, I suggested to him in his office one morning as we were designing the plan for research and development of composite materials. On the night battlefield of the future you could deploy weapons that were invisible even to radar tracking planes flying overhead behind the lines. Shells would start falling, and the enemy wouldn't know where they were coming from until after we had the advantage of five or more unanswered salvos. By then, and with the advantage of surprise, the damage might well be done. If we were using mechanized artillery, we could set up positions, fire a series of quick salvos, redeploy, and set up again.

The secret lay not just in the same Stealth aircraft technology but also in the development of a Stealth ceramic that could withstand tremendous explosive barrel pressures and still maintain an integrity through the arc of its trajectory. The search for just such a molecularly aligned composite ceramic was inspired by the composite material of the Roswell spacecraft. In analysis after analysis, the army tried to determine how the extraterrestrials fabricated the material that formed the hull of the spacecraft but was unable to do so. The search for the kind of molecularly aligned composite began in the 1950s even before General Trudeau took command of R&D, continued during my tenure at Foreign Technology when the early "Stealth" experimentation began at Lockheed that resulted in the F117 fighter and Stealth bomber, and continues right through to today.

The general was also more than interested in the kinds of warheads we would propose for just such a shell, a warhead that did come into use in 1961 and was successfully deployed during the Gulf War. And we had a suggestion for a round that we thought could change the nature of the kinds of battles we projected we'd be fighting against the Warsaw Pact forces, a warhead fabricated out of depleted uranium. This was a way to utilize the stockpile of uranium we foresaw we'd have as a result of spent fuel from commercial nuclear reactors, reactors powering U.S. Navy vessels, and the nuclear reactors the army was developing for its own bases and for delivery to bases overseas.

Depleted uranium was a dense, heavy metal, so dense in fact that conventional armament was no match for a high-speed round tipped with it. Its ability to penetrate even the toughest of tank armor and detonate once it was inside the enemy vehicle meant that a single round fired from one of our own tanks equipped with a laser range finder would disable, if not completely destroy, an enemy tank. Depleted uranium would give us a decided advantage on a European battlefield on which we knew we'd be outnumbered two or three to one by the Warsaw Pact or in China where sheer numbers alone would mean that either we'd be over-whelmed or we'd have to resort to nuclear weapons. The depleted uranium shell kept us from having to go nuclear.

Privately, I suggested to General Trudeau that depleted uranium also fulfilled our hidden agenda. It was another weapon in a potential arsenal we were building against hostile extraterrestrials. If depleted uranium could pene-trate armor, might the heaviness of the element enable it to penetrate the composite skin of the spacecraft, especially if the spacecraft were on the ground? I suggested that it certainly merited development at the nearby Aberdeen Proving Grounds in Maryland, and if it proved worthwhile, it was a weapon we should deploy.

Even though the composite ceramic Stealth round is still an elusive dream in weapons development, the depleted-uranium-tipped warhead saw action in the Gulf War, where it didn't just disable the tanks of the Iraqi Republican Guard, it exploded them into pieces. Fired from the laser range-finder-equipped Abrams tanks, TOW missile launch-ers, or even from Hedgehog infantry support aircraft, the depleted-uranium-tipped warheads wreaked havoc in the Gulf. They were one of the great weapons-development successes of Army R&D that came out of what we learned from the Roswell crash.

HARP—The High-Altitude Research Project

HARP was another project whose need for research and development was suggested to us by the challenge posed by flying saucers. They could outfly our own aircraft, we had no guided missiles that could bring them down, and we didn't have any guns that could shoot them down. We were also exploring weapons systems that had a double or triple use, and HARP, or "the big gun," was one such system. Essentially, Project HARP was the brainchild of Canadian gunnery expert and scientist Dr. Gerald Bull. Bull had studied the threat posed by the German "Big Bertha" in World War I and the Nazi V3 supergun toward the end of World War II. He realized that long-range, high-powered artillery was not only a practical solution to launching heavy-payload shells, it was very affordable once the initial research and development phase was completed. Mass-produced big guns and their ordnance, assembled in stages right on the site, could provide enormous firepower well back from the front lines to any army. They would become a strategic weapon to rain nuclear destruction down on enemy population centers or military staging areas.

Dr. Bull had also suggested that the gun could be retasked as a launch vehicle, blasting huge rounds into orbit, which could then be jettisoned, like the booster stage of a rocket, so the payload warhead could thrust itself into position. This would require a minimum amount of rocket fuel and could effectively push a string of satellites into orbit very quickly, almost like an artillery barrage. If the army needed to put special satellites into orbit in a hurry or, better still, explosive satellites that would pose a threat to orbiting extraterrestrial vehicles, the big gun was one method of accomplishing this mission.

There was still a third potential to the supergun. General Trudeau foresaw the ability of this weapon to launch rounds that could ultimately be placed into a lunar orbit. Especially if hostilities broke out between the United States and USSR or, as we expected, between Earth military forces and the extraterrestrials, we could resupply a military moon base without having to rely on rocket-launch facilities, which would demand long turnaround times and be very vulnerable to attack. A camouflaged supergun, even a series of superguns, would allow us all the benefits of a field artillery or quick-response antiaircraft unit, but with a piece that could launch payloads into space. It was this combination of capabilities that delighted General Trudeau because it enabled one R&D project to help create many different systems.

The United States, Canada, and the British military combined their joint expertise to find ways to develop Dr. Bull's supergun with General Trudeau, I believe, becoming one of Bull's staunchest supporters. But by the time military budget decisions had to be made to fund the weapon, all of the governments' military establishments had become committed to the guided missile and rocket-launched space vehicle rather than a supergun. While the weapon had some potential, the United States, UK, and Canada were too far along with their own missile programs to start up a completely new type of weapon. And in the end, they decided to end the research while still keeping close tabs on Bull's efforts to sell his technology to other powers, especially governments in the Middle East.

Through the 1980s, Gerald Bull, whom I had met at a reception honoring General Trudeau in 1986, entered into negotiations with the Israelis as well as with the Iraqis and perhaps even the Iranians. The decade-long war between Saddam Hussein and Iran proved a fertile sales territory for weapons merchants in general, and particularly for Gerald Bull, who was courted by both sides. In the end, he cut his deal with the Iranians, testing experimental versions of a supergun and planning to build the monster weapon before the British intervened and seized shipments of gun barrel units before they were shipped out of the country. By this time, Dr. Bull may have become a liability to the Iraqis, as well as to the Israelis and to the United States as well, and was shot to death outside his apartment in Belgium before the outbreak of the Gulf War.

Like Jules Verne's character Barbicane in *From the Earth to the Moon,* Bull had a vision of the potential of a long-range artillery piece. Unlike Barbicane, he came very close to proving it a practical way of launching vehicles into space. The murder of Gerald Bull has never been solved, and whatever secrets he still possessed about the assembly of a gun to launch vehicles into space probably died with him in the hallway outside his apartment.

List of Omissions

As I worked through the stack of projects on my desk during the spring months of 1962, I found I was devoting more of my time to the Roswell file and less to some of the other projects under development. It was apparent to me that the treasure trove we'd retrieved from Roswell was beginning to pay off in ways that not even I thought would happen. There were so many army research projects under way, I told my boss, that were not foundering, but sputtering along that could benefit from something similar found in the Roswell wreckage if we could find the match between the two. Night vision, lasers, and fiber-optic communication were obvious, I said to him, but I was sure there were other areas we could find just by looking at the problems posed by what we discovered from Roswell, not just retrieved from the wreckage.

"Make it specific, Phil," the general asked. "What do you mean?"

"If you just look at what we didn't find at the crash site," I said. "That goes a long way to explaining the differences between what we are and what they are. It also shows us what we need to develop if we're going to prepare for long periods of travel in space."

"Can you make me a list?" the general asked. "There are a lot of ongoing research contracts out there that could benefit from a list of things we'd have to concern ourselves with if we're going to be planning for space travel in the next fifty years."

By the time our conversation was finished, General Trudeau had asked me to prepare not only a list of what were called the "omissions" at Roswell but a very brief report detailing the areas where I thought development needed to take place. So I assembled all the reports and information in the Roswell file and began looking for what was missing that I might expect to find at a space traveler's crash site.

There was no mention in any of the reports of any food source or nutrient, and no one discovered any food-preparation units or stored food on board the spacecraft, nor were there any refrigeration units for food preservation. There was no water on the ship either for drinking, washing, or flushing of waste, nor were there any waste- or garbage-disposal facilities. The Roswell field reports said that the retrieval team found something they thought was a first-aid kit because it contained material that a doctor said was for bandaging purposes, but there were no medical facilities nor any medications. And finally, the army retrieval team said there were no rest facilities at all on board the ship; nothing that could be construed as a bunk or a bed.

From this available data the army assumed that this UFO was a reconnaissance craft and could quickly return to a larger or mother ship where all of the missing items might be found. The other explanation Dr. Hermann Oberth came up with was that this was a time/dimensional travel ship that didn't traverse large distances in space. Rather, it "jumped" from one time/space to another or from one dimension to another and instantly returned to its point of origin. But this was just Dr. Oberth's speculation, and he would usually discount any of it the moment he believed I was taking it as fact.

I believed, however, that the EBEs didn't require food or facilities for waste disposal because they were fabricated beings, just like robots or androids, who had been created specifically for space travel and the performance of specific tasks on the planets they visited. Just like our lunar rover in the 1970s, which was a robot, so these creatures had been programmed with specific tasks to perform and carried them out. Perhaps their programming could be updated or altered from a remote source, but they weren't life-forms that required ongoing sustenance. They were the perfect creatures for long voyages through space and for visiting other planets. Human beings, however, weren't robots and did require sustenance. Therefore, it would be necessary to provide for long-term sustenance and waste-disposal needs if humans were going to travel long distances in space.

Other scientists from our R&D ad hoc brain trust suggested that, indeed, this could have only been a scout ship that either got caught in our tracking radars from the 509th or from Alamogordo or was hit by lightning in the fierce electrical storm that night. They believed that the ship was navigated by an electromagnetic propulsion system. Other scientists suggested that even before we could generate the necessary power to drive such a propulsion system, we would have to have developed some form of a nuclear-powered ion drive first. As for the absence of food, scientists suggested that this would pose a major drawback for long-term human space exploration. Thus, in my quick and dirty proposal for General Trudeau, I suggested that the army had to complete the development of at least two items that I knew had been in the R&D system for at least ten years: a food supply that could never spoil and didn't require refrigeration and an atomic drive that could be assembled in space out of components as the power plant for an interplanetary spacecraft.

Irradiated Foods

The general read my notes a few days later, and seemed impressed. He knew from the memo I had left him the night before that I'd be ready to talk about my omissions list the next day, but he didn't say anything to me right away. Instead, he picked up the phone, dialed a number, told someone at the other end that he'd be right over, then looked up at me.

"Go get your hat," he said. "Meet me on the helipad. We've been invited to lunch."

Ten minutes later after the general's helicopter had picked us up, we circled the Pentagon once and were flown over to the Quartermaster Center.

An officer who shall remain anonymous met us at the helipad. He saluted as we got off the chopper. "Thank you for joining us."

He took us inside to a downstairs storeroom where he showed off shelves and shelves of all types of meat, fruit, and vegetables. "Look at this pork," he said. "It's been stored here unrefrigerated for months and it's completely free of trichina worm." He held up a couple of loose eggs and a chicken breast. "Eggs, unrefrigerated, and chicken. Completely free of bacterium salmonella. And it's the same for the seafood."

He escorted us along the shelves of food and, almost like a salesman, presented the virtues of each of the items. The food was wrapped, but not vacuum-sealed, in a clear cellophane to keep it free from dust and surface dirt, but it was not preserved in any manner that I could determine.

"Free of fungus or any spores," he said about the vegetables. "No mold or any insect infestations in the fruit," he said. "And the milk, it's been here on the shelf for over two years and it's not even slightly sour. We've taken great steps to preserve food completely without salting, smoking, refrigeration, freezing, or even canning."

"Does this answer one of your questions, Colonel?" General Trudeau asked as we looked at the stocks of food that seemed completely resistant to spoilage.

The commanding general of the Quartermaster Center joined us in the stockroom. "Pick your lunch, gentlemen," he said and chose a thick steak for himself. "I'm going to have this and, if you don't mind, I'll take the liberty of ordering up the same thing for you, General Trudeau, and you, too, Colonel. How about some potatoes and maybe some strawberries for dessert. All fresh, delicious, and harmless." Then he paused. "And completely bombarded with what some people would call lethal doses of radiation to destroy any bacteria or infestation."

We were escorted upstairs to the commandant's dining room, where we were joined by a number of other officers and civilian research and food-technology experts who described the process of ionizing radiation to destroy the harmful bacteria while preserving the food without canning or smoking. The irradiation process was so complete that if the food were maintained in an antiseptic or dust-free atmosphere, it wouldn't be attacked and would remain uncontaminated. However, because the atmosphere was as dirty as any other atmosphere inside any other building, the food was wrapped in cellophane. Other foods were packaged in a clear plastic wrap and were displayed for visitors like us just as if they were on supermarket shelves.

"We first wanted to determine whether the whole concept of irradiated food was safe," one of the engineers explained. "So our first studies were made with food which was irradiated and then stored in the frozen area. We fed these foods to rats and noticed no harmful effects. Then we did the same thing except this time we increased the radiation to six megarads and then froze the food. Again, no harmful effects."

His presentation continued while we ate, accompanied by charts that showed how the sterilization rate was increased to try to find any harmful effects on rats. Then they tested the irradiated and then frozen food on human volunteers.

"But wait," I asked. "I still don't understand why you irradiated the food and then froze it."

The engineer was waiting for this question because he had his answer already prepared. He acted like he'd been asked it many times before. "Because," he said, "we were testing only for harmful effects from the radiation, not for spoilage, not for taste, not even for harmful effects from the food itself even though we knew it had been sterilized and was tested completely free from bacteria when it was defrosted. What we needed to prove in field trials was the harmlessness to animals and humans of the irradiation process."

Then he described the field trials to prove that irradiation preserved food stored at room temperature. "We selected high-spoilage foods," he said. "Like the meats, chicken, and especially the seafood. We also made composite foods like stews which we fed to rats and dogs along with straight meat and then straight tuna. We first irradiated a sample at three megarads then another sample at six megarads and tested the animals over a period of six months to see whether radiation became concentrated in any of their organs or bones." He paused, letting the dramatic effect of what he was going to say sink in while we were sinking our teeth into the irradiated foods that resulted from the years of experimentation throughout the 1950s. "No toxicological effects whatsoever. And we were very thorough before we tested these foods on human volunteers."

"What's next?" I asked.

"We're setting taste trials of favorite foods at Fort Lee, Virginia, to see how troops in the field respond to this. We think that before the end of the decade we'll have a variety of Meals Ready to Eat for troops in the field who have no benefit of cooking facilities or refrigeration."

General Trudeau looked across the table at me and I nodded. This was perfectly good food that was right up to any quality you'd care to measure.

"Gentlemen," General Trudeau said as he stood. As a three-star general, he was the highest-ranking officer in the room, and when he spoke everyone was silent. "My assistant believes that your work is of utmost importance to the U.S. Army, our nation, and the world, and will contribute to our travel in space. I am of the very same opinion. We are most impressed with your test results and want to help you expand your operation and speed up the testing process. The army needs what you've developed. In the next two weeks, submit to me your supplementary budget to expand your operation and I want it also included into next year's budget." Then he turned to me, nodded, and we thanked the commanding general for lunch and walked out to General Trudeau's helicopter.

"How about that, Phil?" he asked. "I think we checked off some of the items on your list right on the spot."

The pilot helped the general into his seat and I got around on the other side.

"So what do you think?" he asked again.

"I think if we move any faster we'll have the EBEs down here asking for some of our irradiated food," I said.

General Trudeau laughed as we whisked off the helipad and headed back for the short jump to the Pentagon. "Now you have to get to work on finding out what you can about your atomic propulsion system. If NASA ever gets it into its mind to push ahead with building its space station, I'd like the military to have a power source that can keep us up there for a while. If we can get a surveillance window on our visitors, I want it sooner rather than later."

And before the week was out, I was at Fort Belvoir, Virginia, again looking at the developments the army had made in the development of portable nuclear reactors.

Portable Atomics

A challenge posed to us directly by the army's retrieval of the Roswell craft and our further discovery that the craft was not propelled by a conventional engine—either propeller, jet, or rocket—pressed upon us the critical realization that if we were to engage these extraterrestrial creatures in space we would need a propulsion system that gave us a capability for long-distance travel similar to theirs. But we had no such system. The closest form of energy we had that did not rely on a constant supply of fuel was atomic power in a controlled, sustained reaction, and even that was far away from development. However, at the close of the war the army had operational control over atomic weapons because, under Gen. Leslie Groves, director of the Manhattan Project, the army had established the bureaucracy that developed and deployed the atomic bomb.

So for army engineers, struggling to find out how the Roswell spacecraft was powered, atomic power was the easiest form of propulsion to seize upon, in part because it was the most immediate. However, by 1947, a struggle was already breaking out within the Truman administration over who would control nuclear power, a civilian commission or the military. As the nation was making the transition from wartime to peacetime, the specter of a General Groves secretly dictating how and in what manifestation atomic power would be used frightened Truman's advisers. So in the end, President Truman made the decision to turn control of the nation's nuclear program over to a civilian commission. Thus, by 1947, the army was getting out of running the nuclear power business, but that didn't mean that research into the military applications of nuclear power plants stopped. We needed to develop nuclear reactors, not only to manufacture nuclear power propulsion systems for naval vessels and for on-site installation of power-generating stations, but to experiment with ways nuclear power could be made portable in space by assembling systems in orbit from component parts. This would enable us to maintain long-term outposts in space and even to power interplanetary vessels that could serve as a defensive force against any extraterrestrial hostile forces. If this sounds like science fiction, remember, it was 1947, and the nation had barely gotten out of World War II before the Cold War had begun. War, not peace, was on the minds of the military officers who were in charge of the Roswell retrieval and analysis of the wreckage.

The army, I discovered from the "Army Atomic Reactors" reports at Fort Belvoir, not only had a very sophisticated portable reactor program under way, but had already built one in cooperation with the air force for installation at the Sundance Radar Station six miles out of Sundance, Wyoming, early in 1962. This was a highly sophisticated piece of power-generating apparatus that provided steam heat to the radar station, electrical power for the base, and a very precisely controlled separate power supply for the delicately calibrated radar equipment. But this wasn't the first portable power plant, as most people thought it was.

The first portable nuclear reactor plant anywhere was for a research facility in Greenland, under the Arctic ice cap, designed for Camp Century, an Army Corps of Engineers project nine hundred miles from the North Pole. Ostensibly operated by the Army Polar Research and Development Center conducting experiments in the Arctic winter, Camp Century was also a vital observation post in an early-warning system monitoring any Soviet activity at or near the North Pole and any activity related to UFO sightings or landings.

During the years when I was at the White House, the UFO working group had consistently pushed President Eisenhower to establish a string of formal listening posts—electronic pickets staffed by army and air force observers at the most remote parts of the planet—to report on any UFO activity. General Twining's group had argued that if the EBEs had any plans to establish semipermanent Earth bases, it wouldn't be in a populated area or an area where our military forces could monitor. It would be at the poles, in the middle of the most desolate surroundings they could find, or even underneath the ocean. The polar caps seemed like the most obvious choices because during the 1950s we had no surveillance satellites that could spot alien activity from orbit, nor did we have a permanent presence at the two poles. It was thought that we wouldn't be able to put any sophisticated devices at the poles, either, because doing so would require more power than we could transport. However, the army's Nuclear Power Program, developed in the 1950s at Fort Belvoir, provided us with the ability to install a nuclear-powered base anywhere on the planet.

In 1958, work was started on the Camp Century power plant, which was to be constructed beneath the ice in Greenland. Initially this was supposed to be top secret because we didn't want the Soviets to know what we were up to. Ultimately, however, the high security classification proved too unwieldy for the army because too many outside contractors were involved and the logistics, transportation to Thule, Greenland, then installation on skids beneath the ice pack created a cover-story nightmare. So Army Intelligence decided to drop the security classification entirely and treat the entire plan as a scientific information-gathering expedition by its polar research group.

Just like the whole camouflage operation that had protected the existence of the working group, Camp Century provided the perfect cover for testing out a procedure for constructing a prefabricated, prepackaged nuclear reactor under arduous conditions and flying it to its site for final assembly. It also provided the army with a means of testing the performance of the reactor and how it could be maintained at an utterly desolate location in the harshest climate on the planet.

The plant was the first of its kind. It had a completely modular construction that had separately packaged components for air coolers, heat exchangers, switchgear, and the turbine generator. The power plant also had a mechanism that used the recycled steam to melt the ice cap surface to provide the camp's water supply. The entire construction was completed in only seventy-seven days, and the camp remained in operation from October 1960 to August 1963, when the research mission completed its work. The entire operation was successfully taken apart and placed in storage in 1964, and the site of Camp Century was completely restored to its natural state.

I received reports about the camp's operation during the later months of 1962 after General Trudeau had asked me about the feasibility of the army's portable atomics program as a way to instigate research into a launchable atomics program for generating power in orbit. I was so enthusiastic about the success of our portable atomics and the way they provided the research platform for the subsequent development of mobile atomics that I urged the general to provide as much funding as R&D could to enable the Fort Belvoir Army Nuclear Power Program to construct and test as many mobile and portable power plants as possible.

Each power plant gave us a kind of a beachhead into remote areas of the world where the EBEs might have wanted to establish a presence because they believed they could go about it undetected. They were a kind of platform. Once we had demonstrated the ability to protect remote areas of the earth, we'd be in a better position to establish a presence in space.

The atomics program, which was in part a direct outgrowth of the challenge posed to us from our analysis of the Roswell craft, ultimately helped us develop portable atomic power plants, which are now used to power Earth satellites as well as naval vessels. It showed us that we could have portable atomic generators and gave the army a longer reach than anybody might have thought. Ultimately, it allowed us to maintain surveillance and staff remote listening posts. It also provided the basis for research into launching nuclear power facilities into space to become the power plants of new generations of interplanetary vehicles. The portable atomics program allowed us to experiment with ways we would develop atomic drives for our own space-exploration vehicles, which, we believed, would enable us to establish military bases on the moon as well as on the planets near us in the solar system.

And from our successes with atomics, we turned our attention to the development of the weapons we could mount on surveillance satellites in orbit, weapons we developed directly from what we found in the flying saucer at Roswell.

CHAPTER 16

"Tesla's Death Ray" and the Accelerated Particle-Beam Weapon

EMBEDDED IN THE ARMY FIELD REPORTS AND AIR MATERIEL Command engineering evaluations analyzing the Roswell craft were descriptions of how the spacecraft might have utilized a form of energy known as "directed energy," powerful beams of excited electrons that could be precisely directed at any target. We didn't know very much about directed energy back in 1947, or more precisely put, we didn't know how much we knew because in reality we knew a lot. But the information that had been readily available since the 1930s was lying sequestered at a public storage facility, under the authority of the federal government, over on the Lower East Side of Manhattan in the notes of the mysterious inventor Nikola Tesla, whose experiments and reputed discoveries have become the stuff of bizarre but exciting legend.

The laser surgical cutting tool found in the Roswell wreckage was one form of directed-energy beam device whose ability to fire rapidly and with precision revealed that the extraterrestrials had a potential in weaponry far superior to ours. However, if the craft had been brought down by lightning, itself a directed-energy beam of one of the highest magnitudes, then it revealed their vulnerability to bolts of electrons. That stimulated the thinking of army scientists and researchers into the analysis of the potential of a directed-energy beam weapon. Today, fifty years after the crash of the spacecraft at Roswell, these weapons are far more than the device that the Emperor Ming aimed at Earth in the Flash Gordon serials; they are a reality that can be launched on a guided missile, separated from a booster, aimed by an internal computer-guidance system at any incoming device, whether an ICBM warhead or a space vehicle, and fired with devastating effect. This weapon has been a true Army R&D success story.

"The possibilities for benefits to the military are enormous," I wrote to General Trudeau in my 1962 analysis of the potential for directed-energy weapons. "Although, as we have seen, even the most rudimentary of directed energy products, the microwave oven, has more than repaid the initial research and development overhead through consumer product sales, it is the military that will see the greatest benefits from directed energy and is already seeing the potential from it in the applications that are being projected for the laser which is only two years old."

The concept of a weapon that relied on a directed-energy beam, whatever the nature of that beam was, was not a completely new concept to the military community, although its origins were totally shrouded in secrecy. The first test of a directed-energy weapon, a particle-beam accelerator code-named Seesaw whose beam was to be aimed at incoming guided missiles, was first conducted in 1958, two years before the successful demonstration of the laser, by the Advanced Research Projects Agency. Although the test took place the year that I was in Red Canyon, New Mexico, I had known about the project first when I was on the National Security Council at the White House and then again after the successful experiments against a simulated target.

In theory, the particle-beam weapon looked like it would work, assuming the technological development of power generators, electrical storage apparatus, and the computer software to aim and fire the weapon. We already had a rough model for the particle-beam weapon in nature: the lightning bolt, a pure, intense beam of electrons firing between opposite poles and destroying or incapacitating anything it hit that was not grounded. Scientists from Benjamin Franklin to Nikola Tesla have tried to chain the force of lightning as a power source. Now the Advanced Research Projects Agency was experimenting with the theory to apply it to a new and deadly weapon. If they could build the hardware and write the software, the developers at ARPA decided they would be able to generate an intense beam of either electrons or neutral hydrogen atoms, aim it at an incoming target, and fire the particle beam in pulses that would travel near the speed of light and excite the atoms in the target until they literally blew apart. Whatever didn't blow up would be destroyed electronically and rendered useless.

Officially, the project would remain secret until funding could be acquired and the technological development of the components moved far enough along to allow us to build working prototypes. The great fear of the developers at ARPA was that the Soviets, realizing what we were trying to construct, would maximize their effort to build one before we did, rendering our newly developed Atlas ICBM obsolete before it even got to the launching pad.

The Advanced Research Projects Agency was a highly secretive network of defense scientists, members of the industrial defense contractor R&D community, and university researchers operating either under the formula of a government grant or the tacit acknowledgment of the Defense Department that their research would come under government control at some point. ARPA was founded in 1958, in part, I believed, because up to then Army R&D had been a disorganized department barely able to manage the core research necessary to keep us technologically superior to our enemies. This created a gap in research that the Advanced Research Projects Agency was created to fill. Working on military defense-oriented research, many times far in advance of any concrete proposals for the development of a weapons system or a product, ARPA often acted as a forward skirmish line for the development of military weapons or simply facilitated the basic scholarship necessary for the more concrete items to be developed. However, too many times it was in conflict with the military because

ARPA had its own separate agenda, especially after General Trudeau had reorganized the entire military R&D apparatus and refocused it so that it ran like a machine.

In 1969, during the era of large mainframe computers, under a contract to develop a network of networks linking universities, defense contractors, and the military, the ARPANET was born. And in the 1970s after the Advanced Research Projects Agency changed its name to the Defense Advanced Research Projects Agency, or DARPA, it instituted a project to create an "internetting" of all the existing computers on its system, instituting the software protocols that would link networks running on different operating systems. By 1974, the Transmitting Control Protocol/Internet Protocol was born and the ARPANET became the Internet. In the late 1980s, the European Laboratory for Particle Physics launched a hypertext language, originally conceived of by Vannevar Bush, as a search mechanism on the Internet and by 1990 married it to a graphics user interface that combined hypertext and graphics. The World Wide Web was born.

In 1958, when it was first developing the concepts behind the particle-beam weapon, ARPA was only a year old. It was formed in 1957, when I was still at the White House, in response to the Soviet Union's successful launch of Sputnik because the government realized that the United States needed an independent research organization to marshal the resources of the academic, scientific, and industrial communities. ARPA was formed to fund basic research, and even though it didn't have a military orientation at the outset, it quickly became associated with military projects because that was where the government saw the greatest need for basic research into scientific and technical areas.

There was another reason for the formation of ARPA that, at least in theory, had a lot to do with the perceived threats facing the United States and the need for basic research to respond to them. ARPA, because it was a network deep inside the government and ultimately the Department of Defense, could engage in research ostensibly far afield from the immediate needs of the military services whose research and development organizations were part of the command structure. ARPA wasn't. Although it reported to its own higher-ups in the Defense Department and at the

White House, it was not part of a command structure and didn't have to confine itself to the agendas of the heads of the various special military corps.

ARPA didn't just come into existence out of nowhere. Its ancestor, the National Research Council, had been formed under President Wilson to organize and marshal scientific research for defense purposes and as a rival to the Naval Consulting Board, which was run by Thomas Edison, who had gone on record as saying that the country didn't need a Naval Consulting Board at all. He invited scientists he called a bunch of "perfessers" down to his laboratory in New Jersey to walk around the "scrap heap" to see how real inventions were created. University researchers and corporate heads of research and development were naturally appalled at what Edison thought about government-sponsored research for the war effort and rallied around the NRC. If there were government grants to be handed out for basic defense research, the scientists who worked for corporations, who needed help in basic research no matter what its primary purpose was, were anxious to become associated with this new organization.

University researchers argued, through the prestigious National Academy of Sciences, that the National Research Council should be an "arsenal of science" to protect the United States through the application of its great brain trust in academia and industrial contractors to issues of national defense through technology. President Wilson agreed, and the NRC was born. One of the first tasks given to the National Research Council was the development of a submarine defense. Aircraft had not yet made a decisive appearance on the battlefield at the outset of World War I, but the German U-boats were ravaging the Atlantic fleets. The navy was desperately searching for a way to detect submarines, and although Nikola Tesla had submitted his plans for an energy-beam detector that would send low-frequency waves through the water to reflect off any hidden objects, the National Research Council thought the idea too esoteric and looked for a more conventional technology. Tesla's low-energy wave didn't work well in water anyway, but years later Tesla's description of his invention was the basis for one of the most important devices to come out of World War II, "radar."

The National Research Council had established a pattern of government support for basic research when it had an aspect to it that could be developed for military purposes. It was the first time that research scientists from the private sector, corporations, academicians, bureaucrats, and the military were brought together to solve mutual problems. Therefore, the Advanced Research Projects Agency and the Defense Advanced Research Projects Agency, or DARPA, son of ARPA, were natural outgrowths of an ongoing government relationship.

The problem with ARPA was that it was political and had its own agenda. It was not uncommon for conflicts to arise between the Office of the Chief of Research and Development, General Trudeau, who was operating within the military command structure, and ARPA over money and the policy issues that arose between them. The staffs at ARPA and in the Pentagon crossed swords on a number of occasions, and more than once ARPA tried to lay the blame for its own shortcomings and mistakes on the military. During the early years of the Vietnam War, for example, ARPA tried to blame General Trudeau for mistakes in the deployment of Agent Orange. But General Trudeau and R&D weren't responsible at all for Agent Orange. It was ARPA's baby from the start. But when the field reports started coming in on the casualties Agent Orange was causing among our own troops and ARPA said that it would testify before Congress that General Trudeau was responsible, I hit the ceiling. I let the ARPA staff people know that, protocol be damned, I would storm into the congressional committees on military and veterans affairs and raise the roof of the Capitol Building until everyone knew that ARPA was trying to duck responsibility for negligence in the deployment of a bad chemical. ARPA backed down, but the bad blood between us remained.

When the concept of an ARPA was first discussed at the White House, I saw the potential as well as the problem, but I also knew that a secret agenda driving everything was the policy of the UFO working group. ARPA was an asset to them because they could network through the university community and find out who had any information about UFOs that they weren't disclosing to the military, what technology was being developed that had any relation to the problem of UFOs or EBEs, and who in the academic or scientific community were coming up with theories about the existence or intentions of EBEs. In other words, in addition to being a conduit for research and research grants that fit certain government/military profiles, ARPA was another intelligence-gathering agency, but dedicated to the academic and scientific communities. If information was out there, ARPA was going to find it and pay for its development.

Therefore, when the urgency of coming up with a technological challenge to the Soviet space program arose in 1957, it was no surprise to anyone who understood the requirements of a space defense that it would be an organization like ARPA that would be given the mandate to develop that military response. And given the challenge posed by the Soviet satellite program, a particle-beam weapon was the logical direction such a response would take.

The United States had to develop a weapon that theoretically could knock out the Soviet satellites or blind them so they couldn't take any surveillance photos. They had to gather resources in the academic research community to see whether a talent pool existed for the development of such a weapon. At the same time they didn't want to divert military research into exotic weapons while the military was still trying to get its own satellites into orbit. But rather than putting the plan directly into the hands of the military R&D organizations, they followed a course probably initially laid out for them by the protocols of the UFO working group and went outside the formal military to an ad hoc research organization that was not supposed to be involved in direct military research. When I was at the White House, I could see the hand of the CIA behind this, which immediately sent up a red flag for me because I knew that the government was only creating another budget and research grant bureaucracy the CIA would ultimately control.

It was also no surprise that the first type of weapon whose mission was directed against space vehicles and vehicles reentering Earth's atmosphere from space was a directed-energy weapon, an accelerated particle beam, because even though it may sound like something out of a science fiction movie, it had a history that stretched back all the way to the early twentieth century. It's original creator was Nikola Tesla, some of whose papers were still in my own files when I took over the Foreign Technology desk in 1961.

Tesla was theorizing about directed-energy beams, including particle-beam weapons, even before the beginning of the twentieth century. His now famous "death ray" was essentially a version of a particle-beam weapon that he believed would bring peace to the entire world because it could destroy entire cities anywhere in the world, instantly, and render squadrons of airplanes, naval fleets, and even entire armies completely useless. But even before his announcement of his death ray, Tesla was making news and a fortune through his experiments with the wireless transmission of electricity and his directed beam of electrons, which would strip the electrons of specimen material inside a light globe. In the 1890s, Tesla was experimenting with a device that would become the twentieth-century cyclotron, another device that would become television, and he formulated the ideas for what today are the worldwide television and radio networks. Tesla, his background and his history, are important to any history of twentieth-century science and weapons because his thinking was well advanced beyond that of any scientist of his day, including Thomas Edison, and the political implications of what Tesla discovered mixed in with the furious attempts to manage the government cover-up about UFOs and their technological potential in the days and months after the Roswell crash.

Nikola Tesla, the son of a Serbian Orthodox minister, came to the United States from Paris in 1884 to meet and work for the acknowledged genius of his day, Thomas Edison. Although the two men would eventually clash like titans over the advantages of alternating current over direct current, Tesla did manage to get a job at the Edison offices and laboratory on what is now West Broadway, south of West Houston Street in New York City.

The two men were also very different in the way they approached their inventions. Edison was a tinkerer who would come up with an idea, experiment, build and rebuild, and experiment again until it worked. Often, as in the case of his incandescent bulb, he would go through thousands of experiments, discarding each one after it failed, until he finally succeeded. This was Edison's example of initial inspiration and then lots of perspiration until the thing worked and he believed he'd gotten it right.

Tesla, on the other hand, laid the entire project out in his brain, visualizing it in its completeness, and then assembled it from the vision in his mind. It was unnerving to Edison, who often commented to his former assistant Charles Batchelor that Tesla's ability to build something from what amounted to a set of schematics in his own mind was unnatural. Tesla was also a fastidious, formally trained academician who loved to discuss theory while Edison was mostly a self-taught workbench inventor who often worked and slept in the same clothes for days.

It is ironic that the rivalry between the two men who, by the time each of them died, had patented inventions upon which most of modern technological industry is built, spawned two great competing companies—General Electric and Westinghouse—whose own rivalries extend to the present day. The rivalry between Edison and Tesla helped define the nature of the electrical power industry in the United States, the electrical appliance and entertainment industries, and sustained itself from the 1890s through the 1930s when Edison finally died. Tesla himself died in New York in 1943.

Tesla was an acknowledged genius, a prodigy whose predictions and patents marked him to be a man way ahead of his time. Even before Czech playwright Karel Čapek coined the word "robot" in his play *R.U.R.* and American science fiction writer Isaac Asimov invented the term "robotics" in his book of short stories *I Robot,* Nikola Tesla had created the first "automaton" or mechanical soldier and a robotically controlled model boat before the turn of the century. Yet Tesla, a tall, dark, brooding, but well-educated and cultured Serbian, oftentimes turned out to be his own worst enemy. He became a millionaire when he was only thirty-two but ran through enormous sums of money put up by some of the great industrialists and financiers of his day, including George Westinghouse, J. Pierpont Morgan, A. Stanford White, and John Jacob Astor, only to die destitute and penniless in his room at the New Yorker Hotel. This was the man, however, whose ideas the scientists at ARPA turned to when faced not only with the threat of the first Soviet Sputnik orbiting the earth, but the even worse threat that the EBEs, seeing and hearing the Russian satellite, would be convinced that if colonization of the Earth was their goal, it was the Russians who would help them accomplish it. What was Tesla's idea?

Consistently, throughout the 1890s, Tesla wrote and lectured about his theory of the wireless transmission of electrical current. Like Marconi's wireless radio, which revolutionized communication, Tesla's wireless electrical power supply would revolutionize the growth and development of entire cities. Not just as an extrapolation of wireless power but as a theory in its own right, Tesla reported that he had experimented with a beam of electrical energy, directed without wires, that could excite the atoms in a substance to the point where the substance, even though it could resist heat in conventional ovens, would break down. Such a beam weapon, Tesla said, would revolutionize warfare. In theory at least, it was a very similar device, the laser cutting tool, that the Army retrieval team picked out of the scrub at the Roswell crash site.

One of the astounding aspects about the life and career of Nikola Tesla isn't just that he theorized about these projects, he actually experimented with them, many times succeeding in very intriguing ways, and then patented the important inventions that derived from his experiments. But his ideas qua ideas were so radical for the time, so far ahead of anything his contemporaries were thinking, that they were dismissed as either the uncontrolled ravings of a mad scientist or so wildly impractical that they amounted to nothing. Yet, when you review the patents in his name, his descriptions of the systems he designed, and actual results of the public experiments or exhibitions he conducted, you find that even the most lunatic-sounding ideas like his turn-of-the-century plans for a vertical takeoff and landing bomber actually looked as though they should work. In some cases, like his atom smasher, they worked better and more efficiently than the modern equivalents of these machines when they first appeared.

When I realized that at the turn of the century Tesla had actually demonstrated a model of a remotely piloted boat that could be controlled by radio from a distance and deliver torpedoes right into the heart of an enemy fleet, I was amazed that the navy hadn't jumped on the idea in advance of World War I and even more amazed that we hadn't ordered the design from Tesla in World War II when we knew the Germans were already experimenting with one. Yet today, we're spending hundreds of millions of dollars to develop a remotely piloted vehicle similar in concept to the one Tesla had designed almost a hundred years ago at less than a thousandth of today's cost.

And in 1915, Tesla had written the U.S. War Department that in addition to his remotely piloted boat, they should urgently consider his remotely piloted "aerial machines devoid of sustaining planes [wings], ailerons, propellers, and other eternal attachments, which will be capable of immense speeds, and are very likely to furnish powerful arguments for peace in the near future. Such a machine, sustained and propelled entirely by reaction [thrust rocket engines], can be controlled either mechanically or by wireless energy [radio controlled]." Tesla's description of the remote-controlled rocket-powered guided missile, which was even more advanced than the German V2, is the forerunner of today's modern ICBMs whose targeting information can be relayed to them after they're in flight. As a tactical weapon, Tesla had described, over half a century earlier, the army's remotely piloted TOW antitank missile that destroyed Saddam's armored divisions in the Persian Gulf.

Tesla's experiments with particle-beam generation and direction were well under way during the 1890s when he was invited to set up an experimental station that would prove that he could transmit electrical power using the earth's atmosphere as the medium instead of a heavy cable. If power could be so directed, Tesla's backers, who included industrialist George Westinghouse and financier J. P. Morgan, agreed, it would revolutionize the infant electrical power industry and make whoever controlled the source of power rich beyond anyone's imagination. Tesla believed he could control that power and, with about $60,000 from his backers, traveled to Colorado Springs, not coincidentally today's home of the Air Force North American Air Defense Command (NORAD) and the United States Army's Space Command, to build and demonstrate his power-transmission station.

Tesla described his experiments in an article he wrote for the thirtieth-anniversary edition of the *Electrical World and Engineer* in 1904. He said, "Not only was it practicable to send telegraphic messages any distances without wires, as I recognized long ago, but also able to impress upon the entire globe the faint modulations of the human voice, far more still, to transmit power, in unlimited amounts, to any terrestrial distance and almost without any loss." In Tesla's vision, electrical transmission stations would circle the planet, storing and relaying power from station to station so as to provide electrical power to the entire planet without the use of above- or below-the-ground power lines, feeder cables, and transmission lines. He also saw that a network of relay stations could receive and retransmit the world's breaking news stories instantly around the globe to pocket receivers, "a cheap and simple device which might be carried in one's pocket," which would record special messages sent to it. Tesla had described a modern microwave cellular telephone and remote pager system. He also said that with relay stations like this, "the entire Earth will be converted into a huge brain, as it were capable of response in every one of its parts," in other words, an Internet. During his time, Tesla truly made history by showing that energy could be directed as a beam without wires.

In 1899, it was rumored that Tesla was experimenting with a "death ray" in Colorado Springs. But Tesla never owned up to it, and in fact remained uncommunicative about any experiments he had conducted with rays even when English, German, Russian, and American scientists in the 1920s were applying for patents on the invention. In the 1930s, however, Tesla wrote in his monograph that he had made a new discovery that would make war obsolete because every nation would have the same power to destroy each other's military weapons. It would require a large facility to generate the power, but such a facility would be able to stop entire armies and their machines as far away as two hundred miles in all directions. "It will," he wrote, "provide a wall of power offering an insuperable obstacle against any effective aggression."

But it was not at all a death "ray," he said, because, as scientists working as recently as the 1970s realized, rays tend to diffuse over distance and something is necessary to maintain the intensity of the focus. Rather, he said, "My apparatus projects particles which may be relatively large or of microscopic dimensions, enabling us to convey to a small area at a great distance trillions of times more energy than is possible with rays of any kind. Many thousands of horsepower can thus be transmitted by a stream thinner than a hair, so that nothing can resist."

Although Tesla went on to describe how this beam will improve television transmission and the projection of images, he was really describing a directed, accelerated particle-beam weapon that the folks at ARPA were struggling to develop over twenty-five years after Tesla first wrote about it and eleven years after the charred fragments of a directed-energy apparatus as well as the laser tool were discovered in the wreckage of the spacecraft at Roswell, written up by the engineers at the Air Materiel Command, and sequestered for years in my nut file. We were still trying to develop a workable beam when I was in the Pentagon in 1962 and only barely developed a working model in the Reagan administration as part of the Strategic Defense Initiative program.

But for Tesla, his world in the 1930s rushed toward war. Writing J. P. Morgan about his vision of an H. G. Wells nightmare of the destruction of the civilized world through aerial bombardment, Tesla said that his particle-beam weapon could shoot down airplanes in flight and so protect cities. He made proposals to the Russians to develop such a weapon because Stalin was afraid of an invasion from Japan. He also wrote to the British prime minister about the ability of his beam to protect London from attacks by the Germans. But no one thought his energy-beam weapon practical, not even the Westinghouse Company, which, if they had advanced him the money to file for the patents they would probably have controlled, might have been able to develop the weapon before World War II had Tesla been able to complete it.

As it was, Tesla's death ray, his accelerated particle beam in which subatomic particles were excited by an energy field and directed toward a specific target at speeds close to the speed of light, was never developed during his lifetime. However, the mere hint that Tesla's theories might have found their way to the Germans or the Russians so concerned the federal government, especially the FBI, that when Tesla died in January 1943, the FBI immediately seized all his papers, schematics, writings, and designs and turned them over to the Office of Alien Property, where they were officially sealed until released to the Yugoslavian ambassador, who was a representative of Tesla's estate. They remained in storage in Manhattan until the early 1950s, when they were returned to Yugoslavia. Yet even after their return, the Yugoslavian government believed that the FBI had rifled through Tesla's papers when they were in storage and had microfilmed them or photographed them. J. Edgar Hoover denied this, but photostatic copies of photographs of Tesla's papers were in the possession of the Army R&D's Foreign Technology desk when I took over in 1961. How did they get there?

Tesla's property was officially seized by the U.S. government two days after his death. Even though the FBI knew that Tesla had publicly said he'd perfected his death ray— there was no independent verification of this—no steps had been taken by the government to prevent him from transferring his plans for the death ray to foreign powers. Vice President Henry Wallace, however, told the FBI that the government had a critical interest in whatever papers Tesla had and instructed the FBI to seize them any way they could. That was why the FBI directed the Office of Alien Property to enter Tesla's hotel room on January 9, 1943, and take possession. Tesla's other papers that were already in a storage warehouse were seized by the OAP as well.

Over the next couple of weeks in January 1943, after a flurry of diplomatic activity between the Yugoslavian embassy and J. Edgar Hoover's office, the FBI turned the entire matter over to the Office of Alien Property, which also wanted to get out from under the diplomatic tug-of-war between Belgrade and the State Department. The OAP, still reacting to the vice president's instructions that papers that could give aid to the enemy could not leave the country, contacted the chairman of what would become the Office of R&D, the National Defense Research Committee of the Office of Scientific Research and Development, Dr. John Trump. Dr. Trump examined the papers, determined that not much of them were useful, but decided to make photo-copies of a number of papers Tesla wrote during the years preceding his death. Trump also wrote abstracts of those papers, which included an undated monograph by Nikola Tesla entitled "New Art of Projecting Concentrated Non-Dispersive Energy through Natural Media," Tesla's descrip-tion of how he would generate and direct a high-energy beam of electrons at a target. Though dismissed by Trump as unworkable, the paper nevertheless described Tesla's latest thinking about a directed-energy weapon, the acceler-ated particle-beam device.

With the OAP's making photographs and abstracts of Tesla's papers, the entire Tesla property remained in storage until it was sent back to Belgrade in the 1950s. That should have put an end to the matter. However, in 1945, just after the war ended, the Air Technical Service Command at Wright Field outside of Dayton, Ohio, sought copies of the Tesla papers from the Office of Alien Property in Washing-ton and sent a military courier to take possession of them and bring them back to Wright. Although there was some correspondence between the OAP and the Air Technical Service Command over the next two years regarding the disposition of the papers, at least one of Gen. Nathan Twining's officers at the Air Materiel Command contacted the Office of Alien Property in November 1947 to tell them that the AMC at Wright Field had possession of the Tesla papers and would maintain possession of them at least until after January 1, 1948. Thereafter, the papers, including Tesla's own monograph on his accelerated particle-beam weapon, seem to have completely disappeared—until they appeared in my OCRD files in 1961. But that was only one of the copies.

At least one other copy of Tesla's monograph had re-mained in the possession of the working group under General Twining and had made its way to the Advanced Research Projects Agency in Washington over the course of the next ten years. It was pulled out when the working group realized that upon the launch of Sputnik, the United States had absolutely no defense against war in space being initiated by the Russians, nor against the EBEs. We had one vital clue, however, about the only possible process that could interfere with the electromagnetic field drive we suspected the aliens were using: a directed-particle energy-beam weapon that could disrupt the electromagnetic wave formation around the spacecraft and penetrate the antigravity field. And we didn't even have to microwave the spacecraft by exciting the molecules in the composite material. Because the accelerated-particle weapon carried with it a powerful electromagnetic pulse, the effect of this EMP—the same effect that EMPs have on any electrical equipment—was to disrupt the antigravity gravity field by destroying the integrity of the electromagnetic wave of the spacecraft. In this way, without exploding the spacecraft, the particle beam could force it to crash by destroying its ability to counter gravity. In its role as a more conventional weapon against incoming warheads or enemy satellites, besides destroying any electronics within the weapon through its electromagnetic pulse, the particle beam excites the atoms in the target, causes them to disperse, and the target explodes. In this way the particle beam has a dual destructive capability.

Tesla understood that the particle-beam weapon was just like a bolt of lightning, with very much the same destructive power only much more controlled. A lightning bolt is a massive beam of electrons. Scientists have theorized that you can achieve the same destructive force with a beam of protons. Still other scientists have argued that because electrons carry a negative charge and protons a positive charge, they are vulnerable to distortion within the earth's magnetic field because the beam will either be attracted to the opposite charge or repelled by the same charge. In addition, a beam of like particles will contain a natural dispersive force because the like charges in the beam will repel each other. Entire hydrogen atoms are electrically neutral, however, and make a workable beam for any weapon designed to be used outside of the earth's atmosphere because neutral beams can be directed over the very long distances that the beam from a space weapon will have to travel. Also, a neutral beam doesn't require the energy overhead to control dispersion because within a neutral beam the particles are not charged and will not repel each other.

Research and experiments on prototype models of a particle-beam weapon conducted after 1980 defined two basic types of weapons: those that would be used exclusively in space, or exoatmospheric weapons, and those that would be deployed on Earth against targets like incoming missile warheads. These are called endoatmospheric weapons. Each has enough different characteristics to make them separate weapons, but the similarities of a particle-beam weapon are common to both types. For example, as I began work on the development of basic research into particle-beam weapons, my scientists told me that the weapon has to have six basic characteristics that allow it to kill the target.

First, the beam must travel at such a high velocity—near the speed of light—that targets cannot evade it. Even UFOs travel slower than the speed of light so that in a chase, the particle beam will always win. At the same time, the faster the beam travels, the shorter the burst you have to have in order for it to disrupt the target.

Second, the beam has to stay on the target long enough for it to do its damage. We estimated that if we were bringing down an incoming enemy warhead, a powerful beam would disrupt the warhead's ability to detonate almost immediately and destroy it within a few seconds. In space, where distances are greater, the beam would have to stay on the target for a longer period of time, but it, too, would disrupt the wave propagation of the spacecraft after a very short interval. Even if it didn't destroy the spacecraft, it would certainly render it incapable of carrying out any offensive mission.

Third, you have to be able to aim the beam immediately for it to have any effectiveness, especially if you're targeting an incoming multiple reentry warhead vehicle such as the type deployed by the Russians and us. Unless you took out the bus, the vehicle that carries and aims the separate warheads while still in orbit, you'd have to fire the beam at each of the separate vehicles very quickly in succession after they've split up in orbit and begun their separate reentry trajectories. Thus, you'd have to aim and fire, aim and fire, aim and fire, all within a matter of seconds and making sure each target was destroyed. A single fifty-kiloton detonation over New York City, for example, would paralyze the entire American financial industry and immediately change life as we know it for a considerable period of time. A multiple reentry vehicle launching four 60-kiloton warheads from orbit on separate trajectories for detonation over Boston, New York, Washington, and Miami would cripple the United States for the ensuing five to seven years. And the Russians wouldn't have to launch such a missile; it could easily come from China, North Korea, or even one of the Middle East fanatic terrorist countries like Libya with lots of oil money to spend. A particle-beam weapon that could rapidly aim and fire to take out all four warheads either before or immediately upon reentry would effectively protect the United States and deter any country or terrorist group.

Fourth, the beam must penetrate the surface of the target in order for it to cause any real damage to the mechanism inside the warhead. Therefore, once the beam lands on the skin of the target, its excitation of the target's molecules must take place not just on the outer hull or skin but deep inside the vehicle's electronics. Therefore, even if it doesn't explode, it may either break apart into larger pieces or simply seize up and fall to earth as a dud.

Fifth, the particle beam must also be able to kill through its electromagnetic pulse, which will render the target's electronics inoperable by either throwing off its navigation or destroying its detonation program and turning it into a dud. Used as a space weapon, the electromagnetic pulse will have a similar effect on enemy satellites, killing their control programs and rendering their computer guidance and orientation programs inoperable and blinding them completely. Upon enemy spaceships, the pulse would act as a purely defensive weapon that forces the ship to withdraw because its wave propagation device is rendered inoperable.

And sixth, a particle beam, unlike a laser, can operate in any weather and under any atmospheric conditions. Lasers bounce off clouds and fog and are weakened by anything less than perfectly clear weather. Particle beams penetrate and can operate under all conditions.

As the scientists back in the 1950s evaluated what they would have to do to develop a working prototype, they understood the need for a huge power generator to accelerate the particles necessary to generate the beam, some form of target-painting capability not only to acquire the target quickly and aim the weapon but to reaim in case the first shot is a miss. After I left the Pentagon, work continued on the theory underlying this type of weapon but not much was done to assemble the very expensive supporting technologies such as the atomic particle accelerators, targeting computers, high-energy lasers, and a way to make the whole thing portable.

Today, however, low-energy versions of these directed-energy weapons, partly the great-grandchildren of the Tesla beam and partly the descendant of the directed-energy apparatus from the Roswell craft, are currently on the market for installation in police cars as a weapon against fleeing vehicles as a way to shut down a high-speed chase before it even starts. The police officer in the pursuing vehicle aims his directed-energy particle beam at the fleeing vehicle and turns it on. The electromagnetic pulse from the stream of electrons interferes with the target's ignition system in the engine, and the car, deprived of a flow of electrical power to fire the cylinders, rolls to a stop. No more high-speed chases on the 11:00 P.M. news but a more effective and safer way to catch fleeing suspects in their cars. This was a device developed by the military initially and, now deployed out of the Army's Space Command as a missile-mounted kinetic energy beam for destroying enemy satellites, turned over to the law-enforcement community. But its roots go back to the vision of Nikola Tesla and to what scientists believed to be actual pieces of directed-energy technology that we pulled out of the crashed space vehicle at Roswell, reports about which turned up in the nut file carted into my office in the Pentagon in 1961 from the Pentagon basement.

For me the irony has always been in the confluence between the historic work and discoveries of Nikola Tesla and the technology we ascertained the extraterrestrials had developed from our evaluation of the Roswell wreckage. Tesla had experimented with wireless transmission of energy, and the extraterrestrials seemed to have employed a type of wireless transmission of energy for navigational and defensive purposes. Tesla wrote about the theories behind the distortion or manipulation of a gravitational field through the propagation of electromagnetic waves, and the extraterrestrials seemed to have employed just that kind of technology for a propulsion system. And Tesla's descriptions of the theories behind the death ray he claimed to have perfected ultimately became the basis for the defensive weapons we deployed to challenge the hostile intrusions of our airspace by the extraterrestrials. What posed a threat to us at Roswell and what we eventually learned from Tesla's writings became two confluent streams of scientific theory that eventually became the basis of the Strategic Defense Initiative, an antiballistic missile and space vehicle weapon.

While scientists from the 1950s through the 1970s argued over the cost of such a weapon and whether an antiballistic missile weapon would destabilize the otherwise stable world of mutual nuclear deterrence, others who understood the real threat from outer space argued that there were enemies besides the Soviet Union who might someday acquire the technology to launch nuclear missiles against the United States. No one would dare say that we had to defend ourselves against flying saucers. In fact, it wasn't until the election of Ronald Reagan in 1980 that the particle-beam weapon received another pulse of life as part of the hotly debated but ultimately successful strategy of the Strategic Defense Initiative, or "Star Wars." Amid the guffaws from some political quarters and the hand-wringing from people who thought the thing simply cost too much money, President Reagan managed to prevail. Just the strategy of Star Wars itself and the limited deployment and testing of some of the components were enough to put the United States on a wartime footing with the EBEs and show the Soviets that we finally had a real nuclear deterrent.

The full story behind the SDI and the way it changed the Cold War and forced the extraterrestrials to change their strategies for this planet is a story that's never been told. But as spectacular and fantastic as it may sound, the story behind the limited deployment of the SDI is the story of how humanity won its first victory against a more powerful and technologically superior enemy who discovered, to whatever version of shock it experiences, that there was real trouble down on its farm.

CHAPTER 17

Star Wars

TOWARD THE SPRING OF 1962, GENERAL TRUDEAU TOLD ME OF his intention to retire. He was not going to be the commander of U.S. forces in Vietnam, he'd been told. The old man had charged up too many hills during his years in the army, rifle in hand, and fired back in the face of the enemy. Whatever he felt inside him, and General Trudeau was only human and nothing more, he never showed fear. He was unrelenting in the execution of his orders, unyielding when people opposed him, and he never ducked away from a fight. Those who knew him either respected or feared him, but they never discounted him. A West Point graduate, he was born into a generation of U.S. military officers who had absolutely no doubts about what was right and what was wrong, and he marched through two wars and a series of commands, including the head of U.S. Army Intelligence, secure in the knowledge that he was on the right side.

These were great qualities in a wartime commander, but, as both General Trudeau and I found out, they could be the very things that make you vulnerable in a Cold War army of politicians angling for power as they fought an enemy who could not be seen and whose presence was only indirectly felt.

"There are no more Pork Chop Hills, Phil," General Trudeau told me after he had learned that General Maxwell Taylor with the support of the army leadership had passed him over for the South Vietnam command. It meant that this was his last command and that he would retire as lieutenant general. "And I'm afraid this is a war the army's going to fight by means of a political process instead of on the killing field."

"We would win it if we were going there, General," I said, fury welling up in my chest. "You and I know what we learned in Korea."

Maybe the general could see my face getting flushed because he said, "No, we probably would have gotten court-martialed because of what we learned in Korea. Just think what they would do to us if we were to win the war." Then he laughed in a way that told me he was looking forward to his retirement. "We would have made the Communists look bad. You know you can't do that, Phil."

Even as we were speaking that afternoon toward the end of the summer, another Soviet trawler was heaving to at the entrance to the port of Havana, awaiting instructions for the off-loading of its cargo while another one of our surveillance planes was circling high overhead snapping away its photos of the tarpaulins coming off the IRBMs laid out on the ship's afterdeck. I didn't know it yet, but a sequence of events was unfolding that would swirl me into one of the biggest controversies of my life just as the chilling truth about the attempts to colonize our planet and the harvesting of human beings and animals that were still going on made itself all too clear. A showdown was coming. It was just over the horizon. No one could see it, but a handful of us knew that something was stirring the waters just below the surface.

General Trudeau was saying his good-byes and started counting the days until he would change his uniform for civilian clothes and his office in the Pentagon for a corporate executive suite that befitted his experience as the commanding officer of some of our military's most important divisions. He had been at the helm of R&D for six years after having commanded Army Intelligence for three years before that. Although the general didn't explicitly comment much on the incredible facts we had uncovered in the Roswell file because he considered it just part of his job, he did joke about it from time to time with his old friend Senator Strom Thurmond. More than once, I would take the back door into his inner office only to find Senator Thurmond and General Trudeau sitting on his couch and looking me up and down as I walked in.

"Art," Senator Thurmond would drawl, barely hiding his Cheshire cat smile, "what spooky things you think old Phil's been into?"

"You been inside your 'junk file,' Phil?" the general would ask.

"I would guess that you're able to tell the future, Phil," Senator Thurmond said. "With what you're readin' you can predict anything."

"Just acting like a good intelligence officer, Senator," I said, being as correct and noncommittal as possible in the presence of my commanding officer. "My job is to read intelligence and make analyses."

"Well, they ain't got nuthin' on you, Phil," the senator said, and everybody in the room knew exactly what "they" meant even if we weren't allowed to talk about "them" in public.

As for me? I was preparing my files for General Beech, the incoming chief of research and development, knowing that my own retirement would come at the end of 1962. So I would prepare to go silent about Roswell while setting up a run of about six months to push as many projects through as I could, including whatever was left in my nut file. Only I didn't call it a nut file or anything after General Trudeau left. My new boss and I had a tacit agreement not to broadcast anything about Roswell or the files.

As the summer of 1962 came to an end, ominous reports were circulating all through Washington concerning Soviet freighters making their way into Cuban waters. The traffic was intense, but there was no response from our intelligence people on what was happening. The CIA was completely mum, and the word making its way through the Pentagon was that we were getting slapped around by the Soviets and were going to sit still for it. Whatever it was, friends of mine in Army Intelligence were saying, the CIA was going to downplay it because the Kennedy administration didn't want a confrontation with the Soviet Union.

What was it? I kept asking, knowing all the while that the Soviets must have been playing around with something in Cuba and that's why there were so many ships. Were they massing troops there? Was it a series of military exercises? My answer came in a shocking series of photographs, unmistakable surveillance photographs, that were leaked to me by my friends in an office of Army Intelligence so deep inside the Pentagon and so secret that you weren't even allowed to take notes inside the room. I was asked, by officers who may still be alive and therefore shall go unnamed, to take a good look at the photographs they had developed from the spy plancs over Cuba. They said, "Memorize these, Colonel, because nobody can make any copies here." I couldn't believe my eyes as I looked down at the glossies and then ran a magnifying glass over them just to make sure that I wasn't seeing things. Nope, there they were, Soviet intermediate range ballistic missiles of the latest vintage. These babies could take out Washington in just minutes, and yet there they were, sitting outside of hangars only a few miles from our marine base at Guantánamo Bay.

Had Gen. Curtis LeMay seen these photos, I had to ask myself? LeMay, a veteran of Korean bombing runs, should have been drooling over his desk at the prospect of bombing the hell out of Castro just for thinking he could cven park IRBMs so close to U.S. airspace. Yet no reaction from Washington at all. The army had nothing to say, the air force had nothing to say, and my navy friends were simply unresponsive. Somebody was putting the lid on this, and I was getting deeply worried. So I called one of my friends, New York senator Kenneth Keating, and asked him what he knew.

"What do you mean missiles, Colonel Corso?" he asked. "What missiles, where?"

It was October 1962.

"In Cuba, Senator," I said. "They're sitting in Cuba waiting to be deployed on launchers. Don't you know?"

The truth was Senator Keating did not, nor did Representative Mike Feighan, whom I also called. Both legislators knew better than to ask me where I found the photos or who gave them to me, but before they did or said anything, they wanted to know why I believed them to be authentic.

"They come from our best resources," I told them. "I could pick out the missiles myself. I know what they look like. And it's not just a single photo but a series over weeks of tracking the delivery of them on the decks of Soviet freighters. They're unmistakable, very damning."

Senator Keating asked whether I knew for sure that President Kennedy had been informed of the presence of the missiles, but I told him there was no way of knowing. Privately, I would have been shocked if intelligence sources had kept this information away from the President because there were so many intelligence pathways to the Oval Office the President would have found out no matter who tried to keep the information away. So it was pretty clear to me that the administration was trying to keep the news from the American people so that neither the Russians nor the Cubans would be embarrassed and have their backs against the wall.

I also knew that by going to Senator Keating and Representative Feighan I was taking a huge risk. I was leaking information outside the military and executive chains of command to the legislative branch. But, that same April, I had already testified to Senator Dirksen's committee on the administration of the Internal Security Act that it was my belief—and I had proof to back it up—that our intelligence services, particularly the Board of Estimate, had been penetrated by the KGB and as a result we lost a war in Korea that we should have won. The testimony was regarded as classified and was never released. But it made its way to Attorney General Robert Kennedy, who promised me, in a private interview at the Justice Department, that he would personally make sure his brother, the President, read it. Now here it was a little more than six months later and whatever intelligence information the President was getting about a serious Soviet threat to U.S. security, it was clear that unless somebody stopped them, the Russians were going to get away with it. Not on my watch.

President Kennedy had gone up to Hyannis Port, and the vice president, Lyndon Johnson, a friend of Ken Keating's from his days as Senate majority leader, was completely out of the decision-making loop within the White House. The rumors were that because of his association with Bobby Baker, there was going to be an investigation of the vice president and he might return as a member of the ticket in 1964. So Senator Keating didn't recommend going to Lyndon Johnson with this information. Besides, we had to get it right in front of the public so it couldn't be swept away, leaving the White House free to ignore it until it was too late to force the Soviets' hand. This was a gamble, of course, because the whole world could explode in our faces, but I knew that the only way to deal with the Russians was put their noses in it and teach them a lesson. Had we done that in Korea the way MacArthur wanted to, there probably wouldn't have been a Vietnam War.

One of my old friends in the Washington press corps was Paul Scott, the syndicated political columnist whose pieces appeared in the *Boston Globe* and the *Washington Post.* If we gave him the story, it would find its way into the *Globe* and the *Post* at the same time, right in the President's face and forcing him to act. I didn't enjoy this, but there was no other way. So Senator Keating, Mike Feighan, and I coordinated strategy. I called Scott and told him I had seen some photos and had an interpretation he needed to hear. We met, not at the Pentagon, and I described to him the copies of the photos that I had seen and explained, in very general terms and without revealing anything classified about our surveillance apparatus, how they were taken, why they were authentic, and what they meant.

"You understand that when I saw these cylinders," I said to him, drawing on a notepad the tiny barrels in the photos on the deck of a ship, "these are intermediate range ballistic missiles that can hit Washington, New York, or Boston within fifteen minutes after launch. We don't even detect these babies until they're just below orbit and coming down. That gives us maybe five minutes to get under our desks. But with nuclear warheads on them, anybody sitting anywhere near where they detonate is not going to be protected."

"What's the point?" he asked. "Why would the Cubans want to get into a war with the United States?"

"It's not the Cubans," I explained. "It's Soviet blackmail. They're not going to turn a bunch of missiles over to Fidel Castro and put the trigger for a nuclear war in someone else's hand. The Soviets will have complete control, they'll have their own troops on the island, and they'll threaten to launch them if we or anybody tries to throw Castro out."

"Why are you telling me this?" he asked.

"Because," I said hoping for a sense of outrageous indignation in him that would motivate him to action, "the President already knows and won't do anything about it."

I was right; the newspaperman was in shock. He half suspected that Kennedy wanted to avoid any and all confrontation until he made it to his second term, but this was outright capitulation, he said. "He can't get away with it."

"Oh, yes, he can," I warned him. "If we don't get the story out, it goes away. The President's sticking his head in the sand and hoping nobody pulls it out. You have to run this in the *Globe* right when he's in Massachusetts and force him to confront it. He flies back to Washington and it's in the *Post*. Then the Soviets know that he knows and it's all a complete mess."

"But what if this sets off a war," Scott said.

"Over Cuba? Listen, not even Khrushchev's own people are willing to sacrifice Moscow for Havana," I told him. "It's a Russian gambit because the KGB told Khrushchev he could get away with it. He's punishing us for the U2 and the Bay of Pigs. We have to stand up to the Russians right here and now because if we don't the Cold War's over and we lost. It's all about territory, and if we don't defend our own hemisphere, we lose. If we make them back down, humiliate them, we win."

The story ran in the *Boston Globe* and the *Washington Post* within days, forcing the President back to Washington to confront a crisis that would go down in history as one of the defining moments of the Kennedy administration. Robert Kennedy knew that the White House was getting faulty intelligence from the CIA, and John Kennedy knew that he had to strike a middle course between the CIA people who told him everything would be OK if he let Khrushchev off the hook and his own air force chief, Curtis LeMay, who wanted him to invade Cuba.

Very wisely, President Kennedy didn't invade Cuba. He also didn't back down, at least in public. Our blockade of Cuba turned the Russian navy around and humiliated Nikita Khrushchev, whose gambit had failed. President Kennedy traded off some obsolete missiles in Turkey to give Khrushchev something he could take back to the Kremlin. But we knew all along that when we deployed our Polaris submarines in the Mediterranean and North Seas, we'd have more firepower packed and ready to go against the Soviets than we ever had in Turkey, and the Soviets wouldn't even know it was there. Besides, we knew the Turks would never let us fire our missiles against the Russians from their soil. They were afraid that the Russians would use the missiles as an excuse to attack Turkey, but the Kremlin knew that, too, and knew we wanted an excuse to get out of Turkey graciously.

So it worked all the way around, and President Kennedy got the bragging rights to drawing a line right across the ocean where the Russian navy could not cross, firing a shot across their bows in the open ocean, and making them turn around in open water and sail back home. Before the whole world the Russians had backed down. President Kennedy was a hero.

But I had made some powerful new enemies and could see the end of my own career in the army like the distant sign on an empty expressway coming up at eighty miles an hour that reads "Freeway Ends." I now devoted myself to packing away the Roswell files for those whom they would go to after me and writing my own notes for the work that I might find myself in after I left the army. Who could have realized that within months I'd be sitting in an office on Capitol Hill looking across the desk at one of my own successors who was there as the scientific adviser to the secretary of defense. I may have stepped on the toes of some of the most powerful people in Washington, but it was still the good fight and I was, above all, still a soldier in the Cold War and still fighting the stealth war against the strategies of the EBEs, who were becoming more aggressive in their appearances over defense installations, cities, and our manned and unmanned space probes. Even the Russian intelligence services had begun to complain about the mysterious goings-on with their space probes. But they couldn't come right out and tell us the reasons why. We had to figure those out for ourselves.

If the Cold War sounded complex and chaotic in the early 1960s as Kennedy juggled the strategies of Truman and Eisenhower while recognizing that he couldn't trust his own intelligence services, imagine what it was like when you factored in the "other" cold war or, as some have called it, the "real" cold war against the extraterrestrials. It was becoming like the elephant in a room that everybody knows is there but keeps denying it. Its presence is so massive that you have to walk around it. Its trunk swings with such a force that you have to duck when it sweeps over your head. Watch out that the big elephant feet don't crush your toes when he plants them, and you don't want to step too close to the elephant's backside lest you get buried in what comes out.

In other words, dealing with the Soviets was just a big mess that we had to accommodate while we all sat down at the same dinner table. The Soviets and the Americans, pretending to break bread while not blowing up the world. Yet each of us looking for the advantage while we watched one another's hands the entire time. You watch your enemy's hands, he watches your hands, and whatever you can do with your feet you do. Meanwhile your enemy's doing the same thing.

The army's hands were tied by the cover-up, the refusal of the government to let us take on the alien threat with our full resources because we had to pussyfoot around the truth. But more than a few congressmen knew about the cover-up, were as concerned as we were about the intrusions of the EBEs, the human abductions, and the cattle mutilations, and supported the military's agenda for a program of speeded weapons development in space.

We were convinced that whoever the UFO extraterrestrials were, they were tampering with our planet, operating with impudence, and manipulating us constantly and secretly. But it was a secret that had our full compliance because we were unwilling to admit the truth and fight the war. Those of us in the military who knew what was happening also felt that we could be experiencing an invasion that was more of an infiltration. They were compromising our very systems of defense and government, I suggested, and then, by the time the conflict opened up, we would already be open and vulnerable. If the EBEs had been around long enough, I once suggested to General Trudeau, might they have seen the Trojans towing that huge wooden horse the Greeks left for them right through the open gates of their city?

For his part, General Trudeau, in the months before he retired, made a number of appearances before Congress. He argued consistently that the army did have a real place in space and we had a capability in missile defense that he had proven at Los Alamos and at the guided-missile and Redstone command at Huntsville, Alabama. Moreover, the army had been able to use German scientists in the months immediately after the fighting in Europe had ended. It wasn't just a matter of who could get the biggest budget, General Trudeau testified. In fact, he offered in a briefing before the Congressional Committee on Science and Astronautics, if the space effort was to be completely taken away from the army, then it should be given lock, stock, and barrel to the air force. At least, he said, the air force was a military service and had officers and enlisted personnel who knew how to fight. But, at least in the early years, Congress and the President decided that NASA should control the space program. By the end of the 1960s, however, they had reversed that decision and realized that there was a serious military aspect to space exploration.

General Trudeau also had his allies among the major defense contractors we worked with. Not only scientists but members of the boards of directors suspected that the army had an urgency in developing weapons for use in space. Some of them even realized that we must have had a hidden agenda because each of the projects we proposed, like Horizon and the energy weapons, seemed designed for a war with enemies far more powerful and elusive than the Soviets. When he would address industrial groups on matters of technical intelligence and applied engineering, General Trudeau received what I could only call a "knowing" response. He himself once wrote in his unpublished memoirs that when he was invited to give an address to one of the companies we worked with, the people who showed up were the decision makers. He said:

> I think on every occasion that I went out, the chairman of the board was there, the chief executive officer who was usually the president, and an impressive cross section of their senior corporate officers or directors. I might say even when I went to Sperry-Rand, no less a person than General MacArthur honored me by his presence at dinner, and he didn't turn out for many.

General Trudeau was the father of the ballistic missile and the person who, from the 1950s through the 1960s, made sure that our armed forces adapted the ballistic missile for our own use. His presence at Sperry-Rand with MacArthur, his boss in Korea, was all the more important because General MacArthur knew the truth about UFOs and commented that the army was girding itself to fight in space. And he didn't mean fighting the Russians in space, he meant the extraterrestrials.

But we were fighting so deeply immersed in the darkness of our own official denial that the fantastic nature of the truth, the ongoing effects of the truth, and the capitulation of the civilian intelligence services to some crazed blueprint they had for world order based upon an international government sometimes made us doubt our own senses. However, when you looked at what I called the secret history of the United States since 1947, you knew that the invisible elephant was walking through the room. A better analogy is the concept of the black hole. Black holes, the ultradense remains of stars that have collapsed upon themselves, swallow up light and gravity and, compressing them in like a galactic compactor into something that only subatomic particle physicists can describe and that can't actually be "seen." Only their effects can be determined from the way light and gravity seem to behave around them.

So you guess that a black hole might be present in a specific region of space when light and gravity around it bend almost like the way water circulates around the drain at the bottom of your sink. That's what the truth looked like in the region around our Cold War strategy and the development of any ultra-high-tech or exotic weapons. It might have made sense in 1947, but by 1962, the refusal of the government to admit the war it was fighting was getting in the way of actually fighting the war.

Since 1947 and the formation of the working group, each new layer of bureaucracy operating within the black hole of UFO strategy and intelligence gathering found itself more enmeshed in the confusion of what was true and what was false than the previous layer. Like legions of blind soldiers, they bumped into one another in the night, upset one another's plans, and thought that friends were foes and vice versa. In the absence of a clear policy that could be maintained from generation to generation, the strategy for dealing with the EBEs became tangled up in its own web.

After December 1947 when Gen. Hoyt Vandenberg, the air force chief of staff, directed the air force to evaluate and track UFO sightings—this in response to the working group—Project "Sign" began at the Air Technical Intelligence Center. Sign was so critical that even J. Edgar Hoover in 1947 issued Bureau Bulletin 59 ordering that all future reports of UFOs should not be investigated by FBI agents but sent, instead, to the air force.

Although officially not looking for UFOs, the air force Project Sign examined 243 sightings and submitted its report in February 1949. But at the same time Sign was doing its evaluation, the Air Technical Intelligence Center issued its own document called an "Estimate of the Situation." Basically, but naively, the document came to the conclusion that we were dealing with extraterrestrial interlopers who were observing us from UFOs. But General Vandenberg, in the words of one of the officers I later ran into at the Pentagon, "had a cow, and not a mutilated one."

"Colonel," this officer said, "steam was coming out of the old man's ears he was so furious. Just be glad you weren't there."

So I asked this officer why General Vandenberg was so

steamed. After all, he ordered the report in the first place. Why didn't he just agree with General Twining and Admiral Hillenkoetter to ask the President to begin releasing the information?

"Are you crazy?" this officer said. The year was 1956 and I had been sent over from the White House for a briefing at the Pentagon. "Don't you remember what happened when that Orson Welles 'War of the Worlds' broadcast was on the radio? We had near riots in the cities because they thought that thing was real. Can you imagine what would happen if it really happened? If our own government said that flying saucers had landed just like on the radio, only this time we caught one and they're still coming back? Think about it. Riots, looting, people going insane because they thought aliens were destroying the planet."

He was right. And what was worse, the aliens were setting up for some sort of hostile act, whatever it was.

When General Vandenberg read the "Estimate of the Situation," he fumed and ordered the whole report burned to ashes before anyone else could read it. It was one of the last official government assessments of the UFO situation ever to get even close to being distributed before the real cover-up clamped down.

But the grumblings about the absence of government policy concerning UFO reports continued. Project "Grudge" listed and evaluated 244 UFO sightings. Then in 1949 a memo that came out of the CIA's Office of Scientific Investigation was very apprehensive about unexplained sightings of flying objects. Then in 1952 another CIA memo came to light; from the head of the Office of Scientific Investigations Weapons and Equipment Division it also complained about our lack of knowledge and police in the area of UFO sightings. Now even the CIA, it seemed, was at odds with itself at its various levels of bureaucracy over what to do about UFOs. Generals Twining and Vandenberg had had enough. In 1952, the air force formally initiated Project Blue Book. At least if we weren't going to do anything about UFOs publicly, we had to have a way to salve the public's fear about UFO sightings. Blue Book was that salve.

Whatever the working group was supposed to be doing in

1952, it wasn't satisfying the National Security Council, which ordered the CIA to determine whether the existence of UFOs would create a danger for the United States. Of course, the CIA already knew, because two of its intelligence directors had been members of the working group, that UFOs were displaying hostile intentions not only to the United States but to the Soviets, the Italians, and the Scandinavians as well. All of NATO was trying to figure out a response to the UFO threat without triggering a reaction from the Soviets. That was one of the reasons, thirty years later, President Reagan and Mikhail Gorbachev could come to a meeting of the minds about UFOs that ultimately brought an end to the need for a Cold War.

On January 14, 1953, just before the inauguration of President Eisenhower, CIA officials and air force officers met at the Pentagon at the CIA's invitation to discuss the UFO situation and what our working group had learned up to that point. Officiated at first by Dr. H. P. Robertson, a CIA employee and the director of the Weapons Systems Evaluation Group in the office of the secretary of defense, the group also had working group member Dr. Lloyd Berkner, a physicist and one of the directors of the Brookhaven National Laboratories, as one of its members. The Robertson Panel spent the next three days reviewing case histories of UFO sightings assembled for them by Air Force Intelligence and saw two films that contained footage of alleged flying saucers. The panel concluded there was no threat to the United States and recommended that the government should start debunking UFO sightings in general. This, the CIA reported as late as 1988, was the only official government response to UFO sightings.

Just over a year later, the White House agreed that it was necessary to have some sort of policy governing the release of UFO information to the press. In order to keep lower-level officers from releasing unauthorized information—and by unauthorized the National Security Council advising the President meant only that information cleared by the working group—Gen. Nathan Twining, now the air force chief of staff, signed off on Air Force Regulation 200-2, which said that it was permissible to release reports to the media only when the object was identifiable, like swamp gas or a meteorite. But only the Air Technical Intelligence Center could determine which objects were identifiable and which weren't. In other words, only the ATIC could authorize the release of any information about UFOs, and they did so only when the objects were clearly identifiable as common phenomena and not flying saucers.

Throughout the 1950s, I witnessed the government become more and more secretive about UFOs even though privately I thought that they would get better information if they were more open about it. But I was also a military officer and understood the necessity of keeping information confidential until you understood what it was. Besides, the Soviets were making great strides in the race to get into space and we didn't know if they were getting cooperation from the EBEs. There truly was a war on, and I followed orders on the White House staff even as I watched the officers in the cover-up begin to trip over their own feet time and again. The darkness was closing in all around us.

In 1961, the air force began two secret projects that, in effect, had been in operation since 1947 but had not been committed to policy. "Moon Dust" had to do with the establishment of recovery teams to retrieve and recover crashed or grounded "foreign" space vehicles. But for all intents and purposes, as far as the public was concerned the air force was looking for Soviet satellites that had fallen out of the sky and landed on Earth. But in reality the air force was establishing a recovery of UFOs program just like the army had pulled the crashed UFO out of the New Mexico desert fourteen years earlier. Then in Project "Blue Fly," the air force authorized the immediate delivery of foreign crashed space vehicles and any other item of technical intelligence interest to Wright-Patterson Air Force Base in Dayton, Ohio, for evaluation. It was a repeat of General Twining's retrieval of the Roswell space vehicle from the 509th to Wright Field in 1947.

In 1962, one of the assistants to the secretary of defense, Arthur Sylvester, told the press at a briefing that if the government deemed it necessary for reasons of national security, it would not even furnish information about UFOs to Congress, let alone the American public. Now I was at the Pentagon and I fully understood how the air force was moving to take control of the entire UFO situation. NASA had the mandate from the President to manage space exploration, but the military still had to defend against the UFO threat even though we were being hampered at every turn.

Air Force projects "Saint" and "Blue Gemini" years later were outgrowths of USAF 7795, a code number for the USAF's first antisatellite program, an aggressive operation designed to locate, track, and destroy enemy surveillance satellites or, and more importantly, orbiting UFOs. Using the technology we had developed at R&D, the air force, and then the army, was taking the initial steps to defend the U.S. missile system against Soviet attacks from space and defend the planet against UFO intrusions.

"Saint" was an orbital UFO inspector satellite, a version of a standard Agenda B satellite that the CIA had been using, that had an onboard TV camera and tracking and targeting radar system. Its job was surveillance. Find a potential enemy satellite or UFO lurking in orbit and lock onto it with a TV camera and with radar. Once the lock was in place, Blue Gemini, the "killer" satellite, would move in. One of the projects developed by Hughes Aircraft, a prime air defense contractor and satellite builder, Blue Gemini was the military version of NASA's manned Gemini capsule. Its mission, purely and simply, was to swoop in from a higher orbit and kill or disable an enemy satellite or a UFO. If possible, the Blue Gemini would try to "capture" a UFO in orbit by rendering it immobile and waiting for a manned military astronaut mission to "space walk" over and retrieve whatever we could. Both of these weapons, under the cover of other missions, of course, were eventually deployed, and today they form one of the lines of defense in an antimissile and anti-UFO surveillance system.

Saint and Blue Gemini were important first steps in our war against the UFOs. The technology that came out of Army R&D in the 1960s, retrieved from the aliens themselves, led directly to our ability to put up such a defense against the aliens even though in the hours after the crash at Roswell our situation looked completely hopeless. Like many of the products that came out of R&D and were used for military purposes, they had consumer uses. And today, if you look on the small dish digital direct broadcast television satellite antennas that are being marketed all across the country, you'll see Hughes's own brand. It's an example of how technology originally earmarked for the military winds up as the most basic and everyday consumer product.

On December 17, 1969, the secretary of the air force announced the termination of Project Blue Book. He said that Blue Book's review of more than thirteen thousand cases had yielded no information that there was a threat to national security in any way and that, in effect, since every sighting processed by Blue Book had been identified as something earthly and not extraterrestrial, there were, by definition, no such things as unidentified flying objects. Blue Book had done its job and now could report that our skies were safe. But Blue Book had been pure public relations from the start, and the military's evaluation of UFOs continued uninterrupted.

In 1975 and early 1976, air force nuclear weapons repositories at Loring AFB in Maine, the all-important and sensitive Strategic Air Command facility at Minot, North Dakota, and other facilities in Montana, Michigan, and even the Royal Canadian Air Force Base at Falconbridge in Ontario had been seriously encroached upon by UFOs. These weren't just random sightings. UFOs actually conducted surveillance and scanning operations at the bases that resulted in security alerts and classified reports to Washington about the intrusions.

Then NASA finally got a project up and running to scan for radio transmissions from any advanced civilizations whose signals we could pick up. Called the Search for Extraterrestrial Intelligence and endorsed by the late Carl Sagan, SETI, which has since been discontinued, was not only a set of receivers around the world but a set of international protocols governing what would happen if contact was made with an extraterrestrial civilization.

For over fifty years, now, the war against UFOs has continued as we tried to defend ourselves against their intrusions. The Hughes hunter-killer satellites of the 1970s were our first steps in deploying a planetary defense system that held any real threat against the EBEs. When, late in the

1970s, we realized that a directed-energy weapon and high-energy laser were even more effective than exploding satellites, our defensive ability was enhanced even further. We recognized that by applying both the technology we found at Roswell and Tesla's vision of a particle beam to our own antisatellite missiles and laser targeting equipment, we could achieve the rapid aim/rapid fire capability that these type of defenses demanded. But we were still playing cover-up games even though the Russians were now finally acknowledging that maybe cooperation between the superpowers was called for to meet a common threat.

In the 1980s, both President Reagan and Chairman Gorbachev recognized the need for cooperation against a common enemy. While neither officially owned up to the threat of EBEs and alien hostilities, both acknowledged that if the United States and the Soviet Union could lay aside their differences and participate in a shared policy to defend the space around the earth, then both superpowers would benefit. For his part, President Reagan pushed hard for the rapid development and deployment of a space-based defense technology to defend the planet. Called the Strategic Defense Initiative, and derisively dubbed "Star Wars" by the press, the SDI was described in 1985 in President Reagan's own words as "a defensive shield that won't hurt people but will knock down nuclear weapons before they can hurt people."

Briefly, the Strategic Defense Initiative was described by the White House and the military as a space-based defense system to protect the United States from an all-out nuclear attack by the Soviet Union. It would include satellites that could detect a massive nuclear launch within seconds, orbiting lasers to destroy the first wave of missiles, laser-equipped submarines that could defend against the next round of attacks, and a ground-based missile system providing the last line of defense. In addition, the SDI also included what I thought was the best of its weapons, a missile-launched kinetic energy beam weapon that locked onto incoming warheads or low-orbiting space vehicles and knocked out their electronics with a particle beam. The elegant aspect to the kinetic energy beam weapon was that you couldn't really defend against it. Lasers, even high-energy lasers, had their shortcomings in that once a laser beam bounced off a surface, the surrounding energy envelope protected the surface from subsequent pulses. You either knocked out your target right away or shielded it against subsequent hits. But with a particle-beam weapon, you penetrated the surface, just like microwaving a piece of meat, destroyed its electronics to render it useless, and then broke it apart or melted it from within.

Amidst the warnings that the SDI wouldn't work, was a giant unscientific gamble and a corporate giveaway, couldn't provide the massive shield against nuclear missiles, would violate the ABM treaty President Johnson had negotiated with the Russians, and was a giant waste of the taxpayers' money, guess what?

It worked!

We didn't have to shoot down thousands of Soviet incoming warheads, and the Soviets never really cared about the ABM treaty in the first place because they knew they weren't going to launch a first strike and neither would we. We both knew who the real targets of the SDI were, and it wasn't a bunch of ICBM warheads. It was the UFOs, alien spacecraft thinking themselves invulnerable and invisible as they soared around the edges of our atmosphere, swooping down at will to destroy our communications with EMP bursts, buzz our spacecraft, colonize our lunar surface, mutilate cattle in their own horrendous biological experiments, and even abduct human beings for their medical tests and hybridization of the species. And what was worse, we had to let them do it because we had no weapon to defend ourselves.

These creatures weren't benevolent alien beings who had come to enlighten human beings. They were genetically altered humanoid automatons, cloned biological entities, actually, who were harvesting biological specimens on Earth for their own experimentation. As long as we were incapable of defending ourselves, we had to allow them to intrude as they wished. And that was part of what the working group had to deal with. We had negotiated a kind of surrender with them as long as we couldn't fight them. They dictated the terms because they knew what we most feared was disclosure. Hide the truth and the truth becomes your enemy. Disclose the truth and it becomes your weapon. We hid the truth and the EBEs used it against us until 1974 when we had our first real shootdown of an alien craft over Ramstein Air Force Base in Germany.

They had tried to disrupt our space program for years—Mercury, Gemini, Apollo, and even the Space Shuttle. They buzzed our capsules traveling through space, interfered with our transmissions, and pulsed us with EMP bursts just like we used to do to the Soviet surface ships when we would hit them with a radar burst so massive it would send their earphone-wearing radar and sonar techs howling in pain down to the ship's dispensary. But when the EBEs did it to us, we had no response. That was before the SDI.

Once launched and tested, our space-based high-energy lasers, or HELs, acted like the lightning bolts on the nights of July 3 and 4, 1947, that so thoroughly disrupted the electromagnetic wave propagators in the spacecraft flying over Roswell that the pilots couldn't retain control of their own vehicle. We eventually realized that what happened then was that a natural version of an advanced particle-beam burst actually brought a UFO down even as it tried to escape. When we deployed our advanced particle-beam weapon and tested it in orbit for all to see, the EBEs knew and we knew they knew that we had our defense of the planet in place.

Gorbachev, believe it or not, was also pleased because President Reagan guaranteed that the United States would throw its defensive shield around the Soviet Union, too. Sure, the two leaders shook hands and embraced one another in public. What they had achieved together, cooperating when they were supposed to be fighting, was nothing short of miraculous. Whatever we were fighting over became minimally important in the face of a threat from creatures who were so superior to us in technology that we were their farm animals to be harvested as they pleased. But when the United States and USSR agreed, in the early 1980s, not to fight each other over this territory or that territory, to cooperate so as to defeat the common foe, we were unbeatable. Now, as the Space Shuttle docks with the *Mir* and the astronauts and cosmonauts share a toast of vodka from their plastic squeeze tubes and look out into the

darkest reaches of space, they know that there is an electronic shield around them.

Now that the war is just about over and we defend our
beachhead, the truth will ultimately be revealed. The real
truth behind a fifty-year history of a war that looked like the
ultimate defeat for humankind amidst a Cold War that
threatened us with nuclear annihilation can now finally be
told because we prevailed. It was because in the dark hours
just before dawn in July of 1947 the army, only dimly
recognizing that we were on the edge of a potential cataclys-
mic event, pulled the crashed space vehicle out of the desert
and harvested its parts just like the inhabitants of that
vehicle wanted to harvest us. In those moments, even
though we might have fallen over ourselves in the darkness
of the next fifty years, we set in motion the processes that
brought us to an initial resolution with a military power
greater than us. It helped us in our confrontation with the
Russians and, if we don't lose our way, will help us manage
the threats to come. When that truth of alien intervention in
our planet's affairs and our ongoing contact with an alien
culture is finally revealed, it won't be frightening even
though it will be a shock.

The night closes in around you in the desert, exposing
your deepest terrors of childhood bogeymen to the desola-
tion of the landscape and the blackness of the sky. So, even
inside your car you keep on chattering to keep the night
away.

"And that's what I think about all of it, UFOs, the Cold
War, all of it," I told my companion in the car sitting next to
me as we drove south through the New Mexican desert
toward the town of Roswell. "I may be over eighty now, but
that's what I think."

The night was swallowing us up as our car twisted around
the curves on the crowned road surface, still warm and wet
on a summer night from passing thunderstorms, heading
toward lights we knew were over the horizon but still could
not see.

"The Cold War, the missile crisis of 1962, the worldwide
alert in 1973, all history now, don't you think?" I asked.
"Maybe it was a good thing that the aliens forced us to

defend the planet. At least it kept us in a Cold War even though we were using real bullets."

"And what makes you think the Cold War is over, *tovarisch?*" my friend asked as he carefully took out a cigarette, lit it, and blew the smoke out the window. "American cigarettes," he said. "Am I not the most bourgeois decadent person you've ever met? But what would the *Amerikanskis* have done without me?"

And I laughed to myself and counted the million stars across the desert sky as far as I could see. Cattle sleeping near the scrub and sand fences along the side of the lonely state route, a coyote now and then running through the beams of our headlights, and the sound of my friend's breath as he blew the column of smoke into the desert air. It was a night just like this, lightning crackling off in the distance and a thunderclap rolling across the desert floor, a night just like this.

And what looked like a bright shooting star blazed very bright in an arc from south to north and disappeared over a rise as we continued toward Roswell into the darkness of the New Mexico night.

Afterword

Back in the 1950s, I remember watching a television series called *I Led Three Lives* about the exploits of Herbert A. Philbrick, who described the "fantastic but true" story of his life as a member of a Communist Party cell and an undercover operative for the FBI. Years later, when I got to Army R&D, I remember thinking about how my own story was also "fantastic but true" and how what General Trudeau and I did helped to change the course of history. Very few people knew that what was coming out of Foreign Technology during the early 1960s had some basis in a crash of a UFO that "officially" never took place. Lives were distorted, careers destroyed, children frightened into submission by Army Counterintelligence bogeymen, businessmen in Roswell threatened with financial ruination and even worse if anybody told the story of what happened. But they were all loyal Americans, and even though some might have had their doubts about hiding the truth, they went along with what the army wanted.

Many people have criticized the army and the government for maintaining the Roswell cover-up not only at the time but also through the years. For that, I need to say a word in defense of what the army did. It's easy to criticize if you weren't an adult back then or someone who didn't understand the politics that governed our thinking at that point in American history. We had not yet fully made the transition from a nation at war to a nation at peace. And there was Harry Truman, still reeling from his sudden ascendancy to the presidency, toughened into steel by his decision to drop the atomic bombs on Japan, and now faced with the monumental impact of a crash landing of a strange craft on American soil. Was it Soviet? Did it belong to a foreign power? Was it hostile? We simply didn't know and weren't about to say anything until we knew what it was.

Was it a flying saucer? The last time a public announcement of a landing by extraterrestrials took place, even though it was entertainment, panic ensued. In the aftermath of the war and the fears surrounding the Cold War, we didn't want to risk another panic. So the military recommended and the White House agreed to clam up. Just like the secrecy surrounding the Manhattan Project, no word gets out. And for the next fifty years that policy, once put into place, governed the behavior of the U.S. government and the military about the existence of UFOs and the crash at Roswell.

You can also ask how the government was able to keep this secret for so long. Has there been any other cover-up so efficient and thorough that it went on, unbeknownst to succeeding presidents, year after year until it was finally stopped? In fact, there was just such a cover-up, started in the war, but continued as a matter of policy by Truman in 1947, code-named "Shamrock." Secretary of Defense James Forrestal, one of the original members of the UFO working group, convinced his boss President Truman in 1947 to continue working with International Telephone and Telegraph, Western Union, and RCA to make their international communications traffic available for inspection by U.S. military intelligence services. Even though its initial purpose was to monitor any communications of military significance, such as the transmission of military secrets, there were no controls on what was inspected and what was not. This program continued for the next twenty-eight years and kept secret from every president until it was terminated under the Ford administration in 1975.

Does Shamrock mean that UFOs exist? Of course not. But it does reveal the capability of the U.S. government to keep an ongoing operation secret from even the president of the United States, much like the UFO working group also under James Forrestal.

So what do I think about all of this, about what happened and what I did? I believe that because at the time I was so much in the routine of a military intelligence officer, I didn't really stop to think about the implications of UFOs and EBEs. I understood that we were fighting a Cold War with the Soviets and a skirmish war with extraterrestrials. I believed that their intentions were, and still are, hostile, and I believe that we took the steps necessary to develop the weapons that can blunt their threat. In fact, the U.S. military has better, more accurate, and more powerful weapons for killing UFOs than were deployed in the movie *Independence Day*.

We can knock these guys down tomorrow with high-energy lasers and directed particle-beam weapons that come right out of a *Star Wars* movie. And these aren't fiction, they're fact. If you want to know more, pay a visit to the U.S. Army Space Command Website on the Internet. These missile-launched HELs are the pride of our planetary defense system and a direct result of President Reagan's courage in pushing for the Strategic Defense Initiative when everyone said it wouldn't work. And that SDI was a direct result of the work General Trudeau and I did at Army R&D in 1962.

Sometimes things just work the way they're supposed to. Sometimes, once in a very long while, you get the chance to save your country, your planet, and even your species at the same time. And when that time comes, as Davy Crockett once said:

Be sure you're right, then go ahead.

Postscript

OVER THE COURSE OF THE SUMMER OF 1997, SHORTLY AFTER *The Day After Roswell* first appeared in hardcover, a strange and questionable story appeared on the Internet—from a company in New Jersey called the American Computer Company—concerning the development of the transistor. According to a narrative of events, which they subsequently published on their Web site, consultants revealed to them that, in 1947, the army retrieved a downed extraterrestrial spacecraft in New Mexico.

In that alien wreck, the narrative continues, the engineers and the scientists running the analysis of the debris discovered a whole new technology, which included propulsion and computer and communications systems well beyond the current technology of Earth. In September and October of 1947, pieces of this alien technology were taken to Bell Laboratories in Murray Hill, New Jersey, where they were analyzed by Bell's own scientists and engineers. Here, the story continues, at least one piece was discovered to be a vital key to a generation of electronic switching devices well beyond any in use on Earth. The device was composed of the substances silicon and arsenic and was laid out in an array of microscopic circuitry centuries beyond anything that could have been produced in laboratories on Earth. This device, the American Computer Company narrative alleges, became the major focus of an evaluation and subsequently of a reverse engineering project at Bell Labs.

What the Bell Labs researchers discovered was that the alien electronic device they were studying was highly unusual because not only could it switch current on and off, like an electronic gate, it was also a power amplifier. They dubbed the mysterious piece of debris a "Transfer Resistor," because they could make it resist or accept a flow of electrons at much higher or lower currents than were applied to it. This device came to be known as the "transistor," the center of solid-state electronics and, when miniaturized, the key component of the microcomputer industry.

Before 1947, the American Computer Company Web site correctly reports, the transistor never existed. Researchers, people like Bardeen and Shockley, were experimenting with germanium and selenium diodes, but these were not the fully functioning transistors that came into use during the 1950s. After September 1947, the transistor magically seemed to appear at Bell Labs. It was composed of silicon doped with trace amounts of arsenic. This composition, according to the ACC, greatly enhanced the conductive properties of the silicon in a way that no one had ever seen before, even though experiments with electronic circuits had been going on for years. More intriguing, the means to identify what a transistor was, how it functioned, and how to fabricate one were beyond the technology of the time. Even the chemical composition of the silicon used in the 1947 transistor was something that you wouldn't find in nature because it had to be fabricated.

President Truman was reported to be so impressed with the scientific reports of the alien technology that he asked if it were possible to create a device on Earth that could duplicate the technology. According to the report coming out of American Computer, the answer was yes, and the technology was reverse engineered at Bell Labs, who applied for and received patents for the devices, now based on Shockley, Bardeen, and Brattain's research in 1947 and 1948. It could never be revealed, however, that the ultimate source of the material was alien technology retrieved from the crashed Roswell UFO that the army had delivered to Bell. Therefore, the sudden appearance of the transistor required that a cover story be put into place accounting for the years of research that went into the development of the transistor right here on Earth.

Thus, according to sources, both the government and Bell Labs allegedly created a series of press releases in which a two-year history of development was described that resulted in the discovery of the transistor by Drs. Brattain, Shockley, and Bardeen under the management of Bell Laboratories executive John Morton. Subsequently, the official histories of the development of transistor technology were themselves reverse engineered to account for the numerous experiments on diodes and rectifiers to account for the discovery of the transistor even though the effect of the transistor itself and the actual chemical composition of the silicon seem to have miraculously appeared during a two-month window immediately after the Roswell crash. For the next twenty-five years, the only living witness to what actually might have taken place at Bell Laboratories in 1947 was Jack Morton himself, a resident of Neshanic Station, New Jersey, who in the early 1970s was murdered under what the ACC describes as "highly bizarre circumstances." Had Morton, the last eyewitness, become too much of a liability? Was he the man who knew too much?

To read the original story in its entirety, along with continuing updates, you can find the American Computer Company on the Internet at http://compamerica.com/roswell.htm.

APPENDIX A

Project Horizon

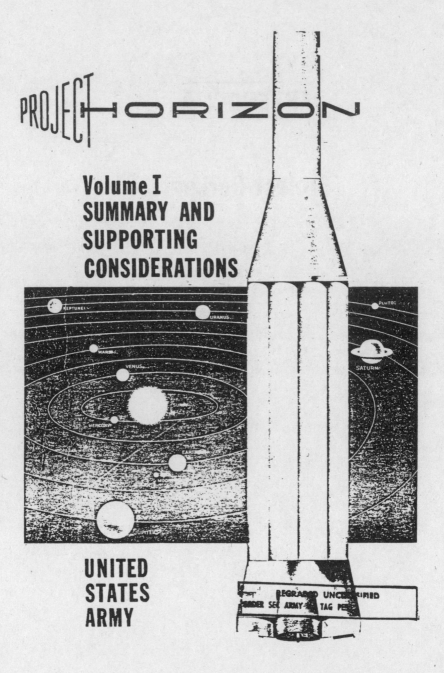

PROJECT HORIZON

Volume I
SUMMARY AND
SUPPORTING
CONSIDERATIONS

UNITED
STATES
ARMY

CRD/1   (S)   Proposal to Establish a Lunar Outpost (C)

Chief of Ordnance   CRD   20 Mar 1959

     1.   (U) Reference letter to Chief of Ordnance from Chief of Research and Development, subject as above.

     2.   (C) Subsequent to approval by the Chief of Staff of reference, representatives of the Army Ballistic Missiles Agency indicated that supplementary guidance would be required concerning the scope of the preliminary investigation specified in the reference. In particular these representatives requested guidance concerning the source of funds required to conduct the investigation.

     3.   (S) I envision expeditious development of the proposal to establish a lunar outpost to be of critical importance to the U. S. Army of the future. This evaluation is apparently shared by the Chief of Staff in view of his expeditious approval and enthusiastic endorsement of initiation of the study. Therefore, the detail to be covered by the investigation and the subsequent plan should be as complete as is feasible in the time limits allowed and within the funds currently available within the office of the Chief of Ordnance. In this time of limited budget, additional monies are unavailable. Current programs have been scrutinized rigidly and identifiable "fat" trimmed away. Thus high study costs are prohibitive at this time.

     4.   (C) I leave it to your discretion to determine the source and the amount f money to be devoted to this purpose.

> Signed
> ARTHUR G. TRUDEAU
> Lieutenant General, GS
> Chief of Research and Development

No contacts with agencies outside the Army will be made until after the results of the preliminary investigation have been presented to the Department of Defense. The findings of the initial investigation will be made through my office to the Chief of Staff. No additional distribution will be made and no public release will be made concerning this project. Because of the sensitive aspects of this proposal it is essential that this project not be disclosed prematurely.

5. Your plan of accomplishment should include full utilization of the other technical services and combat arms to the extent feasible and necessary. In the accomplishment of this investigation the Chief of Engineers will be responsible for the design, construction, and maintenance of the base and the Chief Signal Officer will be responsible for communications and other support for which he is peculiarly qualified. Specific emphasis should be given to the Army-wide capability to contribute to this project. The results of this preliminary investigation are requested by 15 May 1959.

6. Reproduction of this letter to the extent you deem essential is authorized. All copies will be recorded.

1 Incl
  Draft Requirement

ARTHUR G. TRUDEAU
Lieutenant General, GS
Chief of Research and Development

2

Draft

Requirement for a Lunar Outpo _

1. General

    There is a requirement for a manned military outpost on the
moon. The lunar outpost is required to develop and protect potential United
States interests on the moon; to develop techniques in moon-based surveillance of the earth and space, in communications relay, and in operations
on the surface of the moon; to serve as a base for exploration of the moon,
for further exploration into space and for military operations on the moon
if required; and to support scientific investigations on the moon.

2. Operational Concept.

    Initially the outpost will be of sufficient size and contain
sufficient equipment to permit the survival and moderate constructive
activity of a minimum number of personnel (about 10 - 20) on a sustained
basis. It must be designed for expansion of facilities, resupply, and rotation of personnel to insure maximum extension of sustained occupancy. It
should be designed to be self-sufficient for as long as possible without
outside support. In the location and design of the base, consideration will
be given to operation of a triangulation station of a moon-to-earth base
line space surveillance system, facilitating communications with and
observation of the earth, facilitating travel between the moon and the
earth, exploration of the moon and further explorations of space, and to
the defense of the base against attack if required. The primary objective is to establish the first permanent manned installation on the moon.
Incidental to this mission will be the investigation of the scientific,
commercial, and military potential of the moon.

3. Background of Requirement.

    a. References:

        (1) NSC policy on outer space.

        (2) OCB Operations Plan on Outer Space.

    b. Reason for Requirement.

        (1) The national policy on outer space includes the objective
of development and exploiting US outer space capabilities as needed to
achieve scientific, military, and potential purposes. The OCB Operations
Plan to implement this policy establishes a specific program to obtain
scientific data on space environment out to the vicinity of the moon,

Regraded CONFIDENTIAL
13 March 1962.

including the moon's gravitational and magnetic fields and to explore the characteristics of the moon's surface. There are no known technical barriers to the establishment of a manned installation on the moon.

(2) The establishment of a manned base of operations on the moon has tremendous military and scientific potential. Because invaluable scientific, military, and political prestige will come to the nation that first establishes a lunar base, it is imperative that the United States be first.

(3) The full extent of the military potential cannot be predicted, but it is probable that observation of the earth and space vehicles from the moon will prove to be highly advantageous. By using a moon-to-earth base line, space surveillance by triangulation promises great range and accuracy. The presently contemplated earth-based tracking and control network will be inadequate for the deep space operations contemplated. Military communications may be greatly improved by the use of a moon-based relay station. The employment of moon-based weapons systems against earth or space targets may prove to be feasible and desirable. Moon-based military power will be a strong deterrent to war because of the extreme difficulty, from the enemy point of view, of eliminating our ability to retaliate. Any military operations on the moon will be difficult to counter by the enemy because of the difficulty of his reaching the moon, if our forces are already present and have means of countering a landing or of neutralizing any hostile forces that has landed. The situation is reversed if hostile forces are permitted to arrive first. They can militarily counter our landings and attempt to deny us politically the use of their property.

(4) The scientific advantages are equally difficult to predict but are highly promising. Study of the universe, of the moon, and of the space environment will all be aided by scientific effort on the moon. Perhaps the most promising scientific advantage is the usefulness of a moon base for further explorations into space. Materials on the moon itself may prove to be valuable and commercially exploitable.

4. Organizational Concept.

The establishment of the outpost should be a special project having authority and priority similar to the Manhattan Project in World War II. Once established, the lunar base will be operated under the control of a unified space command. Space, or certainly that portion of outer space encompassing the earth and the moon, will be considered a military theater. The control of all United States military forces by unified commands is already established and military operations in space should be no exception. A unified space command would control and utilize, besides the lunar base,

2

operational military satellites and space vehicles, space surveillance systems, and the logistical support thereof. Other space commands might be organized as our operations extended to translunar space.

5. Degree of Urgency.

To be second to the Soviet Union in establishing an outpost on the moon would be disastrous to our nation's prestige and in turn to our democratic philosophy. Although it is contrary to United States policy, the Soviet Union in establishing the first permanent base, may claim the moon or critical areas thereof for its own. Then a subsequent attempt to establish an outpost by the United States might be considered and propagandized as a hostile act. The Soviet Union in propaganda broadcasts has announced the 50th anniversary of the present government (1967) will be celebrated by Soviet citizens on the moon. The National Space policy intelligence estimate is that the Soviets could land on the moon by 1968.

6. Maintenance and Supply Implications.

The maintenance and supply effort to support a lunar base will be high by present standards. Continued delivery of equipment and means of survival will be required and each delivery will be costly. Every conceivable solution for minimizing the logistic effort must be explored. Maximum use of any oxygen or power source on the moon through regenerative or other techniques must be exploited. Means of returning safely to earth must be available to the occupants of the outpost.

7. Training and Personnel Implications.

The number of personnel on the base itself will be quite small, at least initially, but the total number of personnel supporting the effort may be quite large. Until further study is made a realistic qualitative and quantitative personnel estimate cannot be provided. The training requirements of earth based support personnel would resemble those of personnel in long range ballistic missile units and radar tracking systems. For the relatively small number of personnel actually transported to the moon base, training requirements would be exacting in many fields.

8. Additional Items and Requirements.

A complete family of requirements and supporting research and development projects will be necessary to develop all of the supporting equipment to establish a lunar base. Very high thrust boosters, space vehicles, intermediate space stations, space dwellings, clothing and

3

VOLUME I

SUMMARY AND SUPPORTING CONSIDERATIONS (U)

9 JUNE 1959

PROJECT HORIZON REPORT

A U. S. ARMY STUDY FOR THE ESTABLISHMENT
OF
A LUNAR OUTPOST

REGRADED UNCLASSIFIED
ORDER SEC ARMY BY TAG PER 91384

(S) CHAPTER I: INTRODUCTION

A. GENERAL

HORIZON is the project whose objective is the establishment of a lunar outpost by the United States. This study was directed by letter dated 20 March 1959, from the Chief of R&D, Department of the Army, to the Chief of Ordnance. Responsibility for the preparation of the study was subsequently assigned to the Commanding General, Army Ordnance Missile Command. Elements of all Technical Services of the Army participated in the investigation. This report is a limited feasibility study which investigates the methods and means of accomplishing this objective and the purposes it will serve. It also considers the substantial political, scientific and security implications which the prompt establishment of a lunar outpost will have for the United States.

B. JUSTIFICATION

1. The Broad Requirement

The US national policy on space includes the objective of developing and exploiting this Nation's space capability as necessary to achieve national political, scientific, and security objectives. The establishment of a manned outpost in the lunar environment will demonstrate United States leadership in space. It will also provide a basis for further explorations and operations on the lunar surface as well as a supporting capability for other US operations in space.

2. Purpose of the Lunar Outpost

The establishment of a manned US outpost on the moon will:

Demonstrate the United States scientific leadership in outer space.

Support scientific explorations and investigations.

Extend and improve space reconnaissance and surveillance capabilities and control of space.

Extend and improve communications and serve as a communications relay station.

1

Provide a basic and supporting research laboratory for space research and development activity.

Develop a stable, low-gravity outpost for use as a launch site for deep space exploration.

Provide an opportunity for scientific exploration and development of a space mapping and survey system.

Provide emergency staging areas, rescue capability or navigational aid for other space activity'.

3. A Realistic Objective

Advances in propulsion, electronics, space medicine and other astronautical sciences are taking place at an explosive rate. As recently as 1959, the first penetration of space was accomplished by the US when a two-stage V-2 rocket reached the then unbelievable altitude of 250 miles. In 1957, the Soviet Union placed the first man made satellite in orbit. Since early 1958, when the first US earth satellite was launched, both the US and USSR have launched additional satellites, moon probes, and successfully recovered animals sent into space in missiles. In 1960, and thereafter, there will be other deep space probes by the US and the USSR, with the US planning to place the first man into space with a REDSTONE missile, followed in 1961 with the first man in orbit. However, the Soviets could very well place a man in space before we do. In addition, instrumented lunar landings probably will be accomplished by 1964 by both the United States and the USSR. As will be indicated in the technical discussions of this report, the first US manned lunar landing could be accomplished by 1965. Thus, it appears that the establishment of an outpost on the moon is a capability which can be accomplished.

4. Scientific Implications

A wealth of scientific data can be obtained from experiments conducted at a lunar outpost. Without doubt, the scientific community will generate many new and unique applications as man's actual arrival on the moon draws nearer reality. The very absence of knowledge about the moon and outer space is scientific justifications to attempt to breach this void of human understanding.

It is to be expected that civilian efforts to advance science for the sake of science will parallel the military efforts. It is also expected that the National Aeronautics and Space Administration will treat those subjects in greater detail than is either possible or desirable in this study, and that such action will further strengthen the requir⌐ment for earliest possible establishment of an extra-terrestriaι outpost.

5. <u>Political Implications</u>

The political implications of our failure to be first in space are a matter of public record. This failure has reflected adversely on United States scientific and political leadership. To some extent we have recovered the loss. However, once having been second best in the eyes of the world's population, we are not now in a position to afford being second on any other major step in space. However, the political implications of being second in space activities accomplished to date have not been nearly as serious as those which could result from failure to be the first in establishing a manned lunar outpost.

The results of failure to first place man on an extra-terrestrial base will raise grave political questions and at the same time lower US prestige and influence. The Soviet Union has announced openly its intention that some of its citizens will celebrate the 50th anniversary of the October Revolution (1967) on the moon. The US intelligence community agrees that the Soviet Union may accomplish a manned lunar landing at any time after 1965. Judging from past experience, it is not difficult to visualize all manner of political and legal implications which the Soviet Union might postulate as a result of such a successful accomplishment nor the military advantages it might achieve thereby.

6. <u>Security Implications</u>

The extent to which future operations might be conducted in space, to include the land mass of the moon or perhaps other planets, is of such a magnitude as to almost defy the imagination. In both Congressional and military examination of the problem, it is generally agreed that the interactions of space and terrestrial war are so great as to generate radically new concepts.

Admittedly, the security significance of the moon, per se, in the context of offensive and defensive operations, is a matter for con-jecture at this time. From the viewpoint of national security, the primary implications of the feasibility of establishing a lunar outpost is the importance of being first. Clearly the US would not be in a position to exercise an option between peaceful and military applications unless we are first. In short, the establishment of the initial lunar outpost is the first definitive step in exercising our options.

7. Summary

Unquestionably, there are other applications of space (i.e. reconnaisance, meteorology, communications) which will permit an earlier attainment of meaningful accomplishments and demonstrate US interest in space. Individually, however, these accomplishments will not have the same political impact that a manned lunar outpost could have on the world. In the still vague body of fact and thought on the subject, world opinion may view the other applications similar to action on the high seas, but will view the establishment of a first lunar outpost as similar to proprietary rights derived from first occupancy. As the Congress has noted, we are caught in a stream in which we have no choice but to proceed. Our success depends on the decisiveness with which we exercise our current options. The lunar outpost is the most immediate case. It is the basis for other more far-reaching actions, such as further interplanetary exploration.

C. CONCLUSIONS

Four major conclusions summarize the more detailed deductions which may be drawn from the entire report:

1. Political, scientific, and security considerations indicate that it is imperative for the United States to establish a lunar outpost at the earliest practicable date.

2. Project HORIZON represents the earliest feasible capability for the U. S. to establish a lunar outpost. By its implementation, the United States can establish an operations lunar outpost by late 1966, with the initial manned landings to have taken place in the Spring of 1965.

3. The importance of an early decision to proceed with the program, coupled with adequate funding, must be clearly understood. Inordinate delay will have two inescapable results:

a. The program's ultimate accomplishment will be delayed, thus forfeiting the change of defeating the USSR in a race which is already openly recognized as such throughout the world.

4

b. Delayed initiation, followed later by a crash program, which would likely be precipitated by evidence of substantial Soviet progress in a lunar outpost program, will not only lose the advantage of timeliness, but also will inevitably involve significantly higher costs and lower reliability. The establishment of a U. S. lunar outpost will require very substantial funding whether it is undertaken now or ten years hence. There are no developments projected for the predictable future which will provide order of magnitude type price reductions.

4. The U. S. Army possesses the capability of making significant contributions in all aspects of such a program.

D. ORGANIZATION AND CONTENT OF THE REPORT

The Project HORIZON report has been divided into two volumes which are entitled as follows:

Volume I - Summary and Supporting Considerations
Volume II - Technical Considerations and Plans

Volume I is, as indicated, a document which gives a short summary of the other volume, a discussion of non-technical considerations, and a resume of the resources and facilities of the Army Technical Services which can lend support to this program.

Volume II is a technical investigation of the problem. It includes practical preliminary concepts for all elements of the program and, in many cases, relates actual hardware available from current programs to the solution of specific problems. It includes a broad development approach and a funding breakout by fiscal year. Also included are personnel and training requirements for all segments of the operation together with the policy of the US with respect to space and the legal implication of a lunar outpost. This volume was prepared by a unique working group, comprized of a special segment of the Future Projects Design Branch of the Army Ballistic Missile Agency (ABMA), which was augmented by highly qualified representatives of each of the seven Technical Services of the Army. These representatives were carefully selected for the specific task and, during the course of the study, became resident members of the aforementioned ABMA group. The resident representatives of the Technical Services were supported by their respective services with a group of the highest caliber specialists

5

who were made available exclusively to support the project. Thus,
it is believed that the depth of experience, knowledge, and judgement
brought to bear on the problem by this group is commensurate with
the task of accomplishing the report objectives.

Throughout the preparation of the entire report, and especially
within this technical volume, the guiding philosophy has been one of
enlightened conservatism of technical approach. Briefly stated, this
philosophy dictates that one must vigorously pursue research to
"advance the state-of-the-art", but that paramount to successful major
systems design is a conservative approach which requires that no item
be more "advanced" than required to do the job. It recognizes that an
unsophisticated success is of vastly greater importance than a series
of advanced and highly sophisticated failures that "almost worked."
Established engineering principles, used in conjunction with the best
available design parameters, have been applied throughout in order to
remove the elements of science fiction and unrealistic planning.

6

(S) CHAPTER II: TECHNICAL CONSIDERATIONS AND PLANS

A. OBJECTIVES AND SCOPE OF THE STUDY

This p. "t of the study presents applicable technical information which substantiates the feasibility of the expedited establishment of a lunar outpost, and it relates U. S. capabilities and developments to the accomplishment of the task. It is comprehensive in its scope, covering the design criteria and requirements for all major elements of the program including the lunar outpost, the earth-lunar transportation system, the necessary communications systems and the considerable earth support facilities and their operation. The technical assumptions concerning design parameters for this program are realistic yet conservative. Likewise, the assumptions which concern the scope and magnitude of other U. S. programs which will support HORIZON are reasonable and in line with current and projected programs.

B. RESUME OF THE TECHNICAL PROGRAM

The basic carrier vehicles for Project HORIZON will be the SATURN I and II. The SATURN I, currently being developed under an ARPA order, will be fully operational by October 1963. The SATURN II, which is an outgrowth of the SATURN I program, could be developed during the period 1962-1964. The SATURN II will utilize improved engines in the booster and oxygen/hydrogen engines in all of its upper stages.

By the end of 1964, a total of 72 SATURN vehicles should have been launched in U. S. programs, of which 40 are expected to contribute to the accomplishment of HORIZON. Cargo delivery to the moon begins in January 1965. The first manned landing by two men will be made in April 1965. The buildup and construction phase will be continued without interruption until the outpost is ready for beneficial occupancy and is manned by a task force of 12 men in November 1966.

This buildup program requires 61 SATURN I and 88 SATURN II launchings through November 1966, the average launching rate being 5. 3 per month. During this period some 490,000 pounds of useful cargo will be transported to the moon.

During the first operational year of the lunar outpost, December 1966 through 1967, a total of 64 launchings have been scheduled. These will result in an additional 266,000 pounds of useful cargo on the moon.

The total cost of the eight and one-half year program presented in this study is estimated to be six billion dollars. This is an average of approximately $700 million per year. These figures are a valid appraisal and, while preliminary, they represent the best estimates of experienced, non-commercial, agencies of the government. Substantial funding is undeniably required for the establishment of a U. S. lunar outpost; however, the implications of the future impor- tance of such an operation should be compared to the fact that the average annual funding required for Project HORIZON would be less than two percent of the current annual defense budget.

C. OUTPOST

The lunar outpost proposed for Project HORIZON is a permanent facility capable of supporting a complement of 12 men engaged in a continuing operation. The design of the outpost installation herein is based on realistic requirements and capabilities, and is not an attempt to project so far into the future as to lose reality. The result has been a functional and reliable approach upon which men can stake their lives with confidence of survival.

1. Location

The exact location of the outpost site cannot be determined until an exploratory probe and mapping program has been completed. However, for a number of technical reasons, such as temperature and rocket vehicle energy requirements, the area bounded by $\pm$ 20° latitude/longitude of the optical center of the moon seems favorable. Within this area, three particular sites have been chosen which appear to meet the more detailed requirements of landing space, surface conditions, communications, and proximity to varied lunar "terrain. "

A rather extensive lunar mapping program is already underway in order to satisfy existing requirements in Astro-Geodesy. Maps to a scale of 1:5,000,000 and 1:1,000,000 are planned for completion by December 1960 and August 1962, respectively. Larger scale mapping will then be undertaken for several specific site selections.

8

2. Design Criteria

The design of the lunar outpost facilities will, of course, be dominated by the influence of two factors - the lunar environment and the space transportation system capabilities. A few of the more pronounced primary lunar environmental parameters are listed below:

a. Essentially no atmosphere.

b. Surface gravity approximately 1/6 earth gravity.

c. Radius of approximately 1000 miles is about 1/4 that of earth. (This results in a significant shortening of the horizon as compared to earth.)

d. Surface temperature variations between a lunar day and night of +248° F to -202° F.

e. Maximum subsurface temperature at equator is -40°F. These and many other unfamiliar environmental conditions require that every single item which is to be placed on the lunar surface have a design which is compatible with these phenomena. However, a careful determination has been made of man's requirements to live in this environment, and it appears that there is no area which cannot be adequately solved within the readily available state-of-the-art.

3. Outpost Facilities and Their Installation

The first two men will arrive on the lunar surface in April 1965. They will be guided to an area in which the cargo buildup for future construction has already begun. Their landing vehicle will have an immediate return-to-earth capability; however, it is intended that they remain in the area until after the arrival of the advance party of the construction crew. During their stay, they will live in the cabin of their lunar vehicle which will be provided with necessary life essentials and power supplies. For an extended stay, these will be augmented by support from cargo previously and subsequently delivered to the site by other vehicles.

The mission of the original two men will be primarily one of verification of previous unmanned environmental investigations and confirmation of the site selection and cargo delivery.

9

Figure I-1 shows the HORIZON outpost as it would appear in late 1965, after about six months of construction effort. The basic building block for the outpost will be cylindrical metal tanks ten feet in diameter and 20 feet in length. (Details of typical tanks are shown in Fig. I-2.) The buried cylindrical tanks at the left-center of Fig. I-1 constitute the living quarters of the initial construction crew of nine men who will arrive in July 1965. (Details in Fig. I-3.) During the construction period, this force will be gradually augmented until a final complement of 12 men is reached. The construction camp is a minimum facility and will be made operational within 15 days after the beginning of active work at the outpost site. Two nuclear reactors are located in holes as shown in the left portion of Fig. I-1. These provide power for the operation of the preliminary quarters and for the equipment used in the construction of the permanent facility. The main quarters and supporting facilities are shown being assembled in the open excavation to the right-center of the figure. These cylinders will also ultimately be covered with lunar material. Empty cargo and propellant containers have been assembled and are being used for storage of bulk supplies, weapons, and life essentials such as insulated oxygen/nitrogen tanks. Two typical surface vehicles are shown: one is a construction vehicle for lifting, digging, scraping, etc., the other is a transport vehicle for more extended distance trips needed for hauling, reconnaissance, rescue, and the like. In the left background, a lunar landing vehicle is settling on the surface. A lightweight parabolic antenna has been erected near the main quarters to provide communications with earth.

The basic completed outpost is shown in Fig. I-4. Significant additions beyond the items illustrated in Fig. I-1 are two additional nuclear power supplies, cold storage facility, and the conversion of the original construction camp quarters to a bio-science and physical-science laboratory.

A number of factors influenced the decision to locate the main structures beneath the surface. Among these were the uniform temperature available (approximately -40°F), protection from meteoroids, security, good insulating properties of the lunar material, and radiation protection. Each of the quarters and cylinders will be a special double-walled "thermos bottle type" vacuum tank with a special insulating material in the space between the walls. (Vacuum is easily maintained simply by venting the tank to the lunar void.) Despite the ambient subsurface temperature of -40°F, the heat losses from these special tanks will be remarkably low. Investigations show that the

10

Fig. I-1. HORIZON Outpost in Late 1965

11

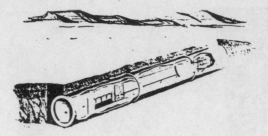

Fig. I-2. Cross Section of Typical Outpost Compartments

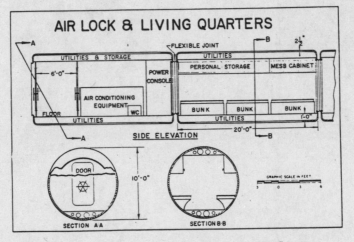

Fig. I-3. Overall View of Initial Construction Camp

13

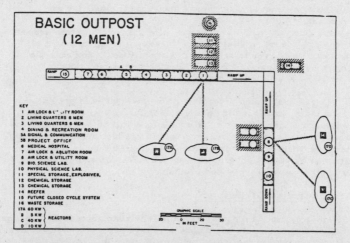

Fig. I-4. Layout of Basic 12-Man Outpost

incidental heat given off by an adequate internal lighting system will nominally supply essentially all of the heat required to maintain comfortable "room" temperature in the outpost quarters.

A suitable atmosphere will be provided within the quarters. The basic gas supply will stem from special insulated tanks containing liquid oxygen or nitrogen. The nitrogen supply needs only to provide for initial pressurization and replacement of leakage losses; whereas, the oxygen is, of course, continuously used to supply bodily needs. However, the weights and volumes of both gases are quite reasonable and presents no unusual problem of supply. Carbon dioxide and moisture will be controlled initially by a solid chemical absorbent and dehumidifier. Such a scheme requires considerable amounts of material; therefore, a carbon dioxide freeze-out system will be installed later.

4. Personnel Equipment

For sustained operation on the lunar surface a body conformation suit having a substantial outer metal surface is considered a necessity for several reasons: (1) uncertainty that fabrics and elastomers can sustain sufficient pressure differential without unacceptable leakage; (2) meteoroid protection; (3) provides a highly reflective surface;

14

(4) durability against abrasive lunar surface; (5) cleansing and sterilization. Figure I-5 shows a cutaway and "buttoned up" concept for such a suit. It should be borne in mind that while movement and dexterity are severe problems in suit design, the earth weight of the suit can be allowed to be relatively substantial. For example, if a man and his lunar suit weigh 300 pounds on earth, they will only weigh 50 pounds on the moon.

A comprehensive program will be undertaken to provide special hand tools, load-handling gear, and dining equipment to meet the unusual requirements. Initially, all food will be pre-cooked; however, as water supplies increase with the introduction of a reclaiming system, dehydrated and fresh-frozen foods will be used. Early attention will be given to hydroponic culture of salads and the development of other closed-cycle food product systems.

5. Environmental Research

In order to corroborate essential environmental data, a series of unmanned experiments are planned. There are early data requirements in the areas of radiation, meteoroid impacts, temperatures, magnetic field, surface conditions, ionization, radio propagation and biological effects.

D. SPACE TRANSPORTATION SYSTEM

1. Flight Mechanics

In choosing appropriate trajectories to use in this program, one must strike a balance between the low-energy paths and the high energy curves. The low energy trajectories give the highest payload capability, but are sensitive to small variations in the injection conditions and can also lead to unacceptably long transit times. The higher energy trajectories are faster and are not as sensitive to deviations in the injection conditions, but they result in payload penalties and higher terminal velocities which in turn require greater braking energy at the termination of the trip. A good compromise appears to be a trajectory which will yield a transit time from earth to moon of approximately 50 to 60 hours.

Several different trajectory schemes will be used in Project HORIZON. They include trajectories for transit: (1) direct from the earth to the moon, (2) from earth to a 96-minute (307 nautical mile

15

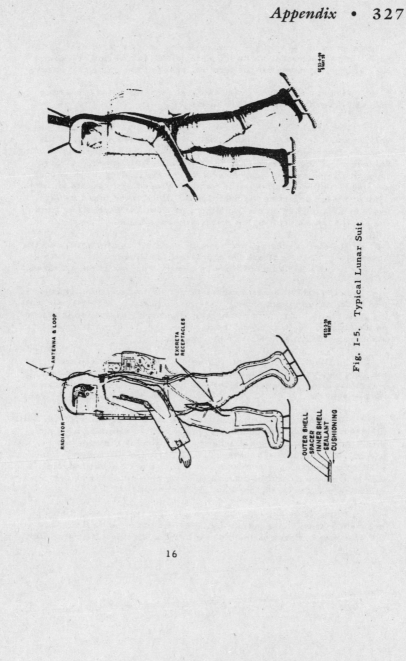

Fig. I-5. Typical Lunar Suit

ANTENNA & LOOP

EXCRETA
RECEPTACLES

RADIATOR

OUTER SHELL
SPACER
INNER SHELL
SEALANT
CUSHIONING

16

altitude) orbit of the earth, (3) from this 96-minute earth orbit to the moon, and (4) direct from the moon to earth. In addition, there are special considerations for the terminal phase of each type trajectory.

Figure I-6 illustrates the two basic schemes of transporting man and cargo from earth to the moon.

The first scheme (1 above) is the direct approach, that is, a vehicle would depart the earth's surface and proceed directly to the lunar surface using a retro-rocket or landing stage for the final landing maneuver. Since the moon has no appreciable atmosphere, a rocket type propulsion system will be required for the landing. The second scheme (2 and 3 above) shown is that for proceeding first into an earth orbit and later departing the orbit for the flight to the lunar surface, again using a landing stage. In either scheme, the flight time from the earth or earth orbit to the moon will be the same.

The direct scheme, which is the most straightforward, has two advantages: first, it offers the shortest flight time from the earth's surface to the lunar surface since an orbital stopover is not required.

In the orbital scheme, much larger payloads can be transported into orbit, assuming the vehicle size to be constant, and by accumulating payloads in orbit, it is possible to transport a payload to the moon on the order of ten times (and more if desired) the capability of a single vehicle flying directly to the moon.

To illustrate this point, it has been assumed in the study that the first men arriving on the moon will be provided with an immediate return capability. Figure I-7 depicts the vehicular requirements for the two schemes.

The direct approach would require a six stage vehicle with a lift-off thrust of 12 million pounds, as compared to a two-million-pound thrust vehicle for the orbital schemes. By placing the upper stage and payload of two-million-pound thrust vehicle into orbit, and with additional vehicles as shown, performing a fuel transfer and checkout operation, the same mission, that of transporting two men to the moon and returning them to earth, could be accomplished.

It should be pointed out, however, that if the United States is to have a manned lunar outpost by 1966, and at the same time provide the first men arriving on the moon with the desired return capability,

17

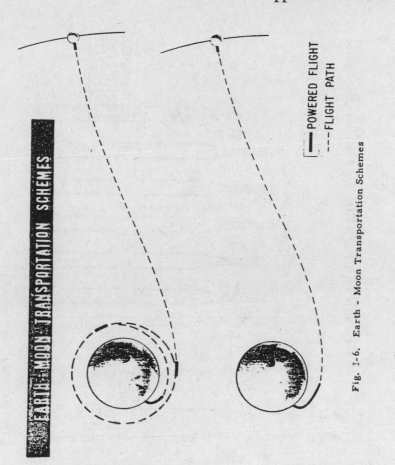

EARTH - MOON TRANSPORTATION SCHEMES

— POWERED FLIGHT
--- FLIGHT PATH

Fig. 1-6. Earth - Moon Transportation Schemes

18

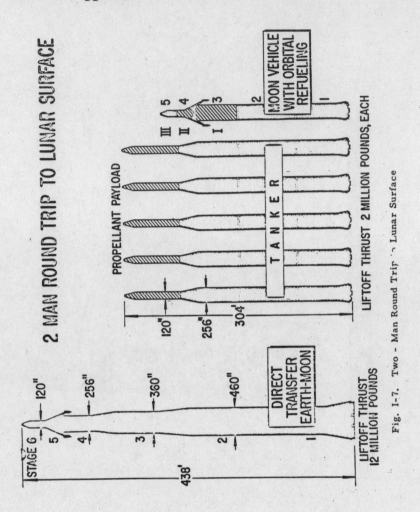

2 MAN ROUND TRIP TO LUNAR SURFACE

Fig. I-7. Two - Man Round Trip to Lunar Surface

19

the orbital approach is mandatory, since a 12-million pound thrust vehicle will not be available to meet the required schedule.

For the return to earth, from either the earth orbit or the lunar surface, aerodynamic braking will be used, since it allows significant overall payload increases when compared to rocket braking. The aerodynamic braking body used for this study is similar in shape to a JUPITER missile nose cone modified by the addition of movable drag vanes at the base of the cone. Though the size varies, the same basic shape was considered for use from the lunar surface to earth as was for use from the 96-minute orbit to the earth's surface. Studies show that, within acceptable limits of entry angle, the vehicle can make a successful descent which is well within the physical tolerances imposed by man's presence, and which can be guided with acceptable accuracy for final recovery. The recent successful flight and subsequent recovery of two primates aboard a nose cone further substantiates the validity of this approach to earth return braking. This test vehicle was fired to IRBM range and, due to the steep re-entry angle, the decelerative forces associated with this operation were many times greater than expected for project HORIZON trajectories.

2. <u>Orbital Carrier and Space Vehicles</u>

Only two basic carrier vehicles are required to carry out Project HORIZON - SATURN I and a further development, SATURN II.

The SATURN I vehicle, shown in Figs. I-8 and I-9 consists of a clustered booster with a lift-off thrust of 1,504,000 pounds, a twin engine second stage of about 360,000 pounds of thrust, and a lox/hydrogen (O_2/H_2) third stage of 30,000 pounds of thrust. The initial performance of this vehicle will enable it to place 30,000 pounds of net payload in a 96-minute orbit and 7,500 pounds of net payload to earth escape velocity. It will be powered by eight North American H-1 engines which are a greatly simplified version of the engine used in JUPITER, THOR, and ATLAS. The second stage is a modified version of the TITAN booster. The third stage is a modified CENTAUR vehicle currently under development by Pratt & Whitney and Convair.

The SATURN II vehicle (Figs. I-10 and I-11) is based on a modified SATURN I booster. The North American H-1 engines of the original version will be replaced by H-2 engines which will up-rate the total thrust by 1/3 to a sea level value of 2,000,000 pounds. The second stage will incorporate two 500,000-pound thrust H_2/O_2 engines, a

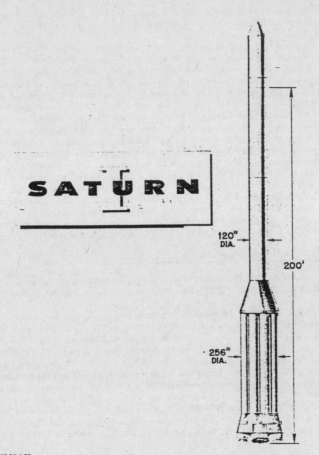

120" DIA.

256" DIA.

200'

GE 52-1-59
9 MAY 1959

Fig. I-8. SATURN I

21

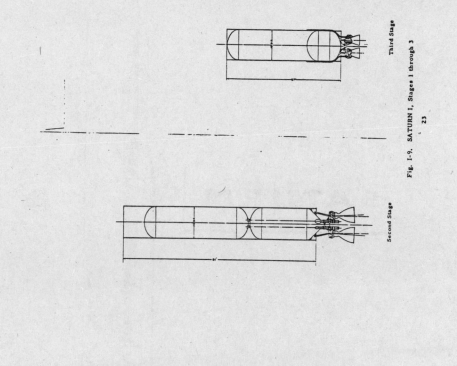

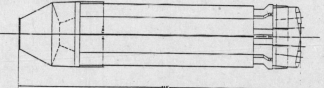

Fig. 1-9.   SATURN I, Stages 1 through 3

23

Third Stage

Second Stage

First Stage (Booster)

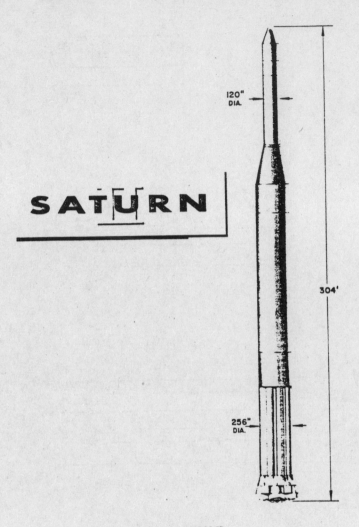

SATURN

120" DIA.

304'

256" DIA.

Fig. I-10. SATURN II

25

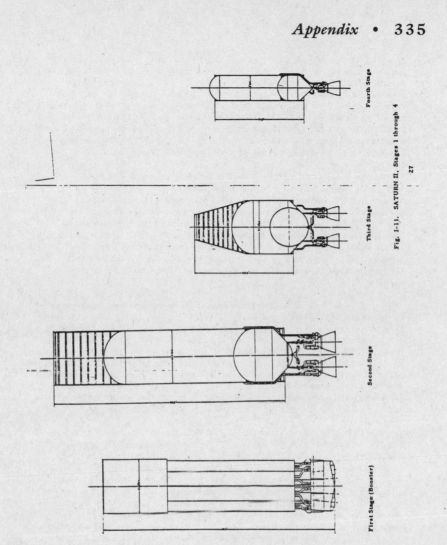

Fig. I-1. SATURN II, Stages 1 through 4

third stage will utilize two 100,000-pound thrust H_2/O_2 engines, a fourth stage will use one such engine. Present feasibility studies inducate a SATURN II payload capability of 70,000 pounds into a 96-minute orbit using three stages and 26,750 pounds to earth escape velocity using four stages. The development of such a vehicle will provide ..e nation a new-optimum vehicle for the utilization of the SATURN booster. The prime requirement for the development of such a vehicle is an expansion of current high-energy O_2/H_2 engine programs to include development of 100 K and 500 K engines.

As mentioned earlier, 6,000 pounds of useful cargo can be soft-landed on the moon with the direct method. As presented herein, only cargo will be transported in this manner, although there is a discussion of how personnel could also be transported to and from the moon utilizing the direct method. The second form of conveyance requires two steps. Initially the required payloads, which will consist of one main lunar rocket vehicle and several additional propellant tankers, will be placed in a 96-minute orbit of the earth. At this time, the propellants in orbit will be transferred to the main lunar rocket vehicle.

Figure I-12 is a conceptual view of the operations in the equatorial earth orbit. The operation in orbit is principally one of propellant transfer and is not as assembly job. The vehicle being fueled is the third stage of a SATURN II with a lunar landing and return vehicle attached. The third stage of the SATURN II was used in bringing the combination into orbit and has thus expended its propellants. This stage is fueled in orbit by a crew of approximately ten men after which the vehicle then proceeds on the moon. It is planned to send all personnel and approximately 1/3 of the cargo to the moon by the orbital method.

Using this orbital system, individual payloads of 48,000 pounds may be soft-landed on the moon. This value is especially significant, since it represents the approximate minimum weight required for a complete earth return vehicle, which is already assembled and loaded with propellants and is capable of returning several men. Thus, in order to provide a preassembled return vehicle on the lunar surface during the time frame under consideration, it is mandatory to go through an initial earth orbit. In addition to providing a large individual payload capability, the orbital transportation system offers other important advantages. Among these are that the total number of firings to deliver the same amount of payload to the moon is less and

29

Fig. I-12. Equatorial Earth Orbit

payloads may be fired for orbital rendezvous at any given pass every day of the month. This alleviates the launch site scheduling problems which are associated with the restricted firing times of direct flights.

There are two versions of the lunar landing vehicle. The first type wil' be used for direct trips from earth to the lunar surface. This vehicle has a gross weight of 26,750 pounds and will soft land some 6,000 pounds of payload. The second vehicle will be used for flights via orbit. It will have a gross weight of 140,000 pounds which gives it a capability of soft landing approximately 48,000 pounds of payload on the moon. Each type of vehicle will have suitable payload compartments to accomplish different mission requirements. The lunar landing vehicle shown in Fig. I-13 has an earth return vehicle as a payload. For such return vehicle payloads, the structure of the expended braking stage will serve as a launching platform when it is time to begin the return journey to earth.

To sustain the orbital station crew and to provide for their safe return to earth, an orbital return vehicle such as shown in Fig. I-14 will be provided. This vehicle may be used in conjunction with another established United States orbital station, or it may be used as a basis for a minimum orbital station needed to support Project HORIZON. It is capable of carrying from 10 to 16 men. It will be carried into orbit by a SATURN I during the first part of the program and replaced by a SATURN II in 1967.

3. Guidance and Control

An investigation of the guidance problems concerned with Project HORIZON indicates that the necessary accuracies and reliabilities can be met by adaptations, combination and slight extensions of known and available guidance hardware and techniques. Final injection velocity, which marks the beginning of the coast phase of the trajectory to the moon, will be controlled by conventional means. Mid-course guidance will assure that the lunar landing vehicle would come within approximately 20 km (11 nautical miles) of the selected point. The terminal guidance system, which would be target oriented, would reduce the three standard deviation error at landing to approximately 1.5 km.

33

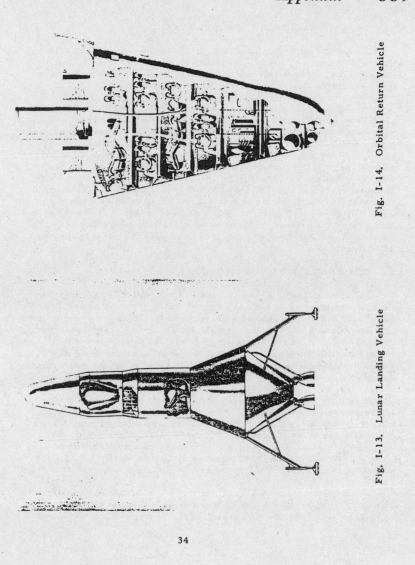

Fig. I-14. Orbital Return Vehicle

Fig. I-13. Lunar Landing Vehicle

34

E. TRANSPORTATION SYSTEM INTEGRATION

The development and integration of the space carriers to support HORIZON have been carefully outlined and various considerations as to compatibility, size, development schedule, and overall mission have been included and discussed in detail in Volume II.

Personnel space transportation requirements to support HORIZON are shown on Fig. I-15. By the end of 1967 some 252 persons will have been transported into an earth orbit, 42 will have continued to the moon, and 26 will have returned from the moon. The orbital station strength is approximately ten; however, the crew will be rotated every several months. The space transportation system will deliver some 756,000 pounds of useful cargo to the lunar surface by the end of 1967. In order to accomplish this, 229 SATURN vehicle firings will be required. A schedule of launching and the broad mission assigned each vehicle is shown in Fig. I-16. It should be noted that, due to the savings incurred by the booster recovery system which will be used, the total number of SATURN boosters required to support the program is not 229 but only 73.

F. COMMUNICATIONS ELECTRONICS

The communications required for Project HORIZON are logically divided into an earth-based and lunar-based complex. Each of these complexes may be considered as having two functions - communications and surveillance. Of particular significance for the earth-based complex is the 24-hour communications satellite system presently under development. As illustrated in Fig. I-17 such a system will provide the capability of constant communications with both space vehicles in transit and the lunar outpost.

In addition to the 24-hour communications satellite system, the current development program of a world-wide surveillance net will provide space surveillance for the United States during the 1960 era. The basic hardware and techniques used in this net are directly applicable to HORIZON. Figure I-18 illustrates schematically how such a world net station could be expanded to support HORIZON by the addition of two additional 85-foot antennas and other equipment.

Communications on the lunar surface will pose special problems due in a large part to the lack of atmosphere and the relatively high curvature of the surface. However, careful investigation reveals no

35

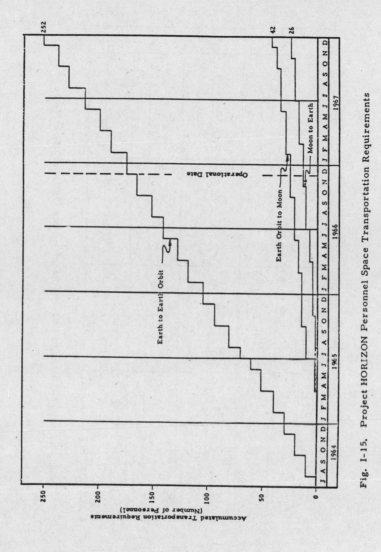

Fig. I-15. Project HORIZON Personnel Space Transportation Requirements

36

PROJECT HORIZON VEHICLE REQUIREMENTS AND LAUNCHING SCHEDULE
Number of Flights for Designated Dates

Vehicle and Mission	1964 J A S O N D	1965 J F M A M J J A S O N D	1966 J F M A M J J A S O N D	1967 J F M A M J J A S O N D	Total Flights
Lunar Soft Landing Vehicle (Direct) SATURN II		1 1 1 1 2 2 2 2 2 2 2 2	2 2 2 2 2 3 2 3 2 3 2 3	3 2 2 3 2 3 2 3 2 2 2 2	73
Earth-Orbit and Return (Manned) SATURN I	1 1	1 1 1 1	1 1 1		16
SATURN II				1 1 1 1 1 1	6
Earth-Orbit (Cargo) SATURN I	1 3 1 3 3	4 3 2 2 3 2 3 3 2 1 1 1	1 1 1 2 3 2 3 3 3 3 3 2	2 2 3 2 2 3 2 2 2 2 3	47
SATURN II	1	1 1 1 1	1 1 1 2 3 3 3 3 3 3 3 2		71
Emergency Vehicles SATURN I		1 1 1	1 1 1	1 1	6
SATURN II		1	1	1 1	10
Orbit-Lunar Soft Landing (Cargo)		1	1	1	4
Orbit-Lunar Soft Landing (Manned)		1 1	1 1	1 1 1	10
Lunar-Earth Return		1 1	1 1 1	1 1	8
Total SATURN I	2 3 2 4	5 5 3 3 4 3 4 3 3 2 1 2	2 1 2 1 2	5 6 5 6 5 6 5 6 5 6 5 4	69
SATURN II	1	1 2 2 2 2 2 3 3 2 4	4 5 5 5 5 6 6 6 6 6 6	5 6 5 6 5 6 5 6 5 6 5 6	160
Total Carrier Vehicles for Project HORIZON	2 3 3 3 4	6 7 5 5 6 5 6 7 6 7 6 6	6 7 7 7 7 7 6	5 6 5 6 5 6 5 6 5 6 5 6	229

Fig. I-16. Project HORIZON Vehicle Requirements and Launching Schedule

37

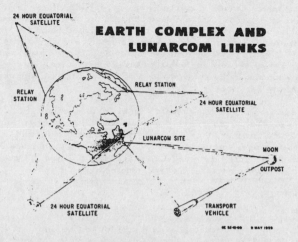

Fig. I-17.   Earth Complex and Lunarcom Links

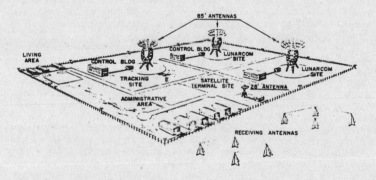

Fig. I-18.   Typical Tracking and Lunarcom Site

38

problems which cannot be solved by an appropriate research program. In a number of areas, current developments appear almost directly applicable; for example, the small helmet-mounted radio currently in production and troop use. A microminiaturized version of this, presently i advanced development, will provide a basis for personal communication between individuals clad in lunar suits. As the lunar outpost expands, radio relay stations will extend the radio horizon as conceived in Figure I-19.

In addition to voice communication between members of the lunar party, a number of other electronic devices will be used at the outpost. These include TV receipt and transmission, transmission of still photographs, homing and location devices, instantaneous self-contained emergency communications packs (for distress signals to earth), infrared detectors, and radar detectors.

G. LAUNCH SITE

A survey was made to determine the adequacy of the Atlantic Missile Range and Pacific Missile Range for the accomplishment of Project HORIZON. The results of this survey indicated that, all things being considered, neither site was suitable. Since a new launch site will be required, a study was made to determine the optimum location and requirements for such a site.

The results of this study are discussed in detail in Volume II and illustrated in Fig. I-20. A total of eight launch pads are required. This facility will support the requirements of HORIZON and would also provide additional capacity for other United States programs.

The equatorial location of the new launch site would provide very real advantages in terms of payload capability, guidance simplicity, and operational launching schedules in terms of increased latitude of appropriate firing times. Two sites stand out when compared to others Brazil and Christmas Island. Both of these locations appear feasible; however, more detailed criterial will have to be established to make the best choice. Cost and early availability may ultimately be the governing factors. It is emphasized that site acquisition and initiation of launch site construction is one of the most critical items in the program with respect to leadtime. For the purposes of this study it has been assumed that the Brazil site would be used.

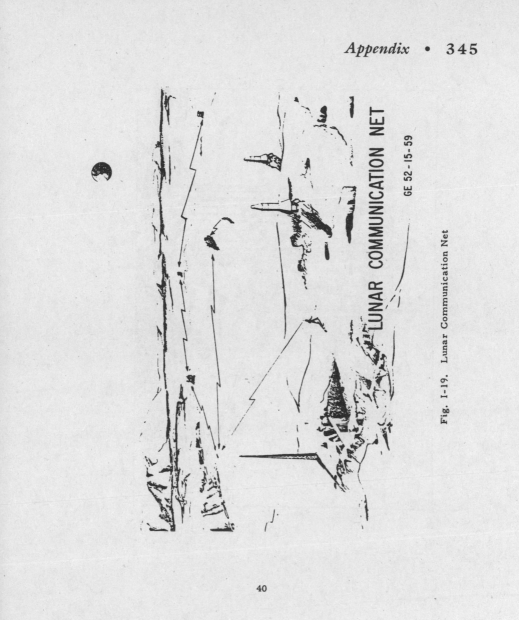

Fig. I-19. Lunar Communication Net

40

Fig. 1-20. Terrestrial Launch Site

41

H. PROGRAM LOGISTICS

The logistic support for Project HORIZON has been studied in overall scope as well as detailed investigations of specific areas such as manufacturing considerations, transportation considerations, personnel, and personnel training.

The results of the studies show very clearly that military participation in the logistic portion for Project HORIZON is not only desirable, but mandatory. No attempt has been made to determine the level of military participation since such items as the world-wide political situation will play an important part in the ultimate decision.

I. RESEARCH AND DEVELOPMENT

Project HORIZON has been divided into six phases which include R&D as well as the operational aspects of the overall program. The schedule for each phase is illustrated on Fig. I-21 and discussed below:

Phase I - The initial feasibility study was completed on 9 June 1959 and is contained in this two volume report.

Phase II - The detailed development and funding plan will require a more detailed study with limited experimentation. This phase will require approximately eight months to complete and will cost $5.4 million.

Phase III - The hardware development and system integration phase constitutes the majority of the development effort. In Phase III all:

Systems (space transportation, communication outpost, etc)

Sub-systems (space vehicles, communications, ground and relay stations, etc.)

Components (rocket engines, communication transmitters & receivers, etc.)

Schemes and procedures (orbital rendezvous, orbital fuel transfer, etc.)

required to accomplish the project objectives will be developed.

43

Phase IV - The construction of the lunar outpost involves the utilization of the systems and procedures developed in Phase II and is in actuality an operational phase of the program. The completion of this phase will accomplish the initial objective of the program - "establish a manned lunar outpost."

Phase V - The initial period of outpost operation will begin in December 1966 and will constitute the first completely operational phase of the program.

Phase VI - The expansion of initial outpost operational capabilities could begin at any time after December 1966. For the purpose of this study it has been assumed to begin in January 1968.

1. Basic and Supporting Research

The importance of a strong basic and supporting research effort in support of a project of this nature cannot be over stated. Typical areas requiring attention are food and oxygen, clothing, chemical, biological, radiological, bio-medical, vacuum conditions, weightlessness, meteoroids, lunar-based systems, moon mapping, explosives in lunar environment, power generation, material and lubricants, liquid hydrogen production and handling, and lunar "soil" mechanics.

2. Project HORIZON Development Program

As mentioned above, a strong basic and supporting research program will be required to accomplish the HORIZON development program, and ultimately the project objectives. The development program for this project is basically covered by the first three phases of the project outlined above, the first of which has been completed. Phase II, the next step in the development program, must be accomplished in the time scale indicated in Fig. I-21 if the United States is to succeed in establishing the first lunar outpost. The development plan, generated in Phase II will spell out in considerable detail the developments required in Phase III, as well as requirements for later phases.

Basically, Phase III will be the development portion of the project. During this phase, all development required to accomplish the project objectives will be satisfied.

44

3. Research and Development Facilities

Several unique facilities will be required to support HORIZON.
Figure I-22 is a view of a large lunar environmental simulator which
will provide a capability for research, development, testing and
training for HORIZON as well as other projects in the national space
program. Figure I-23 illustrates a space flight simulator which will
provide for research and training of effects associated with boost
acceleration, coasting, weightlessness, and braking deceleration. In
addition, medical research facility is located in conjunction with this
site.

PROJECT HORIZON
RESEARCH AND DEVELOPMENT PROGRAM

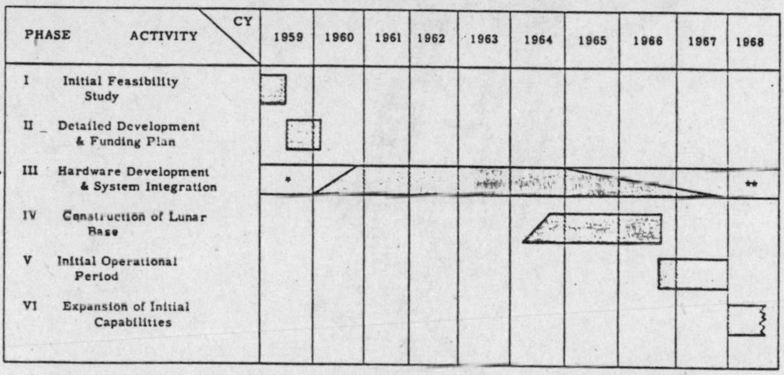

PHASE	ACTIVITY	CY	1959	1960	1961	1962	1963	1964	1965	1966	1967	1968
I	Initial Feasibility Study		▫									
II	Detailed Development & Funding Plan			▫								
III	Hardware Development & System Integration		*									**
IV	Construction of Lunar Base											
V	Initial Operational Period											
VI	Expansion of Initial Capabilities											

* Hardware and Systems being developed for other programs that will have direct application in Project HORIZON.

** Development required for expansion of capability.

Fig. I-21. Organization for Research and Development

45

46

Fig. I-22. Cross Section Through Main Facility LERUT

Fig. I-23.   View of Flight Simulator

47

(S) CHAPTER III: MANAGEMENT AND PLANNING CONSIDERATIONS

A. SCOPE OF OPERATIONS

1. General

Having developed a requirement for the establishment of a manned lunar outpost, we may discuss the operational concepts and facilities necessary to fulfill that requirement. From these, an organizational structure can be evolved. The treatment of the technical concepts and facilities in this chapter will be limited to that detail absolutely necessary to establishment of an organizational/operational structure.

2. Terrestrial Launch Site

In order to accomplish any space mission, a terrestrial launch site will be required. Use of any of the existing sites controlled by the United States has several disadvantages. Among these is the fact that all of these bases are geographically located as to limit firing times to but a few days each month and to require wasteful expenditure of available energy to achieve success. This latter results from the fact that none of the existing launch sites are located close to the equator. Furthermore, once human beings are either placed in orbit or dispatched on planetary missions, there can be no interfering problems regarding scheduling of firings, either regular or emergency; physical space difficulties resulting from supply build-up or other logistic considerations, etc. The terrestrial launch site is expected to evolve into an operational complex supporting both continued R&D and firing by operational units with orbital or other space missions. Existing United States launching complexes are devoted primarily to R&D firings of weapons systems. Most such complexes are rapidly becoming saturated with such firings in the confines of their present areas. It rapidly becomes evident that a separate site will be required in order to support this nation's space efforts in a most economical manner.

There are a great many factors involved in this requirement. They are discussed at length in Chapter V. Three major factors influencing requirements are:

a. Operational need for having an orbital station in an equatorial orbit to simplify the rendezvous problem.

49

b. High payload penalty and complexity of trajectory problem involved in "dog-legging" into equatorial orbit from a non-equatorial launch site.

c. Magnitude of effort requred to implement the objectives of this operation.

In addition, of course, there are other factors influencing the attainment of such a site. For example:

a. Diplomatic and political implications involved at some suitable sites.

b. Military vulnerability and security requirements at all suitable sites. (These are relative choices not necessarily consistent with the best diplomatic or political choice.)

c. Cost: It may be reasonably assumed here, based on the above mentioned factors and detailed technical considerations in Volume II that an equatorial launch site will be selected. It will be the terrestrial site from which this nation dispatches its first man destined to set foot on the lunar surface. This site will provide a capability to conduct additional space missions in fulfillment of other requirements.

For this site to be operational in sufficient time, action is demanded immediately in negotiations required for acquisition. Build-up of facilities must begin at an early date in order to meet the desired operational readiness date.

A terrestrial launch site, which supports the lunar outpost project during the early technical effort, should also support it during the operational phase. There will be practical requirements for the utilization of the launch site for other projects possibly involving military R&D, military operations, and the National Aeronautics and Space Administration. Practical problems thus raised are subsequently treated under organizational considerations.

3. Orbital Station

In order to successfully accomplish lunar soft landings in the time frame under consideration, firings may be undertaken either directly from the earth's surface to the destination or by means of an intermediate station in orbit about the earth. The former approach requires the expenditure of tremendous amounts of energy for relatively small payloads. Therefore, it cannot provide an immediate return capability in the proposed time frame, using the boosters then available. Under those conditions, the orbital station, providing larger payloads and immediate, emergency, return capability from the moon is the most desirable choice for transport of personnel.

During early transit operations through the orbital station, facilities in orbit will be on a minimum essential, austere basis. It will have rendezvous, refueling and launch capabilities but not a vehicle assembly capability. During this period, it will be little more than an interim assembly of fuel tanks and other hardware in orbit. Personnel involved in its operation will utilize their earth-to-orbit-to-earth vehicle as living quarters for the duration of their stay in orbit. Until an orbital station is developed to a higher order of operational autonomy in support of this and perhaps other operations, it will be under the immediate operational control of the terrestrial launch site.

Throughout the operation, assembly of equipment in orbit must be directed toward the eventual establishment of more sophisticated orbital stations. As indicated previously, an early improved station may be constructed from 22 vehicle shells. Prior to any expansion of lunar outpost operations, sufficient tankage will have been placed in orbit to permit construction of two or three such stations. Having more than one station in orbit enhances future operational capability and flexibility by increasing number of possible firing times per month.

Although it is considered premature in this preliminary feasibility study to establish an exact schedule for assembly of more sophisticated orbital stations, the operational requirement must be recognized now. Some considerations which affect implementation of this requirement are that:

a. No other program is likely to make available a similar amount of material, in orbit, without a previously established purpose.

b. The demands of this program will use a considerable fraction of foreseeable or predictable large booster resources,

c. The economy of using otherwise wasted resources to a constructive end.

51

Early attainment of more advanced operational capability in the orbital station will contribute to other space activities as well as to this specific operation. Examples of such contributions are:

    a. Space laboratory, acclimatization, and training capability for personnel.

    b. Space laboratory for equipment.

    c. Materiel storage space.

    d. Low-altitude communication relay

    e. Earth surveillance (perhaps a security consideration in this specific operation).

    f. Space surveillance.

    g. Meteorological surveillance.

    h. Survey/geodesy data collection.

    i. Instrumentation for test of earth-to-space weapon effects.

As the scope of operations at the orbital station increases, so will the interactions with other national space activities increase. therefore, it can be expected to evolve into an independent agency supporting this terrestrial launch site, and possibly others.

    4. Lunar Outpost

This goal of the project is envisioned as falling into several basic areas as follows:

    a. Life Support and Preliminary Exploration.

    In the first outpost phase, lasting from 30 to 90 days, concern of those landed revolves primarily about life support and the human verification of many details of information previously generated by unmanned satellites or probes. Permanent site selection will also depend upon such verification.

52

b. Construction

During the second outpost phase, we find personnel and cargo located in the vicinity of the permanent site capable of contructing habitable structures. There will be a rotation of personnel during this phase which will last approximately 18 months. Maximum tour will not be more than one year. Titular head of the outpost during this period will be one whose primary speciality is construction.

c. Benefical Occupancy and Initial Operational Capability

This is the goal for Project HORIZON as set forth in this study. The outpost at this point can comfortably support 12 men, six of whom will spend a large part of their time in general maintenance and life support.

These volumes have focused on the goal of establishing a lunar outpost capable of supporting 12 people. This represents a large capital expenditure. Once established, the cost is shown decreasing as a result of eliminating the capital expenditure and continuing only the life support resupply. In order to realize a full return on the investment involved, it will obviously be desired to establish additional equipment at the outpost in quantity. For example, the use of the moon as a launching site for manned or unmanned planetary expeditions will be highly desirable. As such requirements multiply it is obvious that construction, equipment, and personnel requirements will also multiply.

There exists an immediate requirement, therefore, to initiate an early industrialized expansion of the outpost giving it a capability of self-regeneration, to the greatest extent possible, from materials at hand. Each returning vehicle will bring physical and biological materials and samples back for analysis. Each sample must be critically analyzed to determine its utility. Methods must then be determined and equipment transported to the lunar outpost which will contribute to a self-regenerative capability. During this secondary/expansion/construction period, the operational outpost will acquire an industrial self-regenerative capability and capabilities will evolve which manifestly justify the entire effort. In addition, this nation will be in the position of having contributed in an early and timely manner to the extension of man's horizon.

53

B. ORGANIZATIONAL AND OPERATIONAL CONCEPTS

1. Ge<ins></ins>neral

As indicated earlier, it is expected that the terrestrial launch site and the orbital station will have applications in both R&D and operational activities of other projects. The potential scientific applications of the lunar outpost cover a broad spectrum of activities.

The scope of activities which must occur at the locations of the essential elements of this specific operation call for a full range of support including military, technical R&D; civilian (NASA) scientific research; operational logistics; operational space activity. This involves full Military Air Transport Service and Military Sea Transportation Service type support plus possibly civil air lift and merchant marine. One or more of these requirements will overlap assigned missions of major existing unified commands extending over broad geographical areas.

There will be requirements for support from and to other elements of government. Such requirements will affect both technical and operational elements of any organization set up for the accomplishment of this specific mission. One case, in point, is support of NASA scientific programs. Examples of other support or guidance requirements from or to governmental departments other than Defense are as follows:

a. Operations Coordinating Board, National Security Council; overall inter-departmental coordination.

b. Central Intelligence Agency, National Security Council; National Intelligence.

c. Department of State; relations with other interested nations.

d. Federal Bureau of Investigation, Department of Justice; security matters.

e. U. S. Coast and Geodetic Survey, Department of Commerce; survey and geodesy.

f. U. S. Geological Survey. Department of the Interior; selenology.

Some would have special responsibilities and delegated authorities peculiar to their particular operational situation. For example, the launch site may have major responsibilities in inter-departmental operations approaching that of one of the existing National Missile Ranges; the orbital station may have a major communications responsibility to the entire project, etc.

Both the project management and terrestrial launch site will require a full range of conventional and space-peculiar operational technical support. Technical support at the launch site must have the capability of cross service support to military and civil departments of government. Technical channels of communication should prevail on technical matters without abrogating or diluting responsibility.

3. Staff Organization

As previously noted, a full range of technical staffing and support is required. However, special space-peculiar operational requirements exist and must be clearly identified and treated in future planning documents. It must be recognized that all planning factors for an operation of this magnitude and significance are not firm particularly during the early stages of feasibility demonstration and for the operational as opposed to the purely technical.

At least in the early stages of operation of the orbital station and the lunar outpost, a different staffing pattern will prevail. Individuals must have a wide range of carefully selected skills. While this poses no insurmountable problems, it does require very careful coordination in all phases of operation from first concept approval until expansion of operations to a considerable degree at some yet undetermined date.

The preceding discussions suggest that early activation, staffing and training of the various agencies is mandatory. Full, optimum, most-economical operations will result from a carefully planned activation program. Waiting until the full requirement is imminent would, in any given instance, delay or hazard some facet of operations.

58

(S) CHAPTER IV: NON-TECHNICAL SUPPORTING CONSIDERATIONS

A. GENERAL

Fro .. the viewpoint of national security, the primary implication of the feasibility of establishment of a lunar outpost is the importance of being <u>first</u>. Clearly, we cannot exercise an option between peaceful and military applications unless we are first.

For political and psychological reasons, anything short of being first on the lunar surface would be catastrophic. Being first will have so much political significance that no one can say at this time what the absolute effects will be. However, it is apparent from past space accomplishments that being second again cannot be tolerated.

B. POLICY

Any new venture of the magnitude of this study creates an immediate requirement for both general and specific policy guidance. Policy is a product of times and circumstances. Man's experience in space matters is short, and the circumstances of his space activities are extensions of all the complex relations which preceded them. Accordingly, we have not evolved a comprehensive body of even controversial, much less agreed, policy.

Both the Executive and the Legislative branches of the United States Government have devoted considerable attention to the subject for approximately one and one-half years. The policy which has evolved from Legislative or Executive action is still quite general. No specific policy directed at the subject of this study was found.

An effort has been made to analyze existing general policy and to summarize it in a form suitable as background for this study. That summary is in Appendix A. There has been no conscious effort at abstraction of points of policy pertinent only to this subject. Rather, the effort was to summarize the general policy. This subject will require an early and continuing effort aimed at development, correlation, and codification of policy.

For the present, then, the policy, as the requirements, must be judged against the background of contemporary international political and military situations. The general policy, however, is sufficiently clear in stating the urgency of the situation.

The intelligence estimates which support statements of national policy credit the Soviet Union with a capability of accomplishing the objectives of this study any time after 1965. Therefore, we may infer a requirement from national policy.

C. POLITICA'., PSYCHOLOGICAL AND SECURITY IMPLICATIONS

1. Political and Psychological

The political and psychological implications of our failure to be first in space are a matter of public record. This failure has reflected adversely on United States military, scientific, and political leadership. To some extent we have recovered the loss. However, once having been second best in the eyes of the world's population, we are not now in a position to afford being second on any other major step in space. We have already stretched our luck in being second with the space probe and sun satellite. However, the political implications of the space activities accomplished to date have not been nearly as serious as those which will result from failure to be first in this operation.

The results of failure to first place man on extra-terrestrial, naturally-occurring, real estate will raise grave political questions and at the same time lower United States prestige and influence in dealing with this and related problems. The Soviet Union has announced openly its intention that some of its citizens will celebrate the 50th anniversary of the present government (1967) on the lunar surface. The United States intelligence community agrees that the Soviet Union may accomplish a manned lunar landing at any time after 1965. Judging from past experience, it is easy to visualize all manner of political and legal implications which the Soviet Union might postulate as a result of such a successful accomplishment. As is so often the case in points of law, the effect is the derivative of the precedent.

There are possibly other applications of space which will permit earlier derivation of meaningful military capabilities than will a successful lunar outpost provided these applications are pursued vigorously. Individually, however, they will not have the same political impact. In the still vague body of fact and thought on the subject, world opinion may be expected to view the other applications similar to actions on the high seas and also to view the establishment of a first lunar outpost similar to proprietary rights derived from first occupancy. As the Congress has noted, we are caught in a stream in which we have no choice but to proceed. Our success depends strongly on the decisiveness with which we exercise our current options. The lunar outpost is the most immediate such case. It is the basis for others more far-reaching such as further inter-planetary exploration.

More detailed coverage of legal and political implications may be found in Appendix B. They are directly related to policy discussions in Appendix A.

2. National Security

Volume II of this study indicates that it has the objective of treating the subject up to and including the establishment and maintenance of a twelve-man outpost of which approximately fifty percent (six men) would have the continued functions of life support operations. This would include operation and maintenance of equipment with perhaps minor technical improvements in the outpost. While it may be granted that this achievement will have been a major national accomplishment from the political and diplomatic viewpoint and will provide the know-how for expansion, it will not satisfy all of the foreseeable national security requirements. It is, therefore, merely a point of departure for security considerations.

The total extent of the military applications, which may evolve after the establishment of the initial outpost, is a function of variables which require operational and/or technical evaluation beyond the scope of this study. Some entail National Security Council type evaluation. Examples are:

(1) Evaluation of the actual or potential threat to the continued operation of the outpost and policy on countering the threat. This must include a study of interactions with other space activities.

(2) Evaluation of the significance of lunar operations within the broader framework of the total national defense.

(3) Military evaluation of the operational and technical requirements to implement any National Security Council policies which are specified.

(4) Cost of implementing military operational and technical requirements.

(5) Utilization of knowledge gained during first phases of out-post operation.

(6) Extent to which national policy requires attainment of specific military or scientific capabilities.

(7) State-of-the-art improvement in rocket booster engines, particularly in specific impulse, thrust, and weight.

APPENDIX B

General Twining's Memo

NND 760168 5.4.73

SECRET

Copy

SAVE

HEADQUARTERS
AIR MATERIEL COMMAND

TSDIN/HMM/ig/6-4100
WRIGHT FIELD, DAYTON, OHIO

IN REPLY ADDRESS BOTH
COMMUNICATION AND EN-
VELOPE TO COMMANDING
GENERAL, AIR MATERIEL
COMMAND, ATTENTION
FOLLOWING OFFICE SYMBOL

TSDIN

SEP 23 1947

SUBJECT: AMC Opinion Concerning "Flying Discs"

TO: Commanding General
        Army Air Forces
        Washington 25, D. C.
        ATTENTION: Brig. General George Schulgen
        AC/AS-2

1. As requested by AC/AS-2 there is presented below the considered opinion of this Command concerning the so-called "Flying Discs". This opinion is based on interrogation report data furnished by AC/AS-2 and preliminary studies by personnel of T-2 and Aircraft Laboratory, Engineering Division T-3. This opinion was arrived at in a conference between personnel from the Air Institute of Technology, Intelligence T-2, Office, Chief of Engineering Division, and the Aircraft, Power Plant and Propeller Laboratories of Engineering Division T-3.

2. It is the opinion that:

a. The phenomenon reported is something real and not visionary or fictitious.

b. There are objects probably approximating the shape of a disc, of such appreciable size as to appear to be as large as man-made aircraft.

c. There is a possibility that some of the incidents may be caused by natural phenomena, such as meteors.

d. The reported operating characteristics such as extreme rates of climb, maneuverability (particularly in roll), and action which must be considered evasive when sighted or contacted by friendly aircraft and radar, lend belief to the possibility that some of the objects are controlled either manually, automatically or remotely.

e. The apparent common description of the objects is as follows:

(1) Metallic or light reflecting surface.

U-39552

SECRET

DOCUMENT

Secret

Basic Ltr fr CG, AMC, WF to CG, AAF, Wash. D. C. subj "AMC Opinion Concerning "Flying Discs".

        (2) Absence of trail, except in a few instances when the object apparently was operating under high performance conditions.

        (3) Circular or elliptical in shape, flat on bottom and domed on top.

        (4) Several reports of well kept formation flights varying from three to nine objects.

        (5) Normally no associated sound, except in three instances a substantial rumbling roar was noted.

        (6) Level flight speeds normally above 300 knots are estimated.

    f. It is possible within the present U. S. knowledge — provided extensive detailed development is undertaken — to construct a piloted aircraft which has the general description of the object in subparagraph (e) above which would be capable of an approximate range of 7000 miles at subsonic speeds.

    g. Any developments in this country along the lines indicated would be extremely expensive, time consuming and at the considerable expense of current projects and therefore, if directed, should be set up independently of existing projects.

    h. Due consideration must be given the following:-

        (1) The possibility that these objects are of domestic origin - the product of some high security project not known to AC/AS-2 or this Command.

        (2) The lack of physical evidence in the shape of crash recovered exhibits which would undeniably prove the existence of these objects.

        (3) The possibility that some foreign nation has a form of propulsion possibly nuclear, which is outside of our domestic knowledge.

3. It is recommended that: -

    a. Headquarters, Army Air Forces issue a directive assigning a priority, security classification and Code Name for a detailed study of this matter to include the preparation of complete sets of all available and pertinent data which will then be made available to the Army, Navy, Atomic Energy Commission, JRDB, the Air Force Scientific Advisory Group, NACA, and the RAND and NEPA projects for comments and recommendations, with a preliminary report to be forwarded within 15 days of receipt of the data and a detailed report thereafter every 30 days as the investi-

-2-

Basic Ltr fr CG, AMC, WF to CG, AAF, Wash. D.C. subj "AMC Opinion Concerning "Flying Discs"

gation develops. A complete interchange of data should be effected.

4. Awaiting a specific directive AMC will continue the investigation within its current resources in order to more closely define the nature of the phenomenon. Detailed Essential Elements of Information will be formulated immediately for transmittal thru channels.

N. F. TWINING
Lieutenant General, U.S.A.
Commanding

-3-

U-39552

APPENDIX C

General Twining's Report

*AFR 200-2
1-5

AIR FORCE REGULATION }
NO. 200-2   }

DEPARTMENT OF THE AIR FORCE
WASHINGTON, *12 AUGUST 1954*

INTELLIGENCE
Unidentified Flying Objects Reporting (Short Title: UFOB)

1. Purpose and Scope. This Regulation establishes procedures for reporting information and evidence pertaining to unidentified flying objects and sets forth the responsibility of Air Force activities in this regard. It applies to all Air Force activities.

2. Definitions:

a. *Unidentified Flying Objects (UFOB)*—relates to any airborne object which by performance, aerodynamic characteristics, or unusual features does not conform to any presently known aircraft or missile type, or which cannot be positively identified as a familiar object.

b. *Familiar Objects*—include balloons, astronomical bodies, birds, and so forth.

3. Objectives. Air Force interest in unidentified flying objects is twofold: First as a possible threat to the security of the United States and its forces, and secondly, to determine technical aspects involved.

a. *Air Defense.* To date, the flying objects reported have imposed no threat to the security of the United States and its Possessions. However, the possibility that new air vehicles, hostile aircraft or missiles may first be regarded as flying objects by the initial observer is real. This requires that sightings be reported rapidly and as completely as information permits.

b. *Technical.* Analysis thus far has failed to provide a satisfactory explanation for a number of sightings reported. The Air Force will continue to collect and analyze reports until all sightings can be satisfactorily explained, bearing in mind that:

(1) To measure scientific advances, the Air Force must be informed on experimentation and development of new air vehicles.

(2) The possibility exists that an air vehicle of revolutionary configuration may be developed.

(3) The reporting of all pertinent factors will have a direct bearing on the success of the technical analysis.

4. Responsibility:

a. *Reporting.* Commanders of Air Force activities will report all information and evidence that may come to their attention, including that received from adjacent commands of the other services and from civilians.

b. *Investigation.* Air Defense Command will conduct all field investigations within the ZI, to determine the identity of any UFOB.

c. *Analysis.* The Air Technical Intelligence Center (ATIC), Wright-Patterson Air Force Base, Ohio, will analyze and evaluate: All information and evidence reported within the ZI after the Air Defense Command has exhausted all efforts to identify the UFOB; and all information and evidence collected in oversea areas.

d. *Cooperation.* All activities will cooperate with Air Defense Command representatives to insure the economical and prompt success of an investigation, including the furnishing of air and ground transportation, when feasible.

5. Guidance. The thoroughness and quality of a report or investigation into incidents of unidentified flying objects are limited only by the resourcefulness and imagination of the person responsible for preparing the report. Guidance set forth below is based on experience and has been found helpful in evaluating incidents:

a. Theodolite measurements of changes of azimuth and elevation and angular size.

b. Interception, identification, or air search

_____
* Regulation supersedes AFR 200-2, 26 August 1953, including Change 200-2A, 2 November 1953.

AFR 200-2
5-7

action. These actions may be taken if appropriate and within the scope of existing air defense regulations.

c. Contact with local aircraft control and warning (AC&W) units, ground observation corps (GOC) posts and filter centers, pilots and crews of aircraft aloft at the time and place of sighting whenever feasible, and any other persons or organizations which may have factual data bearing on the UFOB or may be able to offer corroborating evidence, electronic or otherwise.

d. Consultation with military or civilian weather forecasters to obtain data on: Tracks of weather balloons released in the area, since these often are responsible for sightings; and any unusual meteorological activity which may have a bearing on the UFOB.

e. Consultation with astronomers in the area to determine whether any astronomical body or phenomenon would account for or have a bearing on the observation.

f. Contact with military and civilian tower operators, air operations offices, and so forth, to determine whether the sighting could be the result of misidentification of known aircraft.

g. Contact with persons who might have knowledge of experimental aircraft of unusual configuration, rocket and guided missile firings, and so forth, in the area.

6. ZI Collection. The Air Defense Command has a direct interest in the facts pertaining to UFOB's reported within the ZI and has, in the 4602d Air Intelligence Service Squadron (AISS), the capability to investigate these reports. The 4602d AISS is composed of specialists trained for field collection and investigation of matters of air intelligence interest which occur within the ZI. This squadron is highly mobile and deployed throughout the ZI as follows: Flights are attached to air defense divisions, detachments are attached to each of the defense forces, and the squadron headquarters is located at Peterson Field, Colorado, adjacent to Headquarters, Air Defense Command. Air Force activities, therefore, should establish and maintain liaison with the nearest element of this squadron. This can be accomplished by contacting the appropriate echelon of the Air Defense Command as outlined above.

a. All Air Force activities are authorized to conduct such preliminary investigation as may be required for reporting purposes; however, investigations should not be carried beyond this point, unless such action is requested by the 4602d AISS.

b. On occasions—after initial reports are submitted—additional data is required which can be developed more economically by the nearest Air Force activity, such as: narrative statements, sketches, marked maps, charts, and so forth. Under such circumstances, appropriate commanders will be contacted by the 4602d AISS.

c. Direct communication between echelons of the 4602d AISS and Air Force activities is authorized.

7. Reporting. All information relating to UFOB's will be reported promptly. The method (electrical or written) and priority of dispatch will be selected in accordance with the apparent intelligence value of the information. In most instances, reports will be made by electrical means: Information over 24 hours old will be given a "deferred" precedence. Reports over 3 days old will be made by written report prepared on AF Form 112, Air Intelligence Information Report, and AF Form 112a, Supplement to AF Form 112.

a. *Addressees:*

(1) *Electrical Reports.* All electrical reports will be multiple addressed to:

(a) Commander, Air Defense Command, Ent Air Force Base, Colorado Springs, Colorado.

(b) Nearest Air Division (Defense). (For ZI only.)

(c) Commander, Air Technical Intelligence Center, Wright-Patterson Air Force Base, Ohio.

(d) Director of Intelligence, Headquarters USAF, Washington 25, D. C.

(2) *Written Reports:*

(a) Within the ZI, reports will be submitted direct to the Air Defense Command. Air Defense Command will reproduce the report and distribute it to interested ZI intelligence agencies. The original report together with notation of the distribution effected then will be forwarded to the Director of Intelligence, Headquarters USAF, Washington 25, D. C.

(b) Outside the ZI, reports will be submitted direct to Director of Intelligence, Headquarters USAF, Washington 25, D. C. as prescribed in "Intelligence Collection Instructions" (ICI), June 1954.

b. *Short Title.* "UFOB" will appear at the beginning of the text of electrical messages and in the subject of written reports.

c. *Negative Data.* The word "negative"

2

in reply to any numbered item of the report format will indicate that all logical leads were developed without success. The phrase "not applicable" (N/A) will indicate that the question does not apply to the sighting being investigated.

d. *Report Format.* Reports will include the following numbered items:

(1) Description of the object(s):

(a) Shape.

(b) Size compared to a known object (use one of the following terms: Head of a pin, pea, dime, nickel, quarter, half dollar, silver dollar, baseball, grapefruit, or basketball) held in the hand at about arms length.

(c) Color.

(d) Number.

(e) Formation, if more than one.

(f) Any discernible features or details.

(g) Tail, trail, or exhaust, including size of same compared to size of object(s).

(h) Sound. If heard, describe sound.

(i) Other pertinent or unusual features.

(2) Description of course of object(s):

(a) What first called the attention of observer(s) to the object(s)?

(b) Angle of elevation and azimuth of the object(s) when first observed.

(c) Angle of elevation and azimuth of object(s) upon disappearance.

(d) Description of flight path and maneuvers of object(s).

(e) Manner of disappearance of object(s).

(f) Length of time in sight.

(3) Manner of observation:

(a) Use one or any combination of the following items: Ground-visual, ground-electronic, air-electronic. (If electronic, specify type of radar.)

(b) Statement as to optical aids (telescopes, binoculars, and so forth) used and description thereof.

(c) If the sighting is made while airborne, give type aircraft, identification number, altitude, heading, speed, and home station.

(4) Time and date of sighting:

(a) Zulu time-date group of sighting.

(b) Light conditions (use one of the following terms): Night, day, dawn, dusk.

(5) Locations of observer(s). Exact latitude and longitude of each observer, or Georef position, or position with reference to a known landmark.

(6) Identifying information of all observer(s):

(a) Civilian—Name, age, mailing address, occupation.

(b) Military—Name, grade, organization, duty, and estimate of reliability.

(7) Weather and winds-aloft conditions at time and place of sightings:

(a) Observer(s) account of weather conditions.

(b) Report from nearest AWS or U. S. Weather Bureau Office of wind direction and velocity in degrees and knots at surface, 6,000', 10,000', 16,000', 20,000', 30,000', 50,000', and 80,000', if available.

(c) Ceiling.

(d) Visibility.

(e) Amount of cloud cover.

(f) Thunderstorms in area and quadrant in which located.

(8) Any other unusual activity or condition, meteorological, astronomical, or otherwise, which might account for the sighting.

(9) Interception or identification action taken (such action may be taken whenever feasible, complying with existing air defense directives).

(10) Location of any air traffic in the area at time of sighting.

(11) Position title and comments of the preparing officer, including his preliminary analysis of the possible cause of the sighting(s).

(12) Existence of physical evidence, such as materials and photographs.

e. *Security.* Reports should be unclassified unless inclusion of data required by d above necessitates a higher classification.

8. **Evidence.** The existence of physical evidence (photographs or materiel) will be promptly reported.

a. *Photographic:*

(1) *Visual.* The negative and two prints will be forwarded, all original film, including wherever possible both prints and negatives, will be titled or otherwise properly identified as to place, time, and date of the incident

3

AFR 200-2
8-9

(see "Intelligence Collection Instructions" (ICI), June 1954).

(2) *Radar.* Two copies of each print will be forwarded. Prints of radarscope photography will be titled in accordance with AFR 95-7 and forwarded in compliance with AFR 95-6.

b. *Materiel.* Suspected or actual items of materiel which come into possession of any Air Force echelon will be safeguarded in such manner as to prevent any defacing or alteration which might reduce its value for intelligence examination and analysis.

9. **Release of Facts.** Headquarters USAF will release summaries of evaluated data which will inform the public on this subject. In response to local inquiries, it is permissible to inform news media representatives on UFOB's when the object is positively identified as a familiar object (see paragraph 2b), except that the following type of data warrants protection and should not be revealed: Names of principles, intercept and investigation procedures, and classified radar data. For those objects which are not explainable, only the fact that ATIC will analyze the data is worthly of release, due to the many unknowns involved.

By Order of the Secretary of the Air Force:

Official:

K. E. THIEBAUD
Colonel, USAF
Air Adjutant General

N. F. TWINING
Chief of Staff, United States Air Force

DISTRIBUTON:
8; X:
ONI, Department of the Navy 200
G-2, Department of the Army 10